Homestyle Family Favorites

Annual Recipes ■ 2009

Treasured Dishes for Every Day
and Every Occasion

Printed in the United States of America

Rodale Inc. makes every effort to use acid-free ♾, recycled paper ♻.

Photographs by © Mitch Mandel/Rodale Images

Book design by Christina Gaugler

ISBN-13 978–1–59486–997–6

ISBN-10 1–59486–997–9

2 4 6 8 10 9 7 5 3 hardcover

We inspire and enable people to improve their lives and the world around them

For more of our products visit **rodalestore.com** or call 800-848-4735

Contents

INTRODUCTION

"Food is our common ground, a universal experience."

—JAMES BEARD

Welcome to the *Homestyle Family Favorites Annual Recipes 2009*! Like most people, if you're trying to save a few dollars these days, you're probably eating at home a lot more with your family. In fact, it probably didn't take you long to recall that sitting down at the table together is a great way to share experiences and strengthen family bonds.

With this compendium of delicious recipes, you'll never be at a loss for what to cook, whether you're whipping up a quick-and-easy weekday lunch or dinner or preparing more elaborate food for a festive weekend gathering. All the makings for great meals are here, from appetizers to desserts. And this year, we've added a breads chapter that not only includes quick breads and yeast breads, but lots of muffins and specialty breads (like focaccia) as well.

You'll find plenty of recipes you can make in half an hour or less, such as Chicken Pesto Pizza (page 105) or Cherry-Sauced Pork Chops (page 144), and recipes that need longer to simmer or stew, such as Chicken Cassoulet (page 86) or Round Steak Casserole (page 121).

Looking for a change of pace? In addition to new twists on old standbys like Oven-Fried Chicken (page 70) and Herb-Crusted Leg of Lamb (page 156), you'll also find more creative dishes like Seafood Potpie (page 185) and the easy and tasty Greek Dolmades (page 8). The point is, there is something for every occasion and every taste here.

But this indispensable cookbook is more than just a collection of recipes. It's filled with time-saving cooking tips and helpful cooking strategies, as well as ideas for variations and accompaniments. Plus, you'll find suggestions for emergency substitutions, easy equivalents, and methods for estimating the amount of food you'll need for a party for 12.

How to Use This Book

To make sure there are no unexpected glitches, make sure to read through a recipe completely before you intend to make it so you know in advance what ingredients, utensils, and pans are needed; what the marinating, soaking, and cooking times are; and how many servings a recipe makes. Take note of any ingredients that require advance preparation. For example, some recipes may call for toasted nuts, fresh bread crumbs, precooked beans or rice, or hard-boiled eggs, and you'll want to have them on hand before you begin.

To give you a better idea of how a long a recipe actually takes from start to finish, we've provided "Hands-On Time" and "Total Time." Hands-On Time is the time you spend chopping, stirring, pulsing the food processor, and so on. Total Time includes Hands-On Time plus the time you're, say, doing the laundry while the cake bakes. Since marinating and soaking times can vary considerably, from a few hours to overnight, we've indicated when these are required (in parentheses next to the Total Time) but have not included them in that total number.

Choose Fresh Ingredients

Because we believe that family-style cooking really should be "hands on," the majority of recipes in this book call for fresh ingredients that you prep yourself, whether it's dicing the potatoes, chopping the celery, or mincing the garlic. We urge you to shop locally, enjoying the bounty of farmers' markets for what's in season. That said, we know some home cooks barely have time to shop, much less chop.

Luckily, nearly every supermarket is filled with convenience products designed to make family meals faster and easier for time-challenged cooks. You'll find prewashed greens, prechopped onions and garlic, cheeses already grated or crumbled, and all types of preprepped fruits and vegetables. And while these products can be pricey, it's often a toss-up between your precious time and a few dollars more. We leave it up to you to make the decision of whether to do the slicing and dicing or to go for convenience.

A Final Thought

As the introductory quote attributed to the late food guru James Beard suggests, whatever dishes you choose to cook, food is the common denominator that brings us together. Enjoy the pleasures of family and friends at your table.

Super Starters & Snacks

Bacon-Asparagus Wraps

Hands-On Time: 15 minutes ■ Total Time: 30 minutes

This fast and delicious starter has a lot of visual appeal. One or two bundles could also be a light meal or a stunning side dish to a roast at a dinner party.

- 24 spears asparagus
- 8 slices bacon
- 1 teaspoon olive oil
- 3 tablespoons sesame seeds, lightly toasted
- 1 tablespoon soy sauce

1. Preheat the broiler.
2. Wrap 3 spears of asparagus with a strip of bacon around the middle. Secure with a wooden pick. Repeat with the remaining asparagus and bacon.
3. Place the bundles in a shallow dish and drizzle with the oil, turning to coat. Sprinkle with the sesame seeds, turning the bundles to evenly distribute the seeds. Transfer the bundles to a baking sheet and drizzle with the soy sauce.
4. Broil on the top rack, turning once, for 7 minutes, or until the bacon is cooked and the asparagus is crisp-tender.

Makes 8 servings

Spice things up by adding red pepper flakes, ginger, or orange juice and zest.

For a lower-fat appetizer, use turkey bacon.

Thai Beef on Orange Slices

Hands-On Time: 30 minutes ■ Total Time: 30 minutes

This traditional Thai snack—spicy ground beef served on orange slices—makes an unusual and refreshing appetizer. For authentic flavor, substitute Thai fish sauce for the soy sauce.

- 4 large navel oranges
- 1 teaspoon vegetable oil
- ½ small onion, finely chopped
- 3 cloves garlic, minced
- ½ pound lean ground beef
- 1 small jalapeño pepper, seeded and chopped (wear plastic gloves when handling)
- 2 tablespoons light brown sugar
- 1 tablespoon soy sauce
- ½ teaspoon cider vinegar
- 2 tablespoons finely chopped fresh cilantro

1. Peel the oranges. Cut each crosswise into 4 thick slices. Arrange on a platter.
2. In a medium skillet, heat the oil over medium-high heat. Add the onion and garlic and cook, stirring frequently, for about 3 minutes, or until the onion is soft but not browned. Add the beef and cook, stirring, for about 5 minutes, or until the beef is no longer pink. Add the jalapeño pepper, brown sugar, soy sauce, and vinegar. Cook, stirring frequently, for 3 minutes, or until the liquid evaporates. Add the cilantro and stir well to combine.
3. Top the orange slices with the beef mixture.

Makes 16 servings

Kitchen Tip

To freeze, cool the beef mixture, then pack in a freezer-quality plastic container. Freeze for up to 3 months. To use, thaw overnight in the refrigerator. Microwave on high power for 5 minutes, or until hot, and spoon over the orange slices.

Zucchini Bites

Hands-On Time: 20 minutes ■ Total Time: 55 minutes

Paired with glasses of crisp white wine, these delectable squares will get your dinner party off to an elegant start.

- 2 large eggs
- 5 large egg whites
- 4 cups shredded zucchini
- 1½ cups shredded mozzarella cheese
- 1 cup chopped onions
- ½ cup grated Parmesan cheese
- ½ cup all-purpose flour
- 1 tablespoon chopped fresh dill
- ¼ teaspoon baking powder

1. Preheat the oven to 350°F. Grease a 13" × 9" baking dish.
2. In a large bowl, beat together the eggs and egg whites. Stir in the zucchini, mozzarella, onions, Parmesan, flour, dill, and baking powder.
3. Spoon the mixture into the prepared dish. Bake for 30 to 35 minutes, or until a wooden pick inserted into the center comes out clean. Cool in the pan for 5 minutes. Cut into 24 squares. Serve warm or cold.

Makes 8 servings

Sun-Dried Tomato Zucchini Bites: Place 8 dry-pack sun-dried tomatoes in a cup or small bowl. Cover with boiling water and let soak for about 5 minutes, or until softened. Finely chop and stir into the zucchini mixture. In addition, substitute fresh basil for the dill.

Sizzling Jumbo Shrimp

Hands-On Time: 20 minutes ■ Total Time: 40 minutes

These spicy Cajun-flavored shrimp are so much more interesting than shrimp cocktail. Be sure to offer wooden picks for spearing and then dipping the shrimp in the sauce.

Shrimp

- 16 jumbo shrimp, peeled and deveined
- 2½ teaspoons olive oil
- 2 teaspoons Cajun seasoning

Cilantro-Lime Sauce

- 1 cup packed fresh cilantro leaves
- 1 cup packed fresh parsley leaves
- ½ cup sour cream
- Juice of 1 lime
- 2 cloves garlic, minced
- 1 tablespoon seeded and chopped jalapeño pepper (wear plastic gloves when handling)

1. Preheat the oven to 375°F.
2. *To marinate the shrimp:* Place the shrimp in an 8" × 8" baking dish. Add the oil and seasoning and toss to mix. Let sit at room temperature for 15 minutes.
3. *Meanwhile, to make the sauce:* In a food processor, combine the cilantro, parsley, sour cream, lime juice, garlic, and jalapeño pepper. Process until puréed. Transfer to a serving dish.
4. Bake the shrimp for 10 minutes, or until opaque. Transfer to a serving platter. Serve with the cilantro-lime sauce.

Makes 16 shrimp

Variation

Sizzling Shrimp Pasta Salad: Use leftover shrimp and sauce to create a refreshing luncheon salad. In a large bowl, combine 2½ cups cooked, cooled pasta (such as penne or shells); 5 of the shrimp, halved lengthwise; 1 cup cooked fresh or frozen broccoli florets; ½ red bell pepper, cut into strips; and ½ cup cilantro-lime sauce. Toss to mix. Makes 2 servings.

Spinach and Feta Stuffed Mushrooms

Hands-On Time: 35 minutes ■ Total Time: 55 minutes

Stuffed mushrooms are perennial favorites in Greece and on the American party scene—and rightly so. They are a perfect finger food and can accommodate a wide variety of stuffings. This version includes spinach and tangy feta cheese.

- 2 pounds fresh spinach
- 16 large mushrooms
- 1 large onion, finely chopped
- 1 tablespoon minced garlic
- 2 tablespoons chicken broth
- ¼ cup crumbled feta cheese
- 1 cup fresh bread crumbs
- 2 teaspoons olive oil, plus additional for brushing

1. Preheat the oven to 400°F. Remove the thick stems from the spinach and coarsely chop the large leaves. Shake off any excess water and set the spinach aside in a colander to drain.
2. Carefully remove the stems from the mushrooms. Finely chop the stems and set aside. Place the caps, stemmed side up, on a baking sheet and set aside.
3. In a large nonstick skillet, combine the reserved mushroom stems, onion, garlic, and broth. Cook over medium heat, stirring frequently, for 5 minutes. Reduce the heat to low and add the reserved spinach. Cover and cook for 2 minutes, or until the spinach is wilted.
4. Transfer the mixture to a large strainer and press with the back of a spoon to remove the excess liquid. Transfer to a medium bowl and set aside to cool. Stir in the cheese.
5. Wipe out the skillet with paper towels. Add the bread crumbs and the 2 teaspoons oil. Cook over medium heat, stirring frequently, for about 8 minutes, or until the crumbs are lightly browned. Transfer the crumbs to the bowl with the spinach mixture and stir to combine.
6. Brush the mushroom caps with a little oil inside and out, then fill each cap with the spinach mixture. Bake for 15 to 20 minutes, or until the mushroom caps are softened and the filling is heated through.

Makes 16 stuffed mushrooms

Make-Ahead

You can prepare the fresh bread crumbs ahead of time. Tear 4 or 5 slices of fresh or slightly stale bread into pieces. Place in a blender or food processor and pulse until crumbs form. Store in a covered container until ready to use. You can also prepare the filling and stuff the mushrooms several hours ahead.

Greek Dolmades

Hands-On Time: 55 minutes ■ Total Time: 2 hours (plus chilling)

These rice-stuffed grape leaves are best made a day ahead so the flavors have time to blend.

- 1 jar (16 ounces) grape leaves, rinsed
- 1¼ cups white rice
- 3½ cups reduced-sodium chicken broth
- 5 tablespoons extra-virgin olive oil
- 1 onion, finely chopped
- ½ cup finely chopped fresh parsley
- ½ cup fresh lemon juice
- 2 tablespoons finely chopped fresh dill
- 1 clove garlic, minced
- Salt
- Ground black pepper

1. Using a knife, remove and discard the stems from the grape leaves. Set aside.
2. In a medium saucepan, combine the rice and broth. Bring to a boil. Reduce the heat to low, cover, and simmer for 20 to 25 minutes, or until the liquid is absorbed. Set aside.
3. In a medium nonstick skillet, heat 1 tablespoon of the oil over medium heat. Add the onion and cook, stirring, for 5 to 8 minutes, or until softened but not browned. Stir in the parsley, ¼ cup of the lemon juice, the dill, and garlic.
4. Stir the onion mixture into the rice. Season with salt and pepper to taste.
5. Preheat the oven to 350°F.
6. On a flat surface, place 1 grape leaf, smooth side down, with the stem end toward you. Using a spoon, place about 1½ tablespoons of the rice mixture on the leaf 1" from the stem end. Shape the mixture into a cylinder. Fold the stem end over the filling. Roll over once, then fold in the sides and roll up to enclose the filling. Place in a 13" × 9" glass or ceramic baking dish. Repeat with the remaining grape leaves and rice mixture.
7. Drizzle the bundles with the remaining 4 tablespoons oil and ¼ cup lemon juice. Cover with foil and bake for 30 minutes.
8. Let cool for 10 minutes. Refrigerate for at least 4 hours, basting occasionally with the liquid. Serve chilled.

Makes 30 dolmades

Cajun-Roasted Chickpeas

Hands-On Time: 5 minutes ■ Total Time: 40 minutes

These addictive nibbles can be made ahead and left out at room temperature for unexpected guests or snack attacks.

1 can (15 ounces) chickpeas, rinsed and drained

1 tablespoon olive oil

1½ teaspoons Cajun seasoning

1. Preheat the oven to 400°F.
2. In a medium bowl, toss the chickpeas with the oil and seasoning. Spread in a single layer on a baking sheet. Bake, shaking occasionally, for about 35 minutes, or until golden. Let cool before serving.

Makes 8 servings

Make-Ahead

You can roast the chickpeas up to 3 days in advance. Store in a covered container at room temperature.

Kitchen Tip

You can make a double batch of these tasty little morsels so no one goes without: Simply double the ingredients and bake on two large baking sheets.

Nutri-Note

Chickpeas make for a wonderful nutritious, filling snack. They are low in saturated fat; bursting with fiber; and a good source of protein, folate, and manganese.

Tortellini and Vegetable Kebabs

Hands-On Time: 20 minutes ■ Total Time: 45 minutes

Make these innovative appetizer kebabs party-pretty by alternating different-colored tortellini. Serve additional prepared pesto on the side for dipping, if you like.

- 36 colored cheese-filled tortellini
- ⅓ cup prepared pesto
- 1 tablespoon red wine vinegar
- 1 medium yellow, red, or green bell pepper, cut into 24 pieces
- 12 small white mushrooms, halved
- 12 small red and/or yellow cherry or grape tomatoes

1. Cook the tortellini in a large pot of boiling water according to package directions. Drain and set aside.
2. In a small bowl, combine the pesto and vinegar. Stir well.
3. Alternate the reserved tortellini, pepper, and mushrooms on 12 wooden skewers. Place a tomato on the end of each skewer.
4. Place the skewers on a serving platter. Drizzle the pesto mixture over the kebabs and serve.

Makes 12 servings

Ingredients Note

Look for pear tomatoes, grape tomatoes, and currant tomatoes at good supermarkets and farmers' markets. There are also wonderful-tasting heirloom cherry tomatoes available at many markets.

Kitchen Tip

If you have leftover pesto, it's easy to freeze it for another day: Spoon the pesto into ice cube trays and freeze until solid, then transfer the cubes to a resealable plastic bag and store in the freezer.

Onion and Tomato Quesadillas

Hands-On Time: 30 minutes ■ Total Time: 35 minutes

Traditional Mexican "sandwiches," quesadillas are fun and easy to serve to a crowd. If you don't want to turn on the broiler on a hot summer day, it's easy enough to finish the quesadillas in the microwave oven.

- 2 teaspoons vegetable oil
- 2 medium onions, sliced
- 1 cup chopped tomatoes
- ⅓ cup chopped fresh cilantro or parsley
- 2 tablespoons seeded and chopped jalapeño peppers (wear plastic gloves when handling)
- 8 flour tortillas (12" diameter)
- ¾ cup shredded Monterey Jack cheese

1. Preheat the broiler.
2. In a medium skillet, heat the oil over medium-high heat. Add the onions and cook, stirring, for about 8 minutes, or until very soft and golden brown. Add the tomatoes, cilantro, and peppers and cook, stirring, for 5 minutes.
3. Place 4 tortillas on a large baking sheet. Divide the onion mixture among them. Top with the cheese and then the remaining 4 tortillas.
4. Broil the quesadillas until the cheese melts. (Or place each quesadilla on a microwaveable plate and microwave on high power for 1 minute, or until the cheese melts.) Cut into wedges to serve.

Makes 16 servings

Kitchen Tip

To make shredding soft cheese such as Monterey Jack easier, put the block of cheese in the freezer for about 10 minutes to firm it up slightly.

Quick-Pickled Vegetable Appetizer

Hands-On Time: 15 minutes ■ Total Time: 15 minutes (plus standing and marinating)

Japanese cooks serve homemade pickles as traditional appetizers; it's an interesting way to add variety to family and company meals. We like the colorful combination of radishes, cucumbers, and carrots, but you can substitute any crisp vegetables. You can easily double or triple the recipe.

- 1 cup sliced radishes
- ½ cup peeled and sliced cucumber
- ½ cup diagonally sliced carrot
- ½ teaspoon salt
- 6 tablespoons water
- 2 tablespoons cider vinegar
- 4 lettuce leaves

1. In a medium bowl, toss together the radishes, cucumber, carrot, and salt. Let stand at room temperature for 2 hours. Place the vegetables in a colander and press gently to drain off any liquid. Return the vegetables to the bowl.
2. In a small saucepan, bring the water and vinegar to a boil. Remove from the heat and let cool.
3. Pour the vinegar mixture over the vegetables and toss well. Cover and refrigerate for 24 hours.
4. Serve the pickled vegetables on the lettuce leaves.

Makes 4 servings

Ingredients Note

You can use any large-leaf lettuce to line the serving plate; Bibb, Boston, and romaine are good choices. If you use a tender lettuce, such as Bibb or Boston, the dish can be fun finger food: Encourage guests to wrap a leaf around some of the vegetables and then enjoy the healthy "veggie wrap."

Appetizers That Let You Attend Your Own Party

The following five master appetizer ideas are as quick and easy as they are bright and delicious. Plus they're suitable for entertaining any time of year. Mix and match to create your own favorite combinations; and if you use the variations, you can create 20 different appetizers! Each makes about 8 servings.

Hot-Pepper Olives. Toss 1 pint assorted olives (pitted or unpitted) with 1 tablespoon extra-virgin olive oil, 1 minced garlic clove, and ½ teaspoon red pepper flakes. Variations: Use green olives and add ½ cup chopped roasted peppers and ¼ cup small capers. Or use kalamata olives and add ½ cup chopped toasted walnuts and 1 minced garlic clove. You can also use mixed olives and add 1 cup chopped preserved lemon and ¼ cup chopped fresh parsley.

Lemon Cheese. Mix ½ pound farmer cheese, 1 tablespoon fresh lemon juice, 1 tablespoon lemon zest, and 1 teaspoon sugar. Serve on pumpernickel bread with some of the Hot-Pepper Olives, above, if you have them. Variations: Replace the lemon juice with balsamic vinegar and replace the lemon zest with 1 teaspoon cracked peppercorns. Or replace the lemon juice with wine vinegar and replace the lemon zest with 1 minced garlic clove.

Roasted Peppers Four Ways. Toss the sliced, roasted peppers from a 12-ounce jar with 4 ounces fresh mozzarella cut into fingers, 2 tablespoons chopped fresh basil, 1 minced garlic clove, and

1 tablespoon extra-virgin olive oil. Variations: Toss the peppers with 1 cup pitted black olives and 2 teaspoons chopped fresh oregano. Or toss them with 2 tablespoons orange zest, 1 minced garlic clove, and ¼ cup chopped toasted hazelnuts. Or toss them with 6 ounces slivered, smoked ham and 2 tablespoons capers.

Prosciutto. Paper-thin slices of prosciutto di Parma make an elegant appetizer that requires no work and no time (ask the store to slice it for you). Plan ½ pound prosciutto for 15 to 20 portions. You can also serve prosciutto with bread. It is even better with about ½ cup shaved Parmesan cheese, and better still surrounded by bunches of grapes, melon slices, or halved fresh figs. You can continue to gild the piggy with ¼ cup chopped toasted nuts (hazelnuts are wonderful), ¼ cup chopped fresh mint leaves, or 4 to 6 ounces high-quality candied fruit cut into slivers.

Marinated Shrimp. Heat 3 cups water, the juice of ½ lemon, and ¼ teaspoon *each* salt and ground black pepper to boiling. Add 1 pound peeled and cleaned large shrimp. Stir until the shrimp begin to turn pink, about 1 minute. Remove from the heat, cover, and set aside for 30 seconds. Drain. While the shrimp are still warm, toss them with 1 cup Italian salad dressing and chill. Serve with wooden picks for spearing. Variations: Add 2 tablespoons Dijon mustard, 2 minced garlic cloves, and/or ¼ cup chopped fresh parsley.

Potato Skins

Hands-On Time: 20 minutes ■ Total Time: 1 hour 50 minutes

You can easily double or triple this recipe for a crowd.

2 baking potatoes
3 slices bacon
¼ teaspoon onion salt or garlic salt
¼ teaspoon ground black pepper
⅓ cup shredded Cheddar cheese
2 tablespoons snipped chives
1 cup sour cream

1. Preheat the oven to 400°F.
2. Wash and scrub the potatoes and pat dry. Prick with a fork. Place the potatoes on a baking sheet and bake for 60 to 70 minutes, or until tender. Leave the oven on. Let the potatoes stand at room temperature until cool enough to handle.
3. Meanwhile, in a medium skillet, cook the bacon over medium-high heat until crisp. Transfer to paper towels to cool, and then crumble.
4. Cut each potato in half and scoop out the flesh, leaving a shell about ⅛" thick (if you leave too much potato in the shell, the skins will not crisp). Reserve the flesh for another use. Cut each half lengthwise into 3 wedges. Coat each wedge completely with cooking spray, then sprinkle lightly with the onion salt and pepper.
5. Place the strips on a large baking sheet and bake for 15 to 20 minutes, or until the skins are crisp. Sprinkle evenly with the cheese and crumbled bacon and bake for 2 to 3 minutes longer, or until the cheese is melted and the bacon is warmed.
6. Just before serving, sprinkle the potato skins with the chives. Serve warm with the sour cream.

Makes 4 servings

Make-Ahead

Bake the potatoes up to 1 day ahead, then scoop out and prepare the skins just before the guests arrive.

Artichoke and Leek Pizzas

Hands-On Time: 25 minutes ■ Total Time: 35 minutes

Native to the Mediterranean countries, leeks have been prized by cooks for centuries. This recipe blends their mellow flavor with another Mediterranean favorite, artichoke hearts.

1 slice bacon, chopped

½ onion, finely chopped

1 can (14 ounces) artichoke hearts, drained and coarsely chopped

1 large leek, thinly sliced

Salt

Ground black pepper

1 pound fresh pizza dough or homemade (see Kitchen Tip)

¼ cup shredded mozzarella cheese

2 tablespoons grated Parmesan cheese

1. Preheat the oven to 500°F. Grease a large baking sheet.
2. In a large skillet, cook the bacon over medium heat for about 3 minutes, or until golden. Drain on paper towels.
3. Discard any excess fat from the skillet. Add the onion to the skillet and cook, stirring, for about 3 minutes, or until softened but not brown. Stir in the bacon, artichokes, and leek. Season with the salt and pepper.
4. Divide the dough into 4 pieces. Form each piece into a 6" round and place on the prepared sheet. Top with the artichoke mixture and sprinkle with the mozzarella and Parmesan.
5. Bake the pizzas for 10 minutes, or until the bottoms are crisp and brown.

Makes 4 individual pizzas

Kitchen Tip

To make pizza dough: In a food processor, combine 1¾ cups all-purpose flour, 1 tablespoon rye flour, 1 tablespoon cornmeal, 1 package quick-rise yeast, ½ teaspoon salt, and ½ teaspoon sugar. With the motor running, add ¾ cup warm water (about 125°F) and 1½ teaspoons olive oil. Process until a ball forms, then process for 1 minute to knead. Let rest for 10 minutes.

Appetizer Potato Pancakes

Hands-On Time: 30 minutes ■ Total Time: 30 minutes

These earthy delights are traditional Jewish comfort food. Top with sour cream spiked with prepared horseradish. For brunch, try applesauce or strawberry jam.

- 2 large baking potatoes, scrubbed and shredded
- 1 large egg
- 1 tablespoon all-purpose flour
- 1 tablespoon finely chopped onion
- ½ teaspoon baking powder
- ⅛ teaspoon salt
- Pinch of ground black pepper
- 2 tablespoons vegetable oil, plus additional if needed

1. In a medium bowl, stir together the potatoes, egg, flour, onion, baking powder, salt, and pepper.
2. In a large skillet, heat 1 tablespoon of the oil over medium heat. Carefully drop half of the potato mixture by tablespoons into the skillet. Fry on both sides for about 5 minutes per side, or until golden brown. Remove and drain on paper towels.
3. Repeat with the remaining 1 tablespoon oil and potato mixture.

Makes 10 servings

Kitchen Tip

You can shred the potatoes by hand or in a food processor.

Make-Ahead

Fry the pancakes and freeze them separated by pieces of foil. To serve, preheat the oven to 350°F. Wrap a single layer of pancakes in foil. Bake for 20 minutes, or until crisp.

Layered Bean Dip

Hands-On Time: 5 minutes ■ Total Time: 25 minutes

Layers of black beans, refried beans, salsa, and cheese mingle together for delicious Tex-Mex flavor in this great party dip.

- 1 can (14 to 19 ounces) refried beans
- 1 can (14 to 19 ounces) black beans, rinsed and drained
- ½ cup sour cream
- 1 cup prepared salsa
- ½ cup shredded Mexican blend or Cheddar cheese
- Chopped fresh cilantro (optional)

1. Preheat the oven to 375°F.
2. In an 8" × 8" baking dish, combine the refried beans and black beans. Spread to cover the bottom of the dish. Spread the sour cream over the beans. Top with the salsa and cheese.
3. Cover and bake for 20 minutes, or until hot and bubbly. Garnish with the cilantro, if using.

Makes 2½ cups

Accompaniment

Serve with pita chips or baked tortilla chips.

Variation

To make this a low-cal dip, use fat-free refried beans, reduced-fat sour cream, and reduced-fat cheese.

Ingredients Note

Preshredded cheese is a great time-saver for busy cooks. You can find bags of shredded cheese in the dairy case of larger supermarkets. If you'd like to shred your own, use Cheddar, or a combination of Cheddar, colby, and/or Monterey Jack.

Vegetable Medley with Creamy Curry Dip

Hands-On Time: 15 minutes ■ Total Time: 25 minutes

This colorful appetizer platter is a great example of how frozen veggies can be your best friend when planning a party.

Vegetables

- 1 package (10 ounces) frozen broccoli florets, thawed
- 1 package (10 ounces) frozen sliced carrots, thawed
- 8 radishes, thinly sliced
- 1 celeriac, peeled and thinly sliced

Dip

- 1 cup ricotta cheese
- ¼ cup sliced scallions
- 2 teaspoons mango chutney
- ½ teaspoon curry powder

1. *To make the vegetables:* Bring a large pot of water to a boil over medium-high heat. Add the broccoli and carrots. Cook for 30 seconds, or until the broccoli is bright green. Drain in a colander and rinse under cold water. Pat dry with paper towels. Arrange on a serving platter, leaving space in the center for the dip bowl. Surround with the radishes and celeriac.
2. *To make the dip:* In a blender or food processor, process the ricotta until smooth, scraping down the container as needed. Transfer to a serving bowl. Add the scallions, chutney, and curry powder and stir well to combine.

Makes 4 servings

Ingredients Note

Celeriac, also know as celery root, is a knobby, brown root vegetable with a pleasant crunch and a flavor that tastes like a cross between celery and parsley. Look for celeriac in your supermarket and choose firm, unblemished specimens. To prevent sliced celeriac from browning, soak the slices briefly in a bowl of cold water mixed with 2 tablespoons vinegar.

Make-Ahead

The dip can be made ahead and frozen for up to 2 months. Thaw it overnight in the refrigerator and process briefly in a blender before serving.

Tomato-Basil Tartlets

Hands-On Time: 25 minutes ■ Total Time: 40 minutes

Savory tartlets are a lovely way to begin a dinner party. These feature a creamy filling flavored with sun-dried tomatoes and fresh basil.

- 4 tablespoons unsalted butter, melted, plus additional for the pan
- 4 sheets (17" × 11") frozen phyllo dough, thawed
- ¾ cup cottage cheese
- 3 tablespoons crumbled goat cheese or feta cheese
- 1 large egg
- ¼ cup (1½ ounces) oil-packed sun-dried tomatoes, chopped
- 1 scallion, minced
- 2 tablespoons chopped fresh basil
- 2 cloves garlic, minced
- Cherry tomatoes and basil sprigs (optional)

1. Preheat the oven to 375°F. Grease 12 mini-muffin-tin cups lightly with butter.
2. Place 1 phyllo sheet on a work surface. Brush with melted butter. Top with 3 more sheets, brushing each with butter.
3. Cut the sheets into thirds lengthwise and then into quarters crosswise to get 12 approximate squares. Press each square into a muffin-tin cup to form a shell with jagged edges.
4. Bake the tart shells for 5 to 7 minutes, or until golden.
5. Meanwhile, in a food processor, combine the cottage cheese, goat cheese, and egg. Process until smooth. Add the sun-dried tomatoes, scallion, basil, and garlic. Pulse briefly to mix.
6. Spoon the tomato-basil mixture into the tart shells. Bake for 5 to 7 minutes, or until the filling is heated through. Serve on individual plates decorated with cherry tomatoes and basil sprigs, if you like.

Makes 12 tartlets

Make-Ahead

The tartlet shells can be made ahead and stored in an airtight container for up to 2 days before filling and baking. Or look for prepared phyllo tart shells in the freezer section of your supermarket.

White Bean and Roasted Garlic Spread

Hands-On Time: 25 minutes ■ Total Time: 40 minutes

The sweet, nutty flavor of roasted garlic is a natural companion to creamy white beans.

- 1 head garlic
- 2 cans (19 ounces each) white beans, rinsed and drained
- ¼ cup fresh lemon juice
- 1 tablespoon olive oil
- 4 tablespoons finely chopped red onion
- 4 tablespoons finely chopped green bell pepper
- 2 tablespoons finely chopped fresh parsley
- ¼ teaspoon ground black pepper

1. Preheat the oven to 400°F. Break the garlic head into cloves. Place the unpeeled cloves in a custard cup and cover with foil. Roast for 15 minutes, or until soft when tested with the tip of a knife. Do not allow the garlic to brown. Let cool slightly, then slip off the skins and trim off the hard stem ends.
2. In a food processor, combine the garlic, 1 can of the beans, the lemon juice, and oil. Process until smooth. Transfer to a medium bowl. Stir in the remaining 1 can beans along with 2 tablespoons of the onion, 2 tablespoons of the green pepper, the parsley, and black pepper. Roughly mash the whole beans with a fork.
3. Transfer the spread to a serving bowl and sprinkle with the remaining 2 tablespoons onion and 2 tablespoons green pepper.

Makes 3 cups

Accompaniments

Serve this flavorful mixture as a spread on toast triangles or crackers. Or use it as a stuffing for celery pieces, hollowed-out cherry tomatoes, or Belgian endive leaves.

Spinach Dip

Hands-On Time: 15 minutes ■ Total Time: 45 minutes

This recipe is particularly easy, but do allow at least 30 minutes for the yogurt to drain so the dip will be nice and thick. If you're not fond of lots of garlic, use only 1 or 2 cloves.

- 2 cups plain yogurt
- 1 tablespoon olive oil
- 4 cloves garlic, minced
- 1 cup packed fresh spinach, finely chopped
- ¼ teaspoon fresh lemon juice
- ⅛ teaspoon ground black pepper

1. Spoon the yogurt into a sieve lined with cheesecloth or a yogurt-cheese funnel. Place over a bowl and let drain for 30 minutes.
2. In a large skillet, heat the oil over medium heat. Add the garlic and cook, stirring constantly, for 1 minute. Add the spinach. Cook, stirring, for 2 minutes, or until wilted. Remove from the heat.
3. Stir the yogurt, lemon juice, and pepper into the spinach. Transfer to a shallow serving dish.

Makes 8 servings

Kitchen Tip

To make this a low-fat dip and cut down on the calories, use fat-free yogurt.

Accompaniments

Serve this dip with fresh vegetables such as baby carrots, celery sticks, fennel slices, bell pepper slices, blanched sugar snap peas, and/or mushrooms.

Tangy Lime Dip with Fresh Fruit

Hands-On Time: 10 minutes ■ Total Time: 10 minutes

Fresh fruit makes a lovely appetizer. Here we serve it with a creamy sweet-tart dressing. Feel free to substitute whatever fruit you like that is in season.

- 1 or 2 large limes
- ¼ cup sour cream
- ¼ cup vanilla yogurt
- 2 tablespoons honey
- Fresh fruit, such as cherries, grapes, peaches, plums, and strawberries

1. Grate the zest, avoiding the white pith, from 1 lime. Squeeze enough juice from the zested lime and the other lime, if necessary, to make 3 tablespoons.
2. In a small bowl, whisk together the lime zest, lime juice, sour cream, yogurt, and honey. Place the dip on a platter with your favorite fresh fruits.

Makes 4 servings

Kitchen Tip

Be sure to remove the zest from the lime before squeezing the juice, or squeezing will be a nearly impossible task. Special zesting tools, such as the Microplane grater, are perfect for this job. A medium lime will give about 2 teaspoons of zest, which is just right for this recipe. To get the maximum juice from limes, bring them to room temperature and roll them under your palm to soften the fruit and get the juices flowing.

Ingredients Note

For a supercreamy dip, use plain Greek yogurt, which is now available at many grocery stores. Add a touch of vanilla extract (or not) as desired. Even the fat-free version of Greek yogurt tastes rich!

Sassy Salsa

Hands-On Time: 15 minutes ■ Total Time: 30 minutes

Pickled jalapeño peppers add a slight kick to this versatile salsa. Don't be afraid to add more jalapeños if you like the heat.

- 5 tomatoes, seeded and finely chopped
- 1 small red onion, finely chopped
- ½ cup canned Mandarin orange segments
- ¼ cup thinly sliced celery
- 2 tablespoons chopped green olives
- 1 teaspoon olive oil
- Salt
- 1 lime, halved
- 1 or 2 small pickled jalapeño peppers, chopped (wear plastic gloves when handling)

1. In a large bowl, combine the tomatoes, onion, orange segments, celery, olives, oil, and salt to taste.

2. Squeeze the juice from the lime halves over the top. Add the jalapeño peppers and stir to combine. Cover and let stand for 15 minutes.

Makes 4 cups

Accompaniments

Serve this easy salsa with tortilla chips or toasted pita wedges. For superfast nachos, spoon the salsa over a plate of large restaurant-style tortilla chips, top with grated Jack cheese, and microwave on high for 2 to 3 minutes. The salsa is also good with simple grilled or broiled fish.

Satisfying Soups

Tomato-Orange Soup

Hands-On Time: 10 minutes ■ Total Time: 30 minutes (plus chilling)

Make this delightful cold soup during the dog days of summer. It comes together quickly and can be made ahead.

- 1 teaspoon olive oil
- ½ cup chopped onion
- 1 can (14½ ounces) diced tomatoes
- 1 tablespoon quick-cooking tapioca
- 1¼ cups vegetable broth
- 1 cup water
- ¼ cup orange juice
- ¼ cup 1% milk
- Salt
- Ground black pepper

1. In a large saucepan, heat the oil over medium-high heat. Add the onion and cook, stirring, for about 20 minutes, or until soft. Add the tomatoes, tapioca, and ¾ cup of the broth. Reduce the heat and simmer for about 20 minutes, or until the soup begins to thicken.
2. Transfer the soup to a blender and purée. Add the water, orange juice, milk, and remaining ½ cup broth. Process to blend. Add salt and pepper to taste. Chill before serving.

Makes 4 servings

Ingredients Note

Tapioca is a starch from the root of the cassava plant. The quick-cooking variety is commonly used as a thickener in soups, sauces, and pie fillings. You can find tapioca in the supermarket near the pudding mixes or in the baking section.

Cucumber-Yogurt Soup

Hands-On Time: 15 minutes ■ Total Time: 15 minutes (plus chilling)

This refreshing chilled soup is perfect with a sandwich for a summer lunch. It's supereasy to make, but be sure to plan ahead because it needs to refrigerate for at least 4 hours.

- 2 cups plain yogurt
- 1 cup milk
- 2 large cucumbers, peeled, seeded, and coarsely shredded
- 2 tablespoons lemon juice
- 2 small cloves garlic, minced
- ¼ teaspoon salt

In a medium bowl, stir together the yogurt, milk, cucumbers, lemon juice, garlic, and salt. Cover and refrigerate for 4 to 8 hours to blend the flavors.

Makes 4 servings

Kitchen Tip

Shred the cucumber in a food processor using the shredding disk, or grate it with a coarse grater.

Variations

For a low-fat version, use fat-free yogurt and fat-free milk. For added flavor, stir a small amount of finely chopped scallions, chives, dill, or mint into the chilled soup.

Cream of Winter Squash Soup

Hands-On Time: 30 minutes ■ Total Time: 50 minutes

This vivid soup, with a dash of curry, makes delicious use of hard-shell squash such as butternut and buttercup, both excellent sources of vitamin A.

- 1½ tablespoons unsalted butter
- 1 medium onion, thinly sliced and separated into rings
- 1 small butternut or buttercup squash, peeled, seeded, and coarsely chopped
- 1 can (14½ ounces) chicken broth
- ½ cup cider or apple juice
- ½ cup milk
- Pinch of curry powder
- Pinch of ground black pepper
- Finely chopped fresh parsley

1. In a large nonstick saucepan, melt the butter over medium heat. Add the onion and cook, stirring, for about 5 minutes, or until lightly browned.
2. Add the squash, broth, and cider. Increase the heat to high and bring to a boil. Reduce the heat to low, cover, and simmer for 20 minutes, or until the squash is very tender.
3. In small batches, transfer to a blender or food processor and blend until smooth. Return the puréed soup to the pan.
4. Stir in the milk, curry powder, and pepper. Cook over medium heat, stirring, until heated through. Serve sprinkled with parsley.

Makes 4 servings

Kitchen Tip

To easily peel butternut squash, prick the whole squash several times with a fork and warm in a microwave oven on high power for about 2 minutes, or until the skin is more tender. Slice off the two ends and cut the squash in half near the center, where the neck meets the bulb. Place each half on its widest cut side, and use a thin knife or vegetable peeler to remove the peel in strips running from top to bottom.

Spanish Leek and Potato Soup

Hands-On Time: 40 minutes ■ Total Time: 1 hour 45 minutes

Saffron gives traditional potato-leek soup a distinctly Spanish flavor and lovely golden hue.

- ½ teaspoon saffron threads
- 6 cups chicken broth, heated
- 6 tablespoons unsalted butter
- 6 thin leeks (white part only), thinly sliced
- 1 large onion, finely chopped
- 4 medium all-purpose potatoes, peeled and diced
- Ground black pepper
- 1 cup heavy cream
- 6 drops hot pepper sauce
- 6 tablespoons finely chopped fresh chives

1. In a small bowl, soak the saffron in 2 tablespoons of the broth for 10 minutes.
2. Melt the butter in a 5-quart soup pot over low heat. Add the leeks and onion and cook, stirring, until wilted. Add the potatoes and toss to coat with the butter. Add the saffron liquid, remaining broth, and pepper to taste. Simmer for 45 minutes. Let cool slightly.
3. In batches, purée the soup in a blender. Return the soup to the pot and stir in the cream and hot pepper sauce. Reheat over medium heat until heated through. Serve hot, topped with the chives.

Makes 6 servings

You can also serve the soup cold for a terrific summer lunch. Transfer to a container and let cool, then refrigerate until chilled. You may need to thin the chilled soup with a little bit of milk or water.

Vegetable and Orzo Soup

Hands-On Time: 25 minutes ■ Total Time: 40 minutes

Orzo is a tiny rice-shaped pasta that is truly at home in hearty soups, such as this bowl of garden vegetables and fresh herbs.

- 2 teaspoons olive oil
- 1 medium onion, chopped
- 1 cup chopped carrots
- 1 cup whole kernel corn
- 1 small zucchini or yellow summer squash, finely chopped
- ⅓ cup balsamic vinegar
- 4 cups chicken broth
- 1 cup orzo
- 1 cup canned navy beans, rinsed and drained
- 2 cloves garlic, minced
- ¼ cup minced fresh parsley
- 1 tablespoon honey or sugar
- ½ teaspoon ground black pepper
- ⅛ teaspoon salt
- ⅓ cup grated Parmesan cheese

1. In a large soup pot, heat the oil over medium-high heat. Add the onion, carrots, corn, and zucchini and cook, stirring, for about 5 minutes, or until the onion is soft but not browned.
2. Stir in the vinegar, then add the broth, orzo, beans, and garlic. Bring to a boil. Reduce the heat to medium and simmer for 15 minutes, or until the pasta is tender.
3. Add the parsley, honey, pepper, and salt. Stir well to combine. Sprinkle each serving with cheese.

Makes 4 to 6 servings

Freezing Tip

To freeze, pack the cooled soup in a freezer-quality plastic container. To use, thaw overnight in the refrigerator. Transfer to a saucepan, cover, and reheat over low heat, stirring frequently, for about 15 minutes, or until heated through. Add the cheese after reheating.

Mushroom-Barley Soup

Hands-On Time: 30 minutes ■ Total Time: 55 minutes

A light meal in itself, this soup also makes a good partner for sandwiches, such as turkey breast on peasant bread with honey-mustard and romaine lettuce. Offer apples and Gingerbread Cookies (page 326) for dessert. For a touch of richness, top each portion of soup with a spoonful of plain yogurt or sour cream.

- 1 ounce dried mushrooms, such as porcini
- 1 cup boiling water
- 2 teaspoons olive oil
- 12 ounces fresh mushrooms, sliced (about 4 cups)
- 1 medium onion, chopped
- ¾ cup thinly sliced carrots
- ⅓ cup thinly sliced shallots or scallions (white parts only)
- 2 cloves garlic, minced
- 1¾ cups beef broth
- ⅓ cup quick-cooking barley (1½ ounces)
- 1 bay leaf
- ¼ teaspoon ground black pepper
- 1 tablespoon snipped fresh dill

1. In a medium heatproof bowl, combine the dried mushrooms and boiling water. Set aside for about 5 minutes, or until the mushrooms have softened.
2. Using a slotted spoon, lift the mushrooms from the liquid, reserving the liquid. Set the mushrooms aside to cool. Strain the reserved liquid through a cheesecloth-lined strainer into a small bowl, leaving behind any sediment. Coarsely chop the softened mushrooms.
3. In a large, heavy saucepan, heat the oil over high heat. Add the dried and fresh mushrooms, the onion, carrots, shallots, and garlic. Stir well to coat the vegetables with oil. Reduce the heat to medium-high, cover, and cook, stirring occasionally, for 4 to 5 minutes, or until the fresh mushrooms begin to release their liquid.
4. Stir in the reserved mushroom-soaking liquid, the broth, barley, bay leaf, and pepper. Cover and bring to a boil over high heat. Reduce the heat to medium-low and simmer, covered, for 10 to 15 minutes, or until the barley is tender. Discard the bay leaf. Just before serving, stir in the dill.

Makes 4 servings

Ingredients Note

Barley is wonderful in soups, but you can also cook this flavorful grain as you would rice—steam it, bake it, or prepare it as a pilaf—and serve it as a side dish or main-dish casserole. This recipe uses quick-cooking barley, which cooks in about half the time of regular and does not require soaking.

Corn Chowder with Cheese

Hands-On Time: 40 minutes ■ Total Time: 1 hour 5 minutes

We don't know anyone who doesn't like corn chowder. Adding fresh herbs and sharp Cheddar to the hearty favorite makes it all the better.

- 2½ cups water
- 1 large potato, peeled and cut into ½" cubes
- 1 teaspoon cumin seeds
- ¼ teaspoon dried sage
- 1 bay leaf
- 3 tablespoons unsalted butter
- 1 onion, finely chopped
- 3 tablespoons whole wheat flour
- 1 cup heavy cream, heated
- 2 cups fresh corn kernels (about 2 ears)
- 1 tablespoon finely chopped fresh chives
- 1 tablespoon finely chopped fresh parsley
- 1 teaspoon ground nutmeg
- Ground black pepper
- 1½ cups shredded sharp Cheddar cheese
- ¼ cup fresh lemon juice

1. In a 4-quart soup pot, combine the water, potato, cumin, sage, and bay leaf. Bring to a boil, reduce the heat, and simmer for about 15 minutes, or until the potato is tender.
2. Meanwhile, in a medium skillet, melt the butter over medium-high heat. Add the onion and cook, stirring, for about 5 minutes, or until translucent. Add the flour and mix well. Stirring with a whisk, add the cream. Cook on low heat for 1 minute.
3. Scrape the onion mixture into the soup pot and stir to mix. Add the corn, chives, parsley, and nutmeg. Season with pepper. Simmer the soup over medium heat for 10 minutes. Stir in the cheese and lemon juice and mix well. Cook until all the cheese is melted.

Makes 4 to 6 servings

Brown Rice and Lentil Soup

Hands-On Time: 20 minutes ■ Total Time: 1 hour 5 minutes

Here's a delicious, hearty, and filling soup, loaded with the goodness of lentils, brown rice, and fresh vegetables. Serve with whole grain bread and a green salad for lunch or a light supper.

- 4½ cups reduced-sodium chicken broth
- ¾ cup lentils, rinsed and drained
- ½ cup brown rice
- 1 can (14½ ounces) diced tomatoes
- 2 small carrots, chopped
- ½ small onion, chopped
- ½ stalk celery, chopped
- 2 small cloves garlic, minced
- ½ teaspoon dried basil
- ½ teaspoon dried oregano
- ½ teaspoon dried thyme
- 1 bay leaf
- ¼ cup finely chopped fresh parsley
- 1 tablespoon cider vinegar
- Ground black pepper

1. In a soup pot over medium-high heat, combine the broth, lentils, rice, tomatoes, carrots, onion, celery, garlic, basil, oregano, thyme, and bay leaf. Bring to a boil and reduce the heat to low. Simmer, covered and stirring occasionally, for 45 minutes.
2. Remove from the heat and add the parsley, vinegar, and pepper to taste. Discard the bay leaf. Adjust the seasonings and serve.

Makes 6 to 8 servings

Ingredients Note

Lentils are small dried legume seeds with a distinctive, earthy flavor. The seeds are in the shape of a lens; indeed, the English word *lens* comes from the word *lentils*. Find lentils near the rice and dried beans in your supermarket.

Homemade Stocks

Making your own stock not only helps you save money but also puts you in control of the sodium and fat content of your soups. In these recipes, we have not added salt or black pepper. You can do this to your taste after straining.

Thrift experts encourage saving any leftover bones or scraps from meat and fish to make great stock. Many butchers also give away beef or lamb bones and other great stock ingredients. Look for free fish heads or fish bones at your fish market. Or save your own shrimp shells for flavorful stock; use them in addition to or in place of the fish bones.

Cook stock in an uncovered Dutch oven or stockpot to allow some of the water to evaporate and the flavors to concentrate.

Each of the following recipes will provide you with about 12 cups of stock. You can save time by cooking a double batch and freezing the extra (see Kitchen Tip on the opposite page).

VEGETABLE STOCK

- 14 cups water
- 4 stalks celery (with leaves), chopped
- 4 carrots, chopped
- 1 cup chopped green cabbage
- 1 cup mushrooms
- 1 onion, chopped
- 12 cloves garlic
- 10 sprigs fresh parsley
- 2 bay leaves

1. In a Dutch oven or stockpot, combine the water, celery, carrots, cabbage, mushrooms, onion, garlic, parsley, and bay leaves. Bring to a boil over medium-high heat. Reduce the heat to medium and cook for 1 hour, or until the stock is golden brown.

2. Strain the stock through a colander, pressing the vegetables lightly to extract their flavors. Discard the solids.

Makes 12 cups

CHICKEN STOCK

- 14 cups water
- 4 pounds chicken pieces (thighs, drumsticks, backs, and necks)
- 2 large carrots, quartered
- 2 small onions, roughly chopped (don't bother to peel)
- 6 cloves garlic
- 2 bay leaves

1. In a Dutch oven or stockpot, combine the water, chicken, carrots, onions, garlic, and bay leaves. Bring to a boil over medium-high heat. Skim the foam from the top and reduce the heat to low. Cook for 2 hours, or until the stock has a rich chicken flavor.

2. Strain the stock through a colander, pressing the ingredients to extract their flavors. Save the chicken for another use and discard the other solids. Refrigerate the stock overnight. Defat by skimming off and discarding any solidified fat before using.

Makes 12 cups

FISH STOCK

- 14 cups water
- 2 pounds fish heads or fish bones
- 2 large carrots, quartered
- 2 small onions, roughly chopped (don't bother to peel)
- 6 cloves garlic
- 2 bay leaves

1. In a Dutch oven or stockpot, combine the water, fish heads, carrots, onions, garlic, and bay leaves. Bring to a boil over medium-high heat. Skim the foam from the top and reduce the heat to low. Cook for 2 hours, or until the stock has a rich fish flavor.

2. Strain the stock through a colander, pressing the ingredients to extract their flavors. Discard the solids. Refrigerate the stock overnight. Defat by skimming off and discarding any solidified fat before using.

Makes 12 cups

BEEF STOCK

- 14 cups water
- 3 to 4 pounds meaty beef bones (such as shank or shin, tail, or short ribs) or 2 pounds chuck meat
- 2 large carrots, quartered
- 2 small onions, roughly chopped (don't bother to peel)
- 2 stalks celery, cut into chunks
- 6 cloves garlic
- 10 sprigs fresh parsley
- 2 bay leaves

1. In a Dutch oven or stockpot, combine the water, beef bones, carrots, onions, celery, garlic, parsley, and bay leaves. Bring to a boil over medium-high heat. Skim the foam from the top and reduce the heat to low. Cook for 2 hours, or until the stock has a rich beef flavor.

2. Strain the stock through a colander, pressing the ingredients to extract their flavors. Discard the solids. Refrigerate the stock overnight. Defat by skimming off and discarding any solidified fat before using.

Makes 12 cups

Kitchen Tip

Freeze stock flat: Pour cooled defatted stock into heavy-duty zip-top freezer bags, leaving a small amount of empty space for expansion. Press out the excess air, seal the bag, and wipe off any moisture on the outside of the bag. Lay the bags on a sheet of wax paper on the freezer floor or on a baking sheet so that they freeze flat. Then stand the bags on edge for space-efficient storage. Stock stored this way also defrosts faster than stock stored in plastic tubs.

Seafood and Vegetable Harvest Chowder

Hands-On Time: 50 minutes ■ Total Time: 1 hour 35 minutes

You won't believe how creamy this chowder is—without the use of the usual half-and-half or heavy cream! That's because milk thickened with a little flour gives it all the rich body you could ask for.

- 3 medium red-skinned potatoes, unpeeled
- 1 pound fresh mussels, washed and debearded
- 1 cup bottled clam juice
- 1 cup water
- 2 teaspoons fresh lemon juice
- 2 teaspoons minced garlic
- 2 tablespoons unsalted butter
- ¼ cup all-purpose flour
- 2 cups milk
- ½ cup finely chopped celery
- ½ cup frozen or canned corn kernels
- ½ cup finely chopped green bell pepper
- ¼ cup finely chopped red bell pepper
- ¼ cup finely chopped carrot
- ¼ pound white fish fillet (such as flounder, cod, or haddock), cut into ½" cubes
- ¼ pound small shrimp, peeled, deveined, and halved
- 1 tablespoon finely chopped fresh parsley
- ¼ teaspoon ground black pepper
- Salt

1. Cook the potatoes in a steamer or in a microwave oven until just tender (do not overcook, or they will be mushy). Remove from the heat, let cool briefly, and finely chop (you should have about 2 cups). Set aside.
2. In a large heavy pot or Dutch oven, combine the mussels, clam juice, water, lemon juice, and garlic. Bring to a boil over medium heat, cover, and cook for about 10 minutes, or until the mussels open.
3. Strain the broth from the mussels and reserve. Remove the mussels from the shells and reserve.
4. Wash and dry the pot. Add the butter and melt over medium heat. Stir in the flour to make a smooth paste. Whisk in the reserved mussel broth (if there is sandy sediment at the bottom of the broth, be careful not to add it). Whisk in the milk. Whisk over medium-low heat for about 5 minutes, or until thickened.
5. Add the celery, corn, green and red bell peppers, and carrot. Cook over medium-low heat for 5 to 10 minutes, or until the vegetables are tender.
6. Add the fish, shrimp, parsley, reserved potatoes, black pepper, and salt to taste. Cook for 4 to 5 minutes, or until the fish is opaque and the shrimp cooked through. Add the mussels and heat briefly.

Makes 4 servings

Use clams instead of mussels.

Miami Black Bean Soup

Hands-On Time: 30 minutes ■ Total Time: 50 minutes

This thick, spicy soup reflects its Caribbean heritage with cumin, red pepper flakes, and jalapeño peppers.

- 1 teaspoon olive oil
- 1½ cups finely chopped onions
- 2 stalks celery, finely chopped
- 2 carrots, finely chopped
- 4 cloves garlic, minced
- 3 cans (15 ounces each) black beans, rinsed and drained
- 2½ cups chicken broth
- 2 cups canned crushed tomatoes
- 1½ tablespoons fresh lime juice
- 1½ teaspoons ground cumin
- ½ teaspoon red pepper flakes
- ⅓ cup sour cream
- ⅓ cup finely chopped red, yellow, or green bell pepper
- 2 tablespoons sliced jalapeño peppers (wear plastic gloves when handling)

1. In a soup pot, heat the oil over medium heat. Add the onions, celery, carrots, and garlic and cook, stirring, for about 4 minutes, or until the vegetables begin to soften. Add the beans, broth, tomatoes, lime juice, cumin, and red pepper flakes. Cover and bring to a boil. Reduce the heat and simmer for 15 to 20 minutes, or until the vegetables are tender.
2. Serve garnished with the sour cream, bell peppers, and jalapeños.

Makes 4 servings

Ingredients Note

You can use either yellow or red onions. You'll need 2 medium red onions or 1 large yellow onion to yield 1½ cups of finely chopped onions.

Chicken Soup with Matzo Balls

Hands-On Time: 30 minutes ■ Total Time: 1 hour 10 minutes

This mild-flavored, ultraeasy soup begins with canned chicken broth and boneless chicken breasts. Even the homemade matzo balls are a snap to make.

- 2 large eggs
- ½ cup matzo meal
- 2 cups reduced-sodium chicken broth
- 1 carrot, chopped
- ½ stalk celery, chopped
- ½ cup chopped onion
- ½ pound boneless, skinless chicken breasts
- 3 tablespoons chopped fresh parsley

1. In a small bowl, beat the eggs with a fork until frothy. Slowly beat in the matzo meal. Cover and refrigerate for at least 10 minutes.
2. In a soup pot, bring the broth to a boil over high heat. Add the carrot, celery, onion, and chicken. Reduce the heat to medium, cover, and cook for about 15 minutes, or until the chicken is cooked through.
3. Remove the chicken with a slotted spoon and set aside until cool enough to handle.
4. Dampen your hands with cold water and roll about 1 tablespoon of the matzo mixture between your palms into a ball. Repeat to make 8 balls.
5. Bring the broth back to a gentle boil. Drop the matzo balls into the pot. Cover and cook for about 10 minutes, or until the balls are cooked through.
6. Cut the chicken into bite-size pieces and return to the pot. Stir in the parsley. Cook for about 3 minutes, or until the chicken is heated through.

Makes 4 servings

Ingredients Note

Matzo meal is ground matzo, the unleavened bread traditionally eaten during the Jewish holiday of Passover. You can usually find matzo and matzo meal in the ethnic or kosher section of larger supermarkets.

Mexican Turkey Meatball Soup

Hands-On Time: 30 minutes ■ Total Time: 50 minutes

Sopa de albóndigas—that's the Mexican term for meatball soup. Here garlic, jalapeño pepper, cilantro, and cumin give the turkey meatballs real Mexican flavor; the corn and avocado garnish are also south-of-the-border touches. Fresh bread crumbs make the meatballs light. On page 6, you'll find directions for making your own fresh bread crumbs.

- 3 cloves garlic, minced
- 1 large fresh jalapeño pepper, seeded and coarsely chopped (wear plastic gloves when handling)
- ¾ pound ground turkey
- 1 cup fresh bread crumbs
- 1 large egg
- ¼ cup chopped fresh cilantro
- 1½ teaspoons ground cumin
- ¼ teaspoon salt
- 1 tablespoon vegetable oil
- 1 medium onion, finely chopped
- 2 medium carrots, thinly sliced
- 2 stalks celery, finely chopped
- 8 ounces medium white mushrooms, sliced
- 1 can (28 ounces) whole Italian tomatoes, drained and coarsely chopped, with juice reserved
- 1½ cups chicken broth
- 1½ cups water
- ½ teaspoon freshly ground black pepper
- 1 cup frozen or canned corn kernels
- ½ medium avocado, finely chopped
- Cilantro leaves (optional)

1. In a large bowl, combine the garlic and jalapeño pepper. Transfer 1 tablespoon of the mixture to a cup.
2. Add the turkey, bread crumbs, egg, chopped cilantro, cumin, and ⅛ teaspoon of the salt to the large bowl and stir well to combine. Shape the mixture into 12 to 16 (1½" to 2") meatballs; set aside.
3. In a large saucepan, heat the oil over medium heat. Add the onion, carrots, celery, and reserved 1 tablespoon garlic mixture. Cover and cook for 4 to 5 minutes, or until the vegetables begin to soften. Stir in the mushrooms, cover, and cook for 2 minutes longer.
4. Stir in the tomatoes and their juice, the broth, water, black pepper, and remaining ⅛ teaspoon salt. Increase the heat to high and bring to a boil. Add the meatballs and return to a boil. Reduce the heat to medium-low, cover, and simmer the soup for 10 minutes.
5. Add the corn, cover, and simmer for 2 minutes longer. Spoon the meatball soup into 4 bowls and top each portion with some of the avocado. Garnish with cilantro leaves, if desired.

Makes 4 servings

Hot-and-Sour Turkey Soup

Hands-On Time: 35 minutes ■ Total Time: 1 hour 10 minutes

In this easy variation of Chinese hot-and-sour soup, ground turkey stands in for the traditional pork and tofu.

Broth

- 3½ cups reduced-sodium chicken broth
- 1 tablespoon coarsely chopped fresh ginger
- 1 clove garlic, peeled
- ½ jalapeño pepper, coarsely chopped (wear plastic gloves when handling)
- ½ teaspoon grated lime zest

Soup

- 1 tablespoon olive oil
- ¾ pound lean ground turkey breast
- ½ medium red bell pepper, chopped
- 1 cup sliced white mushrooms
- 3 scallions, sliced
- ½ jalapeño pepper, seeded and minced
- 1½ teaspoons slivered fresh ginger
- 1 clove garlic, slivered
- 2 tablespoons soy sauce
- 2 tablespoons fish sauce
- 2 tablespoons rice wine vinegar
- 2½ cups water
- 1 cup snow peas
- 1 cup bean sprouts
- Juice of ½ lime
- 1 tablespoon toasted sesame oil

1. *To make the broth:* In a large soup pot, combine the broth, chopped ginger, whole garlic clove, chopped jalapeño pepper, and lime zest. Bring to a boil over medium-high heat. Reduce the heat and simmer for about 15 minutes, or until the flavors are concentrated and the liquid has reduced to about 3 cups. Strain the broth through a sieve into a large bowl and set aside. Discard the solids. Wipe out the pot.
2. *To make the soup:* In the same pot, heat the olive oil over medium heat. Add the turkey and cook, stirring frequently to break the meat into small pieces, for about 5 minutes, or until no longer pink.
3. Add the bell pepper, mushrooms, scallions, and minced jalapeño pepper. Cook for 5 minutes, or until softened. Add the slivered ginger and slivered garlic and cook for 2 minutes. Add the soy sauce, fish sauce, and vinegar and cook for 2 minutes longer.
4. Return the reserved broth to the pot along with the water. Cover and simmer, stirring occasionally, for 30 minutes. Remove from the heat, add the snow peas and bean sprouts, and let stand uncovered for 5 minutes (the vegetables will cook in the hot broth). Stir in the lime juice and sesame oil just before serving.

Makes 6 to 8 servings

Vibrant Chicken-and-Rice Soup

Hands-On Time: 15 minutes ■ Total Time: 40 minutes (plus rice cooking)

Who doesn't love chicken-and-rice soup? Our quick and easy variation has a California flavor: accents of avocado, coriander, and lime juice.

- 4 cups water
- 2 cups chicken broth
- 1 onion, finely chopped
- 3 carrots, thinly sliced
- 3 boneless, skinless chicken breast halves, cubed
- 2½ cups cooked rice
- 1 small avocado, cut into cubes
- 2 tomatoes, chopped
- 3 tablespoons finely chopped fresh cilantro
- 3 tablespoons lime juice
- ⅛ teaspoon ground red pepper
- 4 ounces farmer's cheese, crumbled

1. In a large soup pot over medium heat, bring the water, broth, onion, and carrots to a boil. Reduce the heat and simmer for 10 minutes. Add the chicken and simmer for about 10 minutes, or until the chicken is cooked through and the carrots are tender.
2. Stir in the rice, avocado, tomatoes, cilantro, lime juice, and ground red pepper. Heat through but do not boil. Serve sprinkled with the cheese.

Makes 6 servings

Ingredients Note

Farmer's cheese is cottage cheese that has had most of the liquid removed. It is firm and dry with a slightly tangy taste.

Spicy Chicken-Tortilla Soup

Hands-On Time: 25 minutes ■ Total Time: 45 minutes

This slightly spicy chicken soup is just the ticket on a chilly night. Pass the bottle of hot sauce at the table in case your guests want a little more heat.

- 1 can (14½ ounces) diced tomatoes
- 2 teaspoons Worcestershire sauce
- 1½ teaspoons chili powder
- 1½ teaspoons ground cumin
- ½ teaspoon hot pepper sauce
- ¼ teaspoon ground black pepper
- 2 teaspoons olive oil
- 1 pound boneless, skinless chicken breasts, cut into 1" pieces
- 1 medium onion, chopped
- 1 or 2 jalapeño peppers, chopped (wear plastic gloves when handling)
- 2 cloves garlic, minced
- 2 cans (14½ ounces each) reduced-sodium chicken broth
- ¼ cup all-purpose flour
- ½ cup water
- ⅓ cup sour cream
- ⅓ cup chopped fresh cilantro
- 4 ounces tortilla chips, crushed

1. In a food processor or blender, combine the tomatoes, Worcestershire sauce, chili powder, cumin, hot pepper sauce, and pepper. Process to a smooth, thick consistency; set aside.
2. In a large soup pot, heat the oil over medium-high heat. Add the chicken, onion, jalapeño peppers, and garlic. Cook, stirring frequently, for 5 minutes, or until the chicken is no longer pink and the onion is softened. Reduce the heat to low and add the reserved tomato mixture and broth. Simmer for 15 minutes.
3. In a small bowl, whisk together the flour and water until a smooth paste forms. Stir into the soup and raise the temperature if necessary to keep the soup just barely boiling. Simmer, stirring occasionally, for 5 minutes.
4. Remove the soup from the heat and stir in the sour cream until well blended. Stir in the cilantro. Garnish with the tortilla chips and serve.

Makes 8 servings

Sensational Salads

White Bean and Tuna Salad

Hands-On Time: 15 minutes ■ Total Time: 15 minutes

In the northern Italian city of Florence, bean and tuna crostini (toast rounds with savory toppings) are a popular street snack. Make this savory salad a main-dish version of those little bites by serving Italian bread on the side.

Dressing

- 2 tablespoons chicken broth
- 1 tablespoon olive oil
- 1 tablespoon lemon juice
- 2 teaspoons Dijon mustard
- Pinch of ground black pepper
- 2 tablespoons chopped fresh basil

Salad

- 1 can (15½ ounces) great Northern beans or cannellini beans, rinsed and drained
- ½ cup chopped tomatoes
- ⅓ cup finely chopped onion
- 2 cans (6 ounces each) chunk light tuna, drained
- Lettuce leaves

1. *To make the dressing:* In a medium bowl, whisk together the broth, oil, lemon juice, mustard, and pepper. Stir in the basil.
2. *To make the salad:* Add the beans, tomatoes, and onion to the dressing. Gently toss until evenly coated. Add the tuna, breaking into pieces if necessary, and toss again. Serve on lettuce leaves.

Makes 3 servings

Variation

White Bean and Chicken Salad: Substitute 2 cups chopped cooked chicken breast for the tuna.

Barbecue Pig in the Greens

Hands-On Time: 25 minutes ■ Total Time: 25 minutes

Combine your love of barbecue with healthful greens and vegetables in this flavorful salad.

Dressing

- ¼ cup mayonnaise
- ¼ cup barbecue sauce
- 2 tablespoons sour cream
- 2 tablespoons buttermilk or milk
- 1 tablespoon finely chopped onion
- 1 tablespoon fresh lemon juice
- ¼ teaspoon sugar
- ¼ teaspoon ground black pepper

Salad

- 6 cups torn mixed salad greens
- ½ cup quartered cherry tomatoes
- ⅓ cup chopped green or red bell pepper
- ¼ cup sliced celery
- ¼ cup thinly sliced carrot
- ¼ cup shredded Cheddar cheese
- ¼ cup shredded Monterey Jack cheese
- 1½ cups shredded cooked pork loin

1. *To make the dressing:* In a small bowl, whisk together the mayonnaise, barbecue sauce, sour cream, buttermilk, onion, lemon juice, sugar, and pepper. If desired, cover and refrigerate until serving time.
2. *To make the salad:* In a large bowl, combine the salad greens, tomatoes, bell pepper, celery, carrot, and Cheddar and Monterey Jack cheeses. Gently toss until combined.
3. To serve, divide the lettuce mixture among large salad plates. Top with the pork and drizzle with the dressing.

Makes 4 servings

You can substitute shredded cooked lean beef, chicken breast, or turkey breast for the pork.

Warm Chicken and Orzo Salad

Hands-On Time: 30 minutes ■ Total Time: 35 minutes

Pasta salads, which are often party fare, also make delightful family dinners. This one starts with the tried-and-true pairing of chicken and rice, but the "rice" is really orzo, a grain-shaped pasta. The dish tastes best when served warm, but if necessary you can prepare it ahead of time and refrigerate it. Just be sure to take the salad out of the refrigerator a little while before serving time so that it can come to room temperature.

- 6 ounces orzo or other small pasta
- 4 tablespoons extra-virgin olive oil
- ¾ pound boneless, skinless chicken breasts
- 1¾ cups reduced-sodium chicken broth
- ½ cup water
- 4 cups broccoli florets
- ¼ cup packed flat-leaf parsley sprigs
- 2 tablespoons red wine vinegar
- 1 tablespoon Dijon mustard
- ¼ teaspoon salt
- ½ teaspoon ground black pepper
- 1 clove garlic, peeled
- ¼ cup finely chopped, drained roasted red peppers (from a jar)

1. Cook the orzo in a large pot of boiling water according to package directions until al dente. Drain in a colander, rinse briefly under cold running water, and drain again. Transfer the pasta to a large salad bowl.
2. While the pasta is cooking, in a large nonstick skillet, heat 2 tablespoons of the oil over medium-high heat. Add the chicken and cook, turning once, for about 4 minutes, or until browned. Add 1½ cups of the broth and the water and bring to a simmer. Continue to cook the chicken for 6 to 8 minutes, or until cooked through. Using a slotted spoon, transfer the chicken to a cutting board to cool briefly; reserve the broth in the skillet.
3. Return the broth to a boil over high heat. Add the broccoli and return to a boil. Cook for 3 to 5 minutes, or until the broccoli is crisp-tender. Drain the broccoli in a colander, cool briefly under cold running water, and drain again. Add the broccoli to the bowl of orzo.
4. Cut the chicken into 1" cubes and add to the bowl of orzo.
5. In a food processor, combine the parsley, vinegar, mustard, salt, black pepper, and the remaining ¼ cup broth and 2 tablespoons oil. With the processor running, drop the garlic through the feed tube and process the dressing until puréed.
6. Pour the dressing over the pasta mixture. Add the roasted peppers and toss to mix well. Serve warm.

Makes 4 servings

Thai Rice and Turkey Salad

Hands-On Time: 35 minutes ■ Total Time: 1 hour 30 minutes

Balance is the keynote of Thai meals, and menus are carefully planned to touch on five flavors: sweet, hot, sour, salty, and even a touch of bitter. A root called galanga, plus citrusy lemon grass and *nam pla* (a pungent fish sauce), are Thai staples. Here, ginger, lime juice, and anchovy paste stand in for those exotic ingredients.

- 1 cup uncooked converted white rice
- 2½ cups water
- ½ cup chicken broth
- 1 tablespoon grated fresh ginger
- 2 cloves garlic, crushed through a press
- ¾ pound skinless, boneless turkey breast, cut crosswise into strips
- 3 tablespoons no-salt-added peanut butter
- 3 tablespoons fresh lime juice
- 1 teaspoon honey
- ½ teaspoon anchovy paste
- ¼ teaspoon salt
- ¼ teaspoon red pepper flakes
- 2 cups shredded napa cabbage
- 1 large red bell pepper, finely chopped
- ½ cup finely chopped red onion
- 3 tablespoons coarsely chopped fresh mint
- 3 cups small tender kale leaves or spinach
- 2 tablespoons coarsely chopped roasted unsalted peanuts

1. In a heavy medium saucepan, combine the rice and 2 cups of the water and bring to a boil over high heat. Reduce the heat to low, cover, and simmer for 20 minutes, or until the rice is tender and the liquid is absorbed. Spread the rice in a shallow baking pan and place in the freezer for about 10 minutes.
2. Meanwhile, in a medium skillet, combine the remaining ½ cup water with the broth, ginger, and garlic. Cover and bring to a boil over high heat. Reduce the heat to medium and simmer for 5 minutes to blend the flavors. Stir in the turkey strips, cover, and cook, stirring frequently, for 3 to 4 minutes, or until the turkey is cooked through. Using a slotted spoon, transfer the turkey to a plate; cover loosely with a sheet of wax paper to keep it moist.
3. Increase the heat under the skillet to high and return the broth to a boil. Boil rapidly for 5 to 6 minutes, or until the broth is thickened and reduced to about ¼ cup.
4. In a salad bowl, whisk together the peanut butter, lime juice, honey, anchovy paste, salt, and red pepper flakes. Whisk in the reduced broth and continue whisking until smooth (whisk in a few drops of hot water if the mixture becomes too thick). Add the cooled rice and the turkey strips and any juices that have collected on the plate and stir gently. Add the cabbage, bell pepper, onion, and mint and toss to mix.
5. Arrange the kale on a platter. Mound the salad in the center and sprinkle with the peanuts.

Makes 4 servings

Grilled Chicken and Potato Salad over Greens

Hands-On Time: 40 minutes ■ Total Time: 1 hour 15 minutes

In this satisfying main-dish salad, potatoes and chicken soak up a delicious marinade that does double duty as a dressing for crisp salad greens.

- ½ cup olive or vegetable oil
- ⅓ cup white wine vinegar
- 1 shallot, finely chopped
- 2 cloves garlic, minced
- 2 tablespoons Dijon mustard
- 2 tablespoons chopped fresh sage
- ½ teaspoon salt
- ¼ teaspoon ground black pepper
- 2 pounds red potatoes, cut into ¾" chunks
- 1 pound boneless, skinless chicken thighs
- 6 cups salad greens

1. In a medium bowl, whisk together the oil, vinegar, shallot, garlic, mustard, sage, salt, and pepper. Transfer 3 tablespoons of the marinade to a small bowl and set aside.
2. In a large bowl, combine the potatoes and half of the remaining marinade and toss until evenly coated. Add the chicken to the medium bowl with the remaining marinade, turning the chicken until evenly coated.
3. Grease the grill rack. Preheat the grill.
4. Tear two 24" × 18" pieces of foil and stack to make a double layer. Spoon the potato mixture into the center and fold the foil in half so that the seams are along the edges. Seal the edges tightly with double folds. Place the packet on the rack and grill, turning and shaking occasionally, for 30 minutes, or until the potatoes are tender.
5. Remove the chicken from the marinade; discard the marinade. Grill the chicken, turning occasionally, for about 15 minutes, or until no longer pink and the juices run clear. Cut the chicken into strips.
6. Place the greens in a serving bowl and toss with the reserved marinade. Top with the potatoes and chicken.

Makes 4 servings

Potato Salad with Warm Bacon Dressing

Hands-On Time: 20 minutes ■ Total Time: 55 minutes

A piquant dressing of bacon, vinegar, and mustard is the perfect foil to steamed potatoes in this classic German potato salad.

- 2 pounds red potatoes, cut into large chunks
- 2 strips bacon, chopped
- 1 small red onion, chopped
- 1 clove garlic, minced
- ¼ cup chopped fresh parsley
- 3 tablespoons cider vinegar
- 3 tablespoons apple juice
- 1 tablespoon stone-ground mustard
- ⅛ teaspoon salt

1. Place a steamer basket in a medium saucepan with 1" of water. Bring to a boil over high heat. Place the potatoes in the basket, cover, and steam for 15 to 20 minutes, or until tender. Transfer to a large bowl and allow to cool for 10 minutes.
2. Meanwhile, in a medium nonstick skillet set over medium heat, cook the bacon for 3 minutes. Add the onion and garlic. Cook, stirring, for 3 minutes, or until the onion is soft and the bacon is crisp. Reduce the heat to low. Add the parsley, vinegar, apple juice, mustard, and salt. Cook for 2 minutes, or until heated through. Pour over the potatoes. Toss to evenly coat and serve.

Makes 6 servings

Nutri-Note

Onions add more than great flavor to recipes. The versatile vegetable is also a health-promoting powerhouse: It helps decrease the risk of cancer, lowers blood pressure and total cholesterol levels, raises beneficial HDL (high-density lipoprotein) cholesterol, relieves congestion, and reduces inflammation.

Beet and Potato Salad

Hands-On Time: 25 minutes ■ Total Time: 1 hour 10 minutes

Magenta beets are especially beautiful in this bright salad served over lovely green escarole.

1¼ pounds small beets
8 ounces small red potatoes
2 tablespoons red wine vinegar
1 tablespoon extra-virgin olive oil
2 teaspoons chopped fresh parsley
¾ teaspoon Dijon mustard
¼ teaspoon chopped fresh tarragon
¾ cup thinly sliced onion
Salt
Ground black pepper
4 cups torn escarole

1. Place the beets and potatoes in separate saucepans. Cover with cold water and bring to a boil over high heat. Reduce the heat to medium and cook until the vegetables are easily pierced with a knife (20 to 25 minutes for the beets and 15 to 20 minutes for the potatoes). Drain and let stand until cool enough to handle. Peel and slice.
2. In a large bowl, whisk together the vinegar, oil, parsley, mustard, and tarragon. Add the beets, potatoes, and onion; toss to combine. Add salt and pepper to taste.
3. Arrange the escarole on a platter. Top with the vegetables and drizzle with the dressing.

Makes 4 servings

Kitchen Tip

Peeling and slicing cooked beets can leave stubborn stains on your hands. Put on a pair of gloves to avoid the red blotches. And don't store any leftover beets in a plastic container because they will stain the plastic. Instead, put into a disposable zip-top bag and refrigerate.

Black Bean and Corn Salad

Hands-On Time: 15 minutes ■ Total Time: 15 minutes (plus standing)

This is a simple and colorful salad that gets better if it sits for at least a couple of hours. For those who like to add some heat, serve with hot pepper sauce on the side.

Dressing

- ⅓ cup fresh lemon juice
- 3 tablespoons reduced-sodium vegetable or chicken broth
- 2 tablespoons olive oil
- Pinch of salt

Salad

- 1 can (15 ounces) black beans, rinsed and drained
- 1 cup canned corn, drained
- ¼ cup chopped green bell pepper
- 16 grape tomatoes, halved lengthwise
- ½ cup thinly sliced scallions, white and green parts
- ½ cup finely chopped fresh parsley
- ¼ to ½ cup chopped fresh cilantro
- Bibb or Boston lettuce leaves

1. *To make the dressing:* In a medium bowl, whisk together the lemon juice, broth, oil, and salt.
2. *To make the salad:* To the dressing, add the beans, corn, pepper, tomatoes, scallions, parsley, and cilantro. Gently toss until the bean mixture is evenly coated with the dressing.
3. Cover and let stand at room temperature for at least 2 hours to blend the flavors. Refrigerate for longer storage.
4. When ready to serve, line 4 salad plates with lettuce. Spoon the salad on top.

Makes 4 servings

Ingredients Note

If you have more time, you can cook dried black beans instead of using canned. For 2 cups of cooked beans, begin with 1 cup of dried black beans. Sort and rinse the beans, then soak them overnight in plenty of cold water. Drain and place in a saucepan with enough fresh cold water to cover by 2". Simmer for 1 to 1½ hours, or until tender but firm. Drain the beans before using.

Accompaniments

Serve the salad with Oven-Fried Chicken (page 90) or Five-Alarm Shrimp (page 177).

Creamy Caesar Salad

Hands-On Time: 15 minutes ■ Total Time: 15 minutes

Here it is: the classic Caesar salad, but with a simplified dressing for quick prep time. Use your favorite supermarket croutons, or make your own.

- 7 cups torn romaine lettuce
- ¼ cup mayonnaise
- 2 tablespoons grated Parmesan cheese
- 1 tablespoon fresh lemon juice
- 1 tablespoon water
- ½ teaspoon white wine Worcestershire sauce
- ½ teaspoon Dijon mustard
- 1 clove garlic, minced
- ¼ teaspoon anchovy paste
- ¼ teaspoon ground black pepper
- Croutons

1. Place the lettuce in a large bowl and set aside.
2. In a small bowl, whisk together the mayonnaise, cheese, lemon juice, water, Worcestershire sauce, mustard, garlic, anchovy paste, and pepper. Pour over the lettuce and gently toss until the lettuce is evenly coated. Top with croutons and serve.

Makes 6 servings

Ingredients Notes

If you don't have white wine Worcestershire sauce, you can use the regular variety. However, expect the dressing to be a bit darker in color and to have a slightly stronger Worcestershire flavor.

Anchovy paste is sold in tubes and keeps for months in the fridge once opened, so it's a great ingredient to have on hand if you use anchovies infrequently. If you do have a jar of anchovies on hand, use half a fillet, mashed to a paste, in this recipe. And if you like anchovies, don't be afraid to add more!

Salads from the Pantry

There are at least a week's worth of entrée and side salads residing in your kitchen. Frozen vegetables, canned beans, dried pasta, brown rice, pickles, artichoke hearts, peppers, salsa, tuna, and salad dressings are all waiting patiently to become lunch or dinner. Here are three throw-together salads to spark your imagination. Each makes 4 servings.

Succotash Salad. Whisk together ⅓ cup vegetable oil, ¼ cup cider vinegar, 3 tablespoons honey, 2 teaspoons brown mustard, ½ teaspoon salt, and ¼ teaspoon ground black pepper. Add 2 cups *each* canned corn kernels, frozen and thawed lima beans, and chopped ham and ¼ cup finely chopped sweet pickles. Toss to mix.

Chickpea, Tomato, and Onion Salad. Toss together 2 cups canned chickpeas, ⅓ chopped red onion, 1 chopped tomato, 3 tablespoons *each* lemon juice and extra-virgin olive oil, ⅛ teaspoon red pepper flakes, 2 tablespoons finely chopped fresh parsley, ½ teaspoon salt, and ¼ teaspoon ground black pepper. Chill.

Rice and Bean Salad. Toss together 2 cups leftover rice with 2 cups canned black beans, 2 finely chopped jarred roasted red bell peppers, ½ minced garlic clove, ¼ cup *each* olive oil and red wine vinegar, the juice of 1 lime, 1 tablespoon chopped fresh parsley, ¼ teaspoon salt, and ⅛ teaspoon ground black pepper.

Chinese Sesame Slaw

Hands-On Time: 25 minutes ■ Total Time: 25 minutes

Coleslaw gets an Asian update with a fresh dressing and a sprinkling of sesame seeds.

- 5½ cups thinly sliced green cabbage
- 1 large carrot, julienned
- 3 scallions, julienned
- ¼ cup fresh lemon juice
- 1 tablespoon sesame oil
- 1 clove garlic, minced
- ½ teaspoon grated fresh ginger
- 1 tablespoon sesame seeds

1. In a large bowl, combine the cabbage, carrot, and scallions.
2. In a small bowl, whisk together the lemon juice, oil, garlic, and ginger. Pour over the cabbage mixture and toss well to combine.
3. Place the sesame seeds in a dry nonstick skillet. Cook over medium heat, stirring, for about 1 minute, or until lightly toasted. Transfer to a mortar and pound lightly to break up the seeds and release their flavor. Don't crush into a paste. Sprinkle over the salad and serve.

Makes 6 servings

Variation

Turn the slaw into a vegetarian sandwich by adding some shredded cheese and serving stuffed into a whole wheat pita.

Accompaniment

Serve with poached chicken or Pepper-Marinated Flank Steak (page 120).

Nutri-Note

Cruciferous vegetables—including cabbage—may be your best line of defense against certain types of cancer. And because studies suggest they're even more effective when eaten raw, this salad makes extra dietary sense.

Cucumber and Tomato Salad with Sour Cream Dressing

Hands-On Time: 15 minutes ■ Total Time: 15 minutes (plus chilling)

Cucumbers in a sour cream dressing is an old-fashioned American favorite. Add ripe tomatoes and you have a salad made for summer.

2 cucumbers, peeled and very thinly sliced
½ cup sour cream
2 tablespoons fresh lemon juice
Pinch of salt
Pinch of sugar
Dash of ground red pepper
3 tomatoes, sliced

1. In a small bowl, combine the cucumbers, sour cream, lemon juice, salt, sugar, and pepper. Cover and refrigerate for several hours.
2. To serve, spoon the cucumber mixture over the tomatoes.

Makes 6 servings

Accompaniments

Serve this summer salad alongside grilled shrimp kebabs and rice pilaf.

Ingredients Note

If you have small cucumbers and the skin is very thin, there may be no need for peeling. Taste the skin first: If it is bitter, go ahead and peel away.

Kitchen Tip

For the cleanest cuts, use a small serrated knife for slicing tomatoes. If you cut a tomato vertically from stem to end (instead of horizontally), the slices will hold together better.

Steak Salad

Hands-On Time: 25 minutes ■ Total Time: 40 minutes

Even hearty appetites will be well satisfied with this robustly flavored yet surprisingly light main-course salad. It's a natural for a casual summer buffet or potluck.

Salad

- 1½ pounds beef top sirloin or top round steak
- 1 jar (13 ounces) artichoke hearts, drained and quartered
- 8 ounces mushrooms, sliced
- 1 bunch scallions, white and green parts, thinly sliced
- 2 tomatoes, cut into wedges
- 2 tablespoons minced fresh parsley
- Pinch of salt
- Pinch of ground black pepper
- 1 medium head romaine lettuce

Dressing

- ¼ cup tarragon or other herb vinegar
- 1 tablespoon fresh lemon juice
- 2 teaspoons honey
- 2 teaspoons Dijon mustard
- ½ teaspoon salt
- ¼ cup olive oil

1. *To make the salad:* Lightly grease a grill or grill pan and heat to medium-high. Grill the steak, turning once, for 10 to 12 minutes for medium-rare. Transfer to a cutting board and let rest for 5 minutes before cutting into ¼"-thick slices.
2. In a salad bowl, combine the steak, artichokes, mushrooms, scallions, tomatoes, parsley, salt, and pepper. Toss gently to combine.
3. *To make the dressing:* In a blender, combine the vinegar, lemon juice, honey, mustard, and salt. With the machine running, add the oil in a steady stream until combined.
4. To serve, arrange the lettuce on 6 dinner plates, top with the salad, and drizzle with the dressing.

Makes 6 servings

Orange Salad with Honey Vinaigrette

Hands-On Time: 20 minutes ■ Total Time: 20 minutes

This sunny salad, with a generous helping of vitamin C, is especially welcome in the winter, when garden-ripe tomatoes aren't available.

Dressing

- 1½ tablespoons white wine vinegar
- 1 tablespoon water
- 1 tablespoon orange juice
- 1 tablespoon honey
- 2 teaspoons canola oil

Salad

- 2 cups torn red leaf lettuce
- 2 cups torn romaine lettuce
- 2 navel oranges, peeled and cut crosswise into slices
- 1 small red onion, thinly sliced and separated into rings

1. *To make the dressing:* In a small bowl, whisk together the vinegar, water, orange juice, honey, and oil.
2. *To make the salad:* In a medium bowl, toss together the red leaf and romaine lettuce. Transfer to salad plates. Arrange the oranges and onion on top. Drizzle with the dressing and serve.

Makes 4 servings

Accompaniments

The bright flavor of this citrus salad is especially welcome before a hearty dinner, such as Round Steak Casserole (page 121) and Chili-Glazed Mini Meat Loaves (page 123).

Kitchen Tip

For an extra jolt of orange flavor, add a bit of orange zest to the dressing and let it sit for 10 to 15 minutes.

Carrot Salad

Hands-On Time: 15 minutes ■ Total Time: 15 minutes

Chopped apple and raisins combine with an abundance of shredded carrots for a refreshing wintertime salad. For a pretty presentation, serve in "cups" of butter lettuce.

- 3 tablespoons cider vinegar
- 3 tablespoons frozen apple juice concentrate, thawed
- 1 tablespoon canola oil
- 1 tablespoon fresh lemon juice
- 3 cups shredded carrots
- 1 tart apple, peeled, cored, and shredded
- ½ cup raisins
- 3 tablespoons chopped fresh parsley
- ¼ teaspoon salt
- ¼ teaspoon ground black pepper

In a large bowl, combine the vinegar, apple juice concentrate, oil, and lemon juice and stir well. Add the carrots, apple, raisins, and parsley and toss well. Stir in the salt and pepper and serve.

Makes 4 servings

Leftovers

Stuff leftover salad into a pita with turkey slices and a dollop of plain yogurt for a quick sandwich.

Nutri-Note

Your mother was right: Eat your carrots for better vision. Carrots are rich in beta-carotene, which protects against macular degeneration. In addition, beta-carotene is converted to vitamin A in the liver. In your eyes' retinas, the vitamin A is then converted to rhodopsin, a pigment that is necessary for night vision.

Paella Salad

Hands-On Time: 30 minutes ■ Total Time: 30 minutes (plus chilling)

Simply put, paella pleases, whether in the form of the traditional hot Spanish casserole or in this contemporary salad.

Salad

- 1⅓ cups water
- ⅔ cup white rice
- ⅛ teaspoon ground saffron or turmeric
- ½ pound small shrimp, peeled and deveined
- 1½ cups chopped cooked chicken breast
- 1 tomato, chopped
- ½ cup frozen peas, thawed
- ⅓ cup thinly sliced celery
- ¼ cup finely chopped onion
- 1 jar (2 ounces) pimientos, drained and chopped

Dressing

- ¼ cup tarragon vinegar
- 2 tablespoons olive oil
- ¼ teaspoon curry powder
- ⅛ teaspoon dry mustard
- ⅛ teaspoon ground white pepper

1. *To make the salad:* In a medium saucepan, combine the water, rice, and saffron. Bring to a boil and reduce the heat. Cover and simmer for 20 minutes, or until the rice is tender.
2. Meanwhile, place the shrimp in a medium skillet and add cold water to cover. Bring to a boil and reduce the heat to low. Gently simmer for 1 to 3 minutes, or until the shrimp turn pink. Drain.
3. In a large bowl, combine the rice, shrimp, chicken, tomato, peas, celery, onion, and pimientos; toss to mix well.
4. *To make the dressing:* In a bowl, whisk together the vinegar, oil, curry powder, mustard, and pepper.
5. Pour the dressing over the rice mixture and toss. Cover and refrigerate for at least 4 hours.

Makes 4 servings

Couscous Salad with Oranges and Olives

Hands-On Time: 15 minutes ■ Total Time: 15 minutes

This bright, zesty salad combines Moroccan and Mediterranean influences for a refreshing luncheon dish.

- 3⁄4 cup couscous
- 2 tablespoons frozen orange juice concentrate, thawed
- 1 tablespoon fresh lemon juice
- 1 teaspoon Dijon mustard
- 1 teaspoon extra-virgin olive oil
- 1 teaspoon chopped fresh oregano
- 1 teaspoon grated orange zest
- 1 cup boiling water
- 1 orange, peeled, sectioned, and chopped
- 1⁄2 cup chopped fresh parsley
- 1⁄4 cup chopped scallions, white parts only
- 2 tablespoons sliced black olives
- Salt
- Ground black pepper

1. In a large bowl, mix the couscous, orange juice concentrate, lemon juice, mustard, oil, oregano, and orange zest. Stir in the water. Cover and set aside for 5 minutes, or until the liquid has been absorbed.
2. Fluff the couscous with a fork. Stir in the orange, parsley, scallions, and olives; toss to blend. Season with salt and pepper and serve.

Makes 4 servings

Make-Ahead

You can prepare the salad several hours ahead, cover, and refrigerate. Let it come to room temperature before serving.

Ingredients Note

Couscous is granular semolina that is sold in the grain and pasta sections of the supermarket. It is ready in just 5 minutes and makes a quick stand-in for pasta and polenta. For an extra boost of fiber, look for whole wheat couscous.

Marinated Vegetable Salad

Hands-On Time: 40 minutes ■ Total Time: 40 minutes (plus marinating)

Most commercial salad dressings make easy, fast marinades for vegetables and meats. This recipe calls for Italian dressing, but you could use almost any herb-flavored vinaigrette. If you'd like to use fresh brussels sprouts, blanch, halve, and cool them before combining with the other ingredients.

- 1 cup prepared Italian salad dressing
- ¼ cup chopped fresh parsley
- 1 package (10 ounces) frozen brussels sprouts, thawed and halved
- 1 package (9 ounces) frozen artichoke hearts, thawed and quartered
- 2 carrots, thinly sliced on the diagonal
- 1 cucumber, sliced
- 1 cup small broccoli florets
- 1 cup small cauliflower florets
- 1 red bell pepper, chopped
- 2 cups sliced mushrooms

1. In a large bowl, combine the dressing and parsley. Add the brussels sprouts, artichokes, carrots, cucumber, broccoli, cauliflower, and pepper. Stir until coated. Cover and refrigerate for at least 2 hours, stirring occasionally.
2. Just before serving, add the mushrooms and gently stir until coated.

Makes 8 to 10 servings

Ingredients Note

If you can't find frozen artichoke hearts, use canned. Drain and rinse them first.

Nutri-Note

To save calories, you can use fat-free or reduced-fat dressing instead of the full fat. Watch out for commercial dressings that contain sugar, however.

Fruit Salads Fresh from the Tropics

There's an incredible array of tropical and other unusual fruits now available at supermarkets and specialty stores. Some of these fruits, such as kiwifruit, have been widely embraced; others are waiting to catch on. Here are some up-and-comers that you can use to make a really wonderful fruit salad.

- **Asian pear.** It looks like an apple but tastes like a pear, only crisper. It's best eaten chilled.
- **Atemoya.** Also called custard apple, this artichoke-shaped fruit has a creamy white, custardy interior. It also has a sweet taste, something between a pineapple and a mango.
- **Carambola.** With waxy skin and deep ribs, a carambola resembles a long, yellow pepper. When sliced, it looks like yellow stars, hence the nickname "starfruit." It can be used as a garnish or to add pizzazz to fruit salads with an apple-grape-citrus taste.
- **Guava.** Pebbly green on the outside and pink on the inside, guava is great in salads. It can also be puréed and made into delicious tutti-frutti yogurt by combining it with nonfat plain yogurt, freezing it until firm, and then running it through the food processor.
- **Kiwifruit.** This fuzzy, egg-shaped fruit is one of the most familiar of the unusual tropical fruits. Kiwifruit tastes like a cross between strawberry and pineapple.
- **Lychee.** This comes encased in a barklike brown shell that peels off, revealing a pearly white fruit with a grapelike appearance and taste.
- **Mango.** As sweet as it is fragrant, the mango is as close to paradise as you can get without getting on a plane. It looks rather like a large misshapen pear, ranging in color from green (unripe) to orange-red.
- **Papaya.** On the outside, it almost looks like a yellow or orange avocado. On the inside, however, is a beautiful orange-pink flesh with edible peppery black seeds. The seeds can be used to give crunch to a salad. The flesh is good in fruit salads and salsas. It also makes a good meat tenderizer.
- **Passion fruit.** Despite the heady name, passion fruit is ready to eat only when it's purple, shriveled, and ugly. Inside you'll find a gelatinous mass of crunchy seeds and juice. The taste is a delightful combination of citrus, honey, and floral flavors.
- **Persimmon.** This is a smooth orange fruit that comes in two varieties. Hachiya persimmons are acorn-shaped and must be quite soft to be eaten. They have a smooth, creamy texture. Smaller, tomato-shaped Fuyus can be eaten when still firm, even crisp.
- **Tamarillo.** Also called tree tomato, it actually looks more like a plum with either golden yellow or scarlet skin and has a slightly tart taste. It must be peeled with a vegetable peeler or blanched before using. To serve, slice and drizzle it with honey and a dusting of nutmeg.

Minted Fruit Salad

Hands-On Time: 35 minutes ■ Total Time: 35 minutes (plus chilling)

This lovely salad would be a nice addition to a brunch buffet alongside Orange Popovers with Honey Butter (page 296) or slices of French toast. Or serve in small cups at your next barbecue or backyard picnic.

- ½ cup orange juice
- ¼ cup fresh lemon juice
- 2 tablespoons sugar
- 1 tablespoon chopped fresh mint
- 1 pint strawberries, hulled
- 3 kiwifruit, peeled and thinly sliced
- 1 medium cantaloupe, cut into cubes or balls
- 1 medium honeydew melon, cut into cubes or balls

In a large glass or ceramic bowl, mix the orange juice, lemon juice, sugar, and mint. Add the strawberries, kiwifruit, cantaloupe, and honeydew and toss gently. Cover and refrigerate for 2 to 3 hours. Toss gently again before serving.

Makes 8 to 10 servings

Kitchen Tip

For a fancy presentation, garnish this refreshing salad with fresh mint sprigs or edible flowers, such as nasturtiums or violets. Be sure to select blooms that have not been sprayed with pesticides.

Variation

Feel free to substitute other melons here: Casaba, Crenshaw, and Santa Claus melons all work well with the strawberries, kiwifruit, and mint.

Panzanella

Hands-On Time: 30 minutes ■ Total Time: 45 minutes

Panzanella is a classic Italian salad containing bread and the best tomatoes and freshest herbs available. That's why it's typically a height-of-summer dish. Serve the panzanella in a hollowed-out loaf of bread, as we do here, or over lettuce leaves.

Salad

- 1 round loaf rustic country bread, about 7" in diameter
- 4 plum tomatoes, chopped
- ¼ cup chopped red onion
- ¼ cup chopped celery
- ¼ cup sliced scallions, white parts only
- ¼ cup chopped fresh basil
- 1 tablespoon chopped fresh oregano
- Salt
- Ground black pepper

Dressing

- 2 tablespoons extra-virgin olive oil
- 2 tablespoons balsamic vinegar
- Pinch of sugar

1. *To make the salad:* Cut the top off the loaf of bread and pull out all the soft bread inside, leaving a shell. Set the shell aside.
2. Place the bread pieces and the removed top crust on a baking sheet. Sprinkle with water and let stand for about 15 minutes, then squeeze out the moisture. Tear the bread into bite-size pieces.
3. In a large bowl, toss together the bread, tomatoes, onion, celery, scallions, basil, and oregano. Add salt and pepper to taste.
4. *To make the dressing:* In a cup, stir together the oil, vinegar, and sugar. Pour over the salad and toss well.
5. Serve the salad in the bread shell.

Makes 4 servings

Nutri-Note

For a healthier salad, use a whole wheat loaf.

Variations

Add capers or anchovies and chopped hard-boiled egg, if you like.

Rosemary Lentil Salad

Hands-On Time: 35 minutes ■ Total Time: 50 minutes

Healthy protein-packed lentils can be your best friend if you're trying to cut down on your consumption of meat. Here, they combine with a lot of fresh vegetables (including precooked beets) for a nutritional powerhouse of a main-dish salad.

Dressing

- 3 tablespoons olive oil
- 2 tablespoons apple cider vinegar or red wine vinegar
- 1 teaspoon Dijon mustard
- 1 teaspoon finely chopped fresh rosemary or ¼ teaspoon dried
- ½ teaspoon ground coriander
- 1 clove garlic, minced

Salad

- 3 cups chicken broth
- 1 cup lentils
- ¼ cup finely chopped onion
- 1 bay leaf
- ½ cup finely chopped yellow bell pepper
- ¼ cup finely chopped celery
- Green or red lettuce
- 1 cup shredded cooked beets
- 1 cup shredded carrots
- 1 cup shredded zucchini
- 1 cup shredded red radishes

1. *To make the dressing:* In a small bowl, combine the oil, vinegar, mustard, rosemary, coriander, and garlic.
2. *To make the salad:* In a 2-quart saucepan, combine the broth, lentils, onion, and bay leaf. Bring to a boil, reduce the heat, and simmer for about 20 minutes, or until the lentils are tender but not mushy. Discard the bay leaf. Carefully strain the lentils, reserving any remaining broth for another use.
3. In a large bowl, combine the lentils, pepper, and celery. Toss gently to combine. Whisk the dressing to combine well, then pour over the lentils and toss lightly. Chill, if desired.
4. Line 6 serving plates with the lettuce. Divide the lentils, beets, carrots, zucchini, and radishes among the plates and serve.

Makes 6 servings

Kitchen Tip

To cook beets: Scrub them well, trim the stems to ½", and cook in water to cover for about 40 minutes, or until tender. Remove the tops with a paring knife and slip off the skins. Refrigerate whole and shred just before serving.

Plain & Fancy Poultry

Chicken Paprikash

Hands-On Time: 30 minutes ■ Total Time: 30 minutes

A creamy tomato sauce coats chicken and vegetables in this traditional Hungarian dish.

- 8 ounces egg noodles
- 1 pound boneless, skinless chicken breast halves, cut into strips
- ½ teaspoon salt
- ¼ teaspoon ground black pepper
- 2 tablespoons olive oil
- 1 large onion, chopped
- 1 red bell pepper, cut into strips
- 1 tablespoon paprika
- 1 can (14½ ounces) diced tomatoes
- ½ cup sour cream

1. In a large pot of boiling water, cook the egg noodles according to package directions.
2. Meanwhile, season the chicken with the salt and black pepper. Heat 1 tablespoon of the oil in a large skillet over medium-high heat. Add the chicken and cook, stirring occasionally, for 5 minutes, or until just browned. Transfer to a plate and keep warm.
3. Heat the remaining 1 tablespoon oil in the same skillet over medium-high heat. Add the onion, bell pepper, and paprika and cook, stirring occasionally, for 5 minutes. Stir in the tomatoes and chicken. Bring to a boil. Reduce the heat to low, cover, and simmer for 5 minutes, or until the chicken is no longer pink. Remove the skillet from the heat and stir in the sour cream.
4. Place the noodles in a serving bowl and top with the chicken mixture.

Makes 4 servings

Roast Chicken Legs with Basil and Garlic

Hands-On Time: 25 minutes ■ Total Time: 1 hour 15 minutes

These succulent chicken legs are incredibly easy to prepare: Just season with fresh basil, then pop into the oven with garlic and potatoes.

- 4 whole chicken legs (about 2 pounds)
- 8 large fresh basil leaves
- 1 head garlic
- 1 lemon, halved
- 4 baking potatoes, cut lengthwise into spears
- 2 teaspoons olive oil
- ¼ teaspoon ground black pepper
- ¼ teaspoon paprika

1. Preheat the oven to 350°F. Carefully lift the skin on each piece of chicken and slide 2 basil leaves under it. Replace the skin.
2. Separate the garlic into individual cloves. Trim the hard end off each clove and remove the peel. Trim any bruises and discard any cloves that are soft or dark. There should be 12 to 15 whole cloves.
3. Place the garlic in a 13" × 9" baking dish and top with the chicken. Squeeze the juice from half of the lemon over the chicken. Remove the seeds from the remaining lemon half and cut the lemon into 4 pieces. Add these to the baking dish along with the potatoes. Drizzle the chicken and potatoes with the oil. Sprinkle with the pepper and paprika.
4. Bake for 45 to 50 minutes, or until the chicken is no longer pink in the center and the juices run clear.

Makes 4 servings

Accompaniment

Serve with coleslaw or mixed steamed vegetables.

Variations

There are plenty of ways to vary this versatile recipe: Replace the chicken legs with breasts (or use a combination of the two). Use other herbs, including fresh parsley, sage, thyme, or tarragon. Replace the white potatoes with sweet potatoes.

Chicken with Ricotta-Herb Dumplings

Hands-On Time: 45 minutes ■ Total Time: 1 hour 20 minutes

Chicken and dumplings was a treasured Sunday night ritual for many families. Bring back the tradition with our updated version.

- 2 cups water
- 1 cup reduced-sodium chicken broth
- 2 pounds boneless, skinless chicken breast halves, cut into 1" cubes
- 4 medium carrots, thinly sliced
- 2 stalks celery, thinly sliced
- 1 pound green beans, trimmed and halved
- 3 scallions, thinly sliced
- 2 tablespoons cornstarch
- 1 cup milk
- 2 tablespoons chopped fresh dill
- 2 teaspoons chopped fresh thyme or ¼ teaspoon dried
- ¾ teaspoon salt
- ¼ teaspoon ground black pepper
- 1 package (10 ounces) frozen peas, thawed
- 1½ cups ricotta cheese
- ¾ cup all-purpose flour
- 3 tablespoons chopped fresh flat-leaf parsley
- 1 tablespoon unsalted butter, melted
- 1 teaspoon baking powder
- Fresh dill sprigs (optional)

1. In a Dutch oven or large, heavy saucepan, combine 1 cup of the water and the broth and bring to a simmer over medium-high heat. Add the chicken and poach for about 4 minutes, or until firm to the touch. Using a slotted spoon, transfer the chicken to a plate and set aside.
2. Add the carrots and celery to the pan and cook for 3 minutes. Add the green beans, scallions, and remaining 1 cup water and cook for about 3 minutes longer, or until the vegetables are tender. Using a slotted spoon, transfer the vegetables to another plate.
3. In a small bowl, whisk together the cornstarch and milk, then whisk the cornstarch mixture into the hot broth. Add the dill, thyme, ½ teaspoon of the salt, and the pepper and cook, stirring frequently, for 5 minutes, or until thickened.

4. Return the chicken and vegetables to the pan. Add the peas and stir to combine. Reduce the heat to medium, cover, and cook for 5 minutes, or until heated through.

5. While the chicken and vegetables are heating, make the dumpling dough: In a medium bowl, combine the cheese, flour, parsley, butter, baking powder, and remaining ¼ teaspoon salt; mix well with a fork.

6. Drop the dough by ¼-cup portions onto the stew to make 16 dumplings. Cover the pan and cook over medium-low heat for 15 minutes, or until the dumplings are done to your taste (they will be moist). Garnish with fresh dill sprigs, if desired.

Makes 8 servings

Kitchen Tip

For well-shaped, evenly sized dumplings, scoop up the dough with a ¼-cup dry measure (the kind you'd use for flour or sugar).

Friday Night Chicken in the Pot

Hands-On Time: 25 minutes ■ Total Time: 50 minutes

The very words "chicken in the pot" are as comforting to say as the dish is to savor. The chicken pieces cook in a large, heavy saucepan or Dutch oven with carrots, red potatoes, onions, turnips, leeks, and parsnips—all bathed in a rich, steaming broth. You can serve this homey meal any evening, but Friday night often provides a good opportunity for a relaxed family dinner.

- 12 ounces small red potatoes
- 2 medium carrots
- 1 medium parsnip
- 1 medium turnip
- 1 small onion
- 1 medium leek
- 1½ cups water
- 1 cup chicken broth
- 2 pounds skinless chicken legs, thighs and drumsticks separated (4 whole legs)
- 1 bay leaf, preferably imported
- ¼ teaspoon ground black pepper
- ⅛ teaspoon salt
- 1 tablespoon snipped fresh dill

1. Cut the potatoes into ¾" wedges. Peel the carrots, parsnip, turnip (if necessary), and onion. Cut the carrots into ¼"-thick slices. Halve the parsnip lengthwise and cut it into ¼"-thick slices. Cut the turnip and onion into ½" wedges.
2. Halve the leek lengthwise and cut off the root end and the coarser part of the green tops. Hold the leek under cold running water and wash thoroughly. Cut the leek into 1" lengths.
3. In a Dutch oven or large, heavy saucepan, combine the potatoes, carrots, parsnip, turnip, onion, leek, water, broth, chicken, bay leaf, pepper, and salt. Cover and bring to a boil over high heat. Skim off the foam that rises to the surface.
4. Reduce the heat to medium-low, cover, and simmer, turning the chicken pieces occasionally, for 20 minutes, or until the chicken is no longer pink in the center and the vegetables are tender.
5. Discard the bay leaf. Ladle the broth, chicken, and vegetables into bowls and sprinkle with the fresh dill.

Makes 4 servings

Ingredients Note

Good turnips are firm, smooth, and heavy for their size; small turnips are sweeter than large ones. If the turnips come with leaves, cook the greens separately as you would kale.

If turnips are small and tender, they don't need to be peeled. However, larger, older turnips should be pared. Trim a thin slice from the top and root end, and pare the turnip with a vegetable peeler rather than a knife to remove the thinnest possible layer of skin.

Chicken Cassoulet

Hands-On Time: 50 minutes ■ Total Time: 2 hours 20 minutes

Cassoulet is a marvelous bean dish from France. Although traditional recipes call for sausage, goose, and even pork rind, those rich ingredients are not at all necessary. Skinless chicken thighs still give the hearty main course robust flavor. For more authentic flavor, use just ½ pound chicken and add ½ pound sliced cooked pork sausage.

- 2 tablespoons vegetable oil
- 1 pound boneless, skinless chicken thighs, cut into ¾" cubes
- ¾ teaspoon dried thyme
- ¼ teaspoon ground allspice
- ¾ teaspoon ground black pepper
- 1 cup chopped onion
- 3 cloves garlic, minced
- 1½ cups chopped tomatoes
- 1 large carrot, finely chopped
- ½ cup white wine or chicken broth
- Pinch of ground cloves
- 2 tablespoons finely chopped fresh parsley
- 2 cups packed chopped spinach
- 3½ cups cooked great Northern beans
- 1½ cups chicken broth
- ½ cup unseasoned dried bread crumbs

1. Preheat the oven to 350°F. Grease a 2½-quart casserole.
2. In a large nonstick skillet, heat the oil over medium-high heat. Add the chicken and sprinkle with the thyme, allspice, and ½ teaspoon of the pepper. Cook, stirring occasionally, until browned. Transfer to a large bowl.
3. Add the onion and garlic to the pan and cook for about 5 minutes, or until tender. Add the tomatoes, carrot, wine, and cloves. Stir in 1 tablespoon of the parsley and the remaining ¼ teaspoon pepper. Cook for about 10 minutes, or until the carrot is almost tender. Add the spinach and cook until wilted. Add the vegetables to the chicken in the bowl and stir in the beans. Combine well.
4. Transfer the chicken mixture to the prepared casserole. Pour the broth over the mixture just to cover. Mix the bread crumbs with the remaining 1 tablespoon parsley and sprinkle over the chicken. Bake for about 1½ hours, or until the crumbs are golden brown.

Makes 6 servings

Baked Chicken Barbecue

Hands-On Time: 20 minutes ■ Total Time: 1 hour

Oven-baked barbecue is a Southern specialty quite distinct from both suburban backyard grilling and large-scale open-pit smoking. In this lighter adaptation, chicken legs take the place of the more usual short ribs baked in a tangy tomato sauce made with raisins, molasses, and vinegar. Don't worry too much about overcooking the chicken: Most people prefer oven-barbecued meats "falling off the bone" tender.

- 2 tablespoons vegetable oil
- 1 medium red bell pepper, cut into thin strips
- 1 medium green bell pepper, cut into thin strips
- 1 small onion, halved and sliced
- 2 cloves garlic, crushed through a press
- 2 cans (8 ounces each) tomato sauce
- ¼ cup raisins
- 3 tablespoons molasses
- 4 teaspoons cider vinegar
- ½ to 1 teaspoon hot pepper sauce
- 1 teaspoon dry mustard
- ½ teaspoon ground black pepper
- ¼ teaspoon salt
- 2 pounds chicken legs, thighs and drumsticks separated (4 whole legs)

1. Preheat the oven to 425°F. Grease a roasting pan.
2. In a heavy medium saucepan, heat the oil over medium-high heat. Add the red and green bell peppers, onion, and garlic and cook, stirring frequently, for about 5 minutes, or until crisp-tender. Stir in the tomato sauce, raisins, molasses, vinegar, hot pepper sauce to taste, mustard, black pepper, and salt and bring to a boil.
3. Place the chicken pieces in the prepared pan. Spoon the sauce over the chicken and turn to coat. Bake the chicken, turning the pieces and basting occasionally with the sauce, for 25 to 35 minutes, or until the chicken is no longer pink in the center and the juices run clear.

Makes 4 servings

Accompaniments

Cornbread and coleslaw are the classic accompaniments to barbecue.

Make-Ahead

Cook the chicken a day ahead, cover with foil, and refrigerate. Reheat covered, adding a little water if necessary.

Baked Chicken with Root Vegetables

Hands-On Time: 45 minutes ■ Total Time: 1 hour 25 minutes

Degreasing the pan juices is an important step in this recipe. The best tool for the job is a gravy separator, a clear cup with a spout that begins at the base (rather than the top). When you pour in fatty pan juices, soup, or sauce, the fat rises to the top, allowing the defatted juices to be poured out through the spout.

- 1⁄4 cup mixed fresh herbs (such as tarragon, basil, parsley, and mint), minced
- 2 cloves garlic, minced
- 2 teaspoons grated lemon zest
- 1 broiler-fryer chicken (2 1⁄4 pounds), cut into 8 serving pieces
- 3 tablespoons fresh lemon juice
- 8 ounces small red potatoes, quartered
- 3 medium carrots, cut into 2" pieces
- 2 medium turnips, peeled and cut into 1" pieces
- 1 small fennel bulb, trimmed and quartered
- 3 large shallots, halved
- 1⁄2 cup reduced-sodium chicken broth
- 1⁄2 teaspoon salt
- 1⁄4 teaspoon ground black pepper

1. Preheat the oven to 375°F. Line a large roasting pan with foil.
2. In a small bowl, combine the herbs, garlic, and lemon zest. Spread 2 tablespoons of this mixture under the skin of the chicken. Stir the lemon juice into the remaining herb mixture and set aside.
3. Arrange the chicken pieces on a rack at one end of the prepared roasting pan. Spread the potatoes, carrots, turnips, fennel, and shallots on the rack at the other end of the pan. Brush the chicken with half of the lemon-herb mixture. Drizzle the vegetables and chicken evenly with the broth, then sprinkle with the salt and pepper.
4. Bake the chicken and vegetables for 15 minutes. Baste the chicken with the remaining lemon-herb mixture. Increase the oven temperature to 400°F, and continue to bake for 25 minutes longer, or until the chicken is browned and no longer pink in the center.
5. Transfer the chicken and vegetables to a platter. Pour the juices remaining in the pan into a gravy separator. Pour the degreased pan juices over the chicken and vegetables.

Makes 4 servings

Kitchen Tip

If you don't have a gravy separator, use this trick for skimming the fat with a spoon: Pour the pan juices into a tall container, such as a glass measuring cup, rather than trying to skim them in the pan. This way, the fat will rise to the top in a deep layer, which is easier to remove.

Oven-Fried Chicken

Hands-On Time: 15 minutes ■ Total Time: 50 minutes

No need to bring out the deep-fryer—you can bake these slightly spicy, crisp-crusted chicken parts in the oven. Dipping the drumsticks and thighs in seasoned yogurt helps keep the meat moist and adds a bit of tang.

- 1 cup unseasoned dried bread crumbs
- ½ cup plain yogurt
- 2 cloves garlic, crushed
- 2 teaspoons cider vinegar
- ½ teaspoon hot pepper sauce, or to taste
- 2 pounds skinless chicken legs, drumsticks and thighs separated (4 whole legs)
- 1 tablespoon vegetable oil

1. Preheat the oven to 450°F. Grease a jelly-roll pan. Spread the bread crumbs on a shallow plate.
2. In a large bowl, stir together the yogurt, garlic, vinegar, and hot pepper sauce. Add the chicken pieces and turn to coat well. One piece at time, dredge the chicken pieces in the bread crumbs to coat evenly. Arrange the chicken in a single layer on the prepared pan.
3. Drizzle the oil over the chicken. Bake for 30 to 35 minutes, or until the chicken is browned and no longer pink in the center, and the juices run clear.

Makes 4 servings

Ingredients Note

The ½ teaspoon of hot pepper sauce is only a suggestion—you can certainly use more if you'd like a little additional heat.

Chicken Parmesan Strips

Hands-On Time: 15 minutes ■ Total Time: 50 minutes

These cheesy chicken tenders are soaked in milk for extra juiciness. Kids love them!

- 1 pound chicken tenders
- ½ cup milk
- ⅓ cup seasoned dried bread crumbs or cereal crumbs
- 3 tablespoons grated Parmesan cheese
- 2 teaspoons chopped fresh parsley
- ¼ teaspoon ground black pepper
- 1 tablespoon vegetable oil

1. Preheat the oven to 400°F. Grease a baking sheet.
2. Place the chicken in a shallow bowl. Pierce in several places with a fork. Pour the milk over the top. Cover and refrigerate for at least 15 minutes.
3. In another shallow bowl, combine the bread crumbs, cheese, parsley, and pepper. Remove the chicken from the milk mixture and dredge in the bread crumb mixture, turning to coat well. Place on the prepared baking sheet and drizzle with the oil.
4. Bake for 10 minutes. Turn the chicken pieces and bake for 10 minutes longer, or until the chicken is no longer is pink.

Makes 4 servings

Ingredients Note

Chicken tenders are the tenderloin of the chicken, cut from the breast. If your market doesn't have tenders, buy boneless breasts and cut them into long strips.

Grilled Lime Chicken and Salsa

Hands-On Time: 35 minutes ■ Total Time: 1 hour 15 minutes (plus marinating)

Convenient boneless chicken breasts are marinated in lime juice, then quickly grilled and served with homemade salsa. If you have salsa left over, use it as a dip for baked tortilla chips or as a topping for broiled fish.

- 5 to 6 boneless, skinless chicken breast halves (4 ounces each)
- ¼ cup frozen apple juice concentrate, thawed
- ¼ cup plus 1 teaspoon lime juice
- 2 tablespoons vegetable oil
- 6 plum tomatoes, seeded and chopped
- ½ cup spicy vegetable juice
- ¼ cup chopped fresh cilantro
- 4 scallions, minced
- ¼ teaspoon salt
- ¼ teaspoon hot pepper sauce

1. Place the chicken in a single layer in a shallow baking pan. In a small bowl, stir together the apple juice concentrate, ¼ cup of the lime juice, and the oil. Pour over the chicken. Cover and refrigerate for 4 to 24 hours.
2. In a medium bowl, stir together the tomatoes, vegetable juice, cilantro, scallions, salt, hot pepper sauce, and remaining 1 teaspoon lime juice. Cover and refrigerate for at least 30 minutes.
3. Grease a grill rack. Preheat the grill to medium-hot.
4. Remove the chicken from the marinade; discard the marinade. Place the chicken on the grill rack and grill, uncovered, for 8 minutes. Turn the chicken and grill for 7 to 10 minutes longer, or until the chicken is no longer pink. Serve with the salsa.

Makes 4 servings

Kitchen Tip

To broil the chicken instead of grilling it, grease the rack of a broiling pan. Remove the chicken from the marinade and place on the rack. Broil 4" from the heat for 5 minutes. Turn the chicken and broil for 4 to 6 minutes longer, or until the chicken is tender and no longer pink.

Chicken Piccata with Escarole

Hands-On Time: 30 minutes ■ Total Time: 40 minutes

Piccata is a classic Italian dish of chicken or veal cutlets that are quickly sautéed, then served with a lemony pan sauce. We like to serve piccata with wilted escarole and cherry tomatoes.

- 4 boneless, skinless chicken breast halves (5 to 6 ounces each)
- ½ teaspoon dried thyme, crumbled
- ¼ teaspoon ground black pepper
- 1½ tablespoons olive oil
- 2 cloves garlic, minced
- 5 cups loosely packed cut-up escarole
- 1 cup halved cherry tomatoes
- ⅛ teaspoon salt
- 2 teaspoons cornstarch dissolved in ½ cup chicken broth
- ½ teaspoon grated lemon zest
- 1 tablespoon fresh lemon juice
- 2 teaspoons unsalted butter

1. Season both sides of the chicken breasts with the thyme and pepper. In a large skillet, heat 1 tablespoon of the oil over medium-high heat. Add the chicken and cook, turning once, for about 10 minutes, or until cooked through. Transfer the chicken to a warm platter and cover loosely with foil.
2. Add the remaining ½ tablespoon oil to the skillet and heat over medium-high heat. Add the garlic and cook, stirring constantly, for 30 seconds, or until fragrant. Add the escarole, increase the heat to high, and cook, tossing frequently, for 2 to 3 minutes, or until the greens begin to wilt. Add the tomatoes and cook for 2 to 3 minutes longer, or until the tomatoes are warm and soft and the escarole is completely wilted. Add the salt, then transfer the vegetables to the warm platter.
3. In the same skillet, whisk together the cornstarch mixture, lemon zest, and lemon juice and bring to a boil over high heat, stirring constantly. Simmer, stirring, for 1 to 2 minutes, or until the sauce is slightly thickened and bubbly. Add the butter and any juices that have collected on the platter and return to a boil, stirring. Cook just until the butter melts and the sauce has thickened. Pour the sauce over the chicken and vegetables and serve.

Makes 4 servings

Thai Curried Chicken and Vegetables

Hands-On Time: 40 minutes ■ Total Time: 40 minutes

The mild flavor of coconut milk contrasted with the zip of green curry paste makes a lively sauce that is delicious tossed with rice noodles and vegetables.

- 8 ounces thin rice noodles or thin spaghetti
- 4 cups small broccoli florets
- 2 tablespoons olive oil or vegetable oil (approximately)
- 1 pound boneless, skinless chicken thighs, cut into strips
- 1 large onion, cut into wedges
- 1 red bell pepper, cut into 1" pieces
- 3 cloves garlic, minced
- 1 tablespoon finely chopped fresh ginger
- 1 can (14 ounces) light coconut milk
- ⅓ cup chicken broth
- 2 tablespoons Thai fish sauce or reduced-sodium soy sauce
- 1 tablespoon green curry paste

1. In a large pot of boiling water, cook the noodles according to package directions, adding the broccoli during the last 3 minutes of cooking. Drain the noodles and broccoli together and place in a large bowl, adding a small amount of oil to keep the noodles from sticking.
2. Meanwhile, in a large nonstick skillet or wok, heat 1 tablespoon of the oil over medium-high heat. Add the chicken and cook, stirring and adding more oil if necessary, for about 8 minutes, or until browned. Transfer to a plate and keep warm.
3. Heat the remaining 1 tablespoon oil in the same skillet over medium-high heat. Add the onion, pepper, garlic, and ginger. Cook over high heat, stirring occasionally, for 3 minutes. Add the chicken along with the coconut milk, broth, fish sauce, and curry paste and bring to a boil. Reduce the heat to low and simmer, stirring occasionally, for about 4 minutes, or until the chicken is no longer pink and the vegetables are crisp-tender.
4. Add the mixture to the bowl with the noodles and broccoli and toss to combine.

Makes 4 servings

Kitchen Tip

The array of Thai ingredients in supermarkets is sure to add zest to many dishes. Try different curry pastes, sauces, and noodles (rice noodles come in different thicknesses). Be sure to use Thai light coconut milk and not cream of coconut, which is too thick and sweet for savory dishes.

Zesty Chicken with Corn Salsa

Hands-On Time: 15 minutes ■ Total Time: 25 minutes

Chili powder and ground cumin add zing to chicken breasts. Served atop a flavorful salsa, this dish is delicious every day, yet pleasing enough for company.

- 2 teaspoons chili powder
- 2 teaspoons light brown sugar
- 1 teaspoon ground cumin
- 4 boneless, skinless chicken breast halves (5 to 6 ounces each)
- 2 tablespoons olive oil
- 1 cup canned corn, drained
- ½ small red bell pepper, chopped
- ½ small cucumber, seeded and chopped
- ½ cup red kidney beans, rinsed and drained
- 3 tablespoons fresh lime juice
- ¼ teaspoon salt

1. In a cup, combine the chili powder, brown sugar, and cumin. Rub both sides of the chicken breasts with the spice mixture.
2. In a large skillet, heat the oil over medium heat. Add the chicken and cook, turning occasionally, for about 12 minutes, or until no longer pink.
3. Meanwhile, in a medium bowl, combine the corn, pepper, cucumber, beans, lime juice, and salt.
4. Evenly divide the corn salsa among 4 plates. Top each with a chicken breast and serve.

Makes 4 servings

Ingredients Note

Chili powder is a blend of dried chile peppers, garlic, cumin, coriander, cloves, and oregano. The color of chili powder can vary from light red to a dark red that is almost brown. These differences cause color changes in your dish, but the great flavor will be the same.

California Chicken

Hands-On Time: 25 minutes ■ Total Time: 40 minutes

Lemon zest and fresh herbs add a big flavor bonus to breaded chicken. You can experiment with your own herb combinations for different twists.

- 1 tablespoon whole grain mustard
- 1 large egg
- 1 cup fresh bread crumbs
- ⅓ cup grated Parmesan cheese
- 1 teaspoon grated lemon zest
- 4 boneless, skinless chicken breast halves (5 to 6 ounces each), pounded to ½" thickness
- 1 bunch watercress, trimmed, or 1 small head leaf lettuce
- 3 large plum tomatoes, chopped
- ¼ cup finely chopped red onion
- ¼ cup chopped fresh basil
- 1 tablespoon balsamic vinegar
- 2 teaspoons extra-virgin olive oil
- ⅛ teaspoon salt

1. Preheat the oven to 350°F. Grease a broiler pan and rack.
2. In a shallow bowl, beat the mustard and egg lightly with a fork. In another shallow bowl, combine the bread crumbs, cheese, and lemon zest. Dip the chicken into the mustard mixture, turning to coat, and then dredge in the bread-crumb mixture, pressing the mixture onto both sides. Place the chicken on the rack in the prepared pan.
3. Bake, turning once, for 20 minutes, or until no longer pink.
4. In a medium bowl, combine the watercress, tomatoes, onion, basil, vinegar, oil, and salt. Evenly divide the salad among 4 plates. Top each with a chicken breast and serve.

Makes 4 servings

Szechuan Stir-Fry

Hands-On Time: 35 minutes ■ Total Time: 35 minutes

Prepared stir-fry sauce makes this meal superfast. The ground red pepper adds fire to the sauce—if you prefer a milder dish, you can eliminate it.

- 1 cup white rice
- 5 tablespoons prepared stir-fry sauce
- 1 pound boneless, skinless chicken breasts, cut into 1" pieces
- 1 tablespoon grated fresh ginger
- ⅛ teaspoon ground red pepper
- 2 tablespoons vegetable oil
- 1 package (8 ounces) sliced mushrooms
- 4 ounces snow peas
- 1 medium red or yellow bell pepper, cut into strips
- ¾ cup chicken broth
- 1½ teaspoons cornstarch

1. Prepare the rice according to package directions, adding 1 tablespoon of the stir-fry sauce to the water.
2. Meanwhile, in a medium bowl, combine the remaining 4 tablespoons stir-fry sauce, the chicken, ginger, and ground red pepper. Toss to coat.
3. In a large skillet, heat 1 tablespoon of the oil over medium-high heat. Add the chicken and cook, stirring occasionally, for 6 minutes, or until no longer pink. Transfer to a plate and keep warm.
4. In the same skillet, heat the remaining 1 tablespoon oil over medium-high heat. Add the mushrooms, snow peas, and bell pepper. Cook, stirring occasionally, for 8 minutes, or until crisp-tender.
5. In a small bowl, whisk together the broth and cornstarch until dissolved. Add to the skillet and bring to a boil over high heat. Return the chicken to the skillet. Continue cooking, stirring occasionally, for 2 minutes, or until the sauce thickens and the chicken is heated through.
6. Evenly divide the rice among 4 plates and top with the chicken.

Makes 4 servings

Chicken with Black Beans and Rice

Hands-On Time: 35 minutes ■ Total Time: 35 minutes

Don't be alarmed by the long ingredient list—this family-friendly skillet dinner actually comes together quite quickly. And if you take a second glance, you'll notice that most of the ingredients are already in your cupboard.

- 1 cup white rice
- 2 tablespoons olive oil
- 1 pound boneless, skinless chicken thighs, cut into strips
- 3 scallions, cut into 1" pieces
- 1 red bell pepper, chopped
- ½ teaspoon dried oregano
- ¼ teaspoon chili powder
- 1 cup chicken broth
- 1 can (15 ounces) black beans, rinsed and drained
- ½ can (28-ounce) whole peeled tomatoes
- 1 can (4 ounces) chopped mild green chiles, rinsed and drained

1. Prepare the rice according to package directions.
2. Meanwhile, in a large skillet, heat 1 tablespoon of the oil over medium-high heat. Add the chicken and cook, stirring occasionally, for about 5 minutes, or until browned. Transfer to a plate and keep warm.
3. Heat the remaining 1 tablespoon oil in the same skillet over medium-high heat. Add the scallions, red pepper, oregano, and chili powder. Cook, stirring occasionally, for 5 minutes, or until the vegetables are crisp-tender.
4. Stir in the chicken, broth, beans, tomatoes, and chiles, using a spoon to break up the tomatoes. Bring to a boil. Reduce the heat to low, cover, and simmer for 5 minutes, or until the chicken is no longer pink. Stir in the rice.

Makes 4 servings

Southwestern Chicken Sauté

Hands-On Time: 20 minutes ■ Total Time: 30 minutes

Chicken is topped with a superchunky warm "salsa" of tomatoes, corn, and chiles in this spicy entrée. A quick chile rub gets the chicken off to a flavorful start, and then more of the chile mixture goes into the sauce. Chili powder is a spice blend, but ground red pepper is unadulterated heat: Leave it out if you prefer a milder dish.

- 1 tablespoon chili powder
- 1¼ teaspoons ground cumin
- ¼ teaspoon salt
- ⅛ teaspoon ground red pepper
- 4 boneless, skinless chicken breast halves (5 to 6 ounces each)
- 2 teaspoons olive oil
- ½ cup chicken broth
- 1 tablespoon cider vinegar
- 8 ounces plum tomatoes, diced
- 1 cup frozen corn kernels
- 1 can (4 ounces) chopped mild green chiles, rinsed and drained
- ¼ cup chopped fresh cilantro
- 1 lime, cut into 8 wedges

1. In a cup, mix the chili powder, cumin, salt, and pepper. Rub both sides of the chicken breasts with 1 tablespoon of the spice mixture.
2. In a large, heavy nonstick skillet, heat the oil over medium-high heat. Add the chicken and cook, turning once, for 4 to 6 minutes, or until the spice coating is browned and the surface of the chicken is opaque. (The chicken will finish cooking later.) Transfer the chicken to a plate.
3. Add the broth, vinegar, and remaining spice mixture to the skillet. Increase the heat to high and bring to a boil, stirring to get up any browned bits from the bottom of the skillet. Boil for 1 to 2 minutes, or until the liquid is slightly reduced.
4. Return the chicken to the skillet, adding any juices that have collected on the plate. Add the tomatoes, corn, and chiles and bring to a simmer. Spoon the corn-and-tomato mixture over the chicken and reduce the heat to medium. Cover and simmer, stirring once or twice, for 5 minutes, or until the chicken is no longer pink in the center and the flavors are blended. Transfer the chicken and vegetables to individual plates and sprinkle with the cilantro. Serve with the lime wedges.

Makes 4 servings

Ingredients Note

Cilantro, also known as coriander or Chinese parsley, looks something like flat-leaf parsley. If you're not sure which is which when you find them side by side at the market, crush a leaf between your fingers—the aroma of cilantro is unmistakable.

Crispy Cajun Chicken

Hands-On Time: 40 minutes ■ Total Time: 40 minutes

Brown sugar and Cajun seasonings come together with a sweet smack that'll have you loving every finger-licking bite of these drumsticks.

- ¼ cup ketchup
- 2 cloves garlic, minced
- 2 tablespoons light brown sugar
- 1 tablespoon chili powder
- 1 tablespoon fresh lime juice
- 1 teaspoon ground cumin
- ½ teaspoon mustard powder
- ¼ teaspoon ground red pepper
- 8 skinless chicken drumsticks (about 1 pound total)

1. Grease the grill rack. Preheat the grill to medium-hot.
2. In a medium bowl, combine the ketchup, garlic, brown sugar, chili powder, lime juice, cumin, mustard powder, and pepper until blended.
3. Place the chicken on the rack and grill, turning occasionally, for 15 minutes. Brush the chicken with the seasoning and grill for about 15 minutes longer, or until no longer pink in the center and the juices run clear.

Makes 4 servings

Accompaniment

For a fun meal in the summer, serve with grilled corn on the cob with a Peach Tart (page 319) for dessert.

Kitchen Tip

If you can't find skinless drumsticks, it's easy to skin them yourself if you use paper towels to get a good grip: Hold the skinny end of the drumstick with a paper towel, then grab the loose skin at the wide end with another paper towel in your other hand and pull down.

Enchilada Casserole

Hands-On Time: 25 minutes ■ Total Time: 45 minutes

Classic Mexican enchiladas cook up wonderfully as a casserole. It's very filling, so be sure to bring your appetite!

- 1 tablespoon olive oil or vegetable oil
- 1 pound ground chicken
- 1 can (14 to 19 ounces) red kidney beans, rinsed and drained
- 1 avocado, pitted and diced
- 1 jar (16 ounces) salsa
- 1½ cups shredded Monterey Jack cheese
- 8 corn tortillas (6" diameter)
- 1 scallion, sliced

1. Preheat the oven to 375°F. Grease a 12" × 8" baking dish.
2. Heat the oil in a large skillet over medium-high heat. Add the chicken and cook, stirring occasionally, for about 6 minutes, or until no longer pink.
3. In a large bowl, combine the chicken, beans, avocado, 1½ cups of the salsa, and 1 cup of the cheese.
4. On a work surface, fill each tortilla with ⅔ cup of the chicken mixture. Roll up and place, seam side down, in the prepared baking dish.
5. Spoon the remaining ½ cup salsa over the tortillas. Sprinkle with the remaining ½ cup cheese and the scallion. Cover with foil and bake for 15 minutes. Remove the foil and bake for 5 minutes longer, or until heated through.

Makes 4 servings

Bird Basics

Supermarkets stock a variety of chickens, which are classified according to size. Here's a look at what you'll find.

- **Broilers.** The smallest of the chickens, broilers are all-purpose birds that weigh less than 2½ pounds. They can be used in virtually any recipe and are often sold cut up.
- **Capons.** Young roosters that were castrated and then fattened up, capons usually weigh between 6 and 10 pounds each. A large percentage of their weight is in tender breast meat.
- **Cornish hens.** These are small hybrid chickens that weigh up to 2½ pounds. They have tender, delicate meat. The smaller Cornish hens tend to be enough to make a single serving. These birds are also called Cornish game hens and Rock Cornish hens.
- **Fryers.** Slightly larger than broilers, these weigh between 2½ and 3 pounds. Fryers are also considered all-purpose birds. They can be roasted whole, but they are more commonly cut into parts.
- **Roasters.** Young birds weighing between 3 and 5 pounds, roasters are sold whole and should be cooked that way, too. They can be roasted in the oven or grilled or smoked outdoors.
- **Stewers.** Older birds weighing between 4½ and 7 pounds, these are very flavorful. They are also the least tender and are used for making soups and stews.

Chicken Pesto Pizza

Hands-On Time: 10 minutes ■ Total Time: 20 minutes

A prebaked pizza shell is the secret to this quick and easy dish—great for those rushed weeknights! Or serve as an appetizer the next time you have company.

1 (12") prebaked pizza shell

⅓ cup prepared pesto

1 cup cooked chicken strips

1 roasted red pepper, cut into small strips

½ cup canned artichoke hearts, rinsed, drained, patted dry, and quartered

½ cup crumbled goat cheese

1. Preheat the oven to 450°F. Place the pizza shell on a baking sheet.
2. Evenly spread the pesto over the crust. Arrange the chicken, pepper strips, and artichokes over the pesto. Top with the cheese.
3. Bake for 10 minutes, or until the pizza is heated through and the crust is crisp.

Makes 4 servings

Accompaniments

Serve with Creamy Caesar Salad (page 62) or Orange Salad with Honey Vinaigrette (page 68).

Ingredients Note

If you have leftovers from a roasted chicken, this is a great way to put them to use. If you don't have leftovers, pick up roasted chicken at the deli counter or a rotisserie chicken from the prepared foods section of your supermarket.

Basic Poultry Roasting Time & Temperature Chart

The most accurate measurement of doneness for poultry is the internal temperature at a specific location on the bird as registered on a meat thermometer, either the conventional model or the instant-read type. This method of testing is best because the shape, age, and tenderness of poultry influence how fast it cooks, and so does the oven temperature.

TYPE OF POULTRY	OVEN TEMPERATURE	WEIGHT	DONENESS	ROASTING TIME
TURKEY				
Breast, bone-in	350°F	4–6 lb	165°F*	1–1½ hr
Breast, boned & tied	350°F	4–5 lb	165°F**	1–1½ hr
Thigh	375°F	½–1½ lb	180°F***	¾–1¼ hr
Whole, unstuffed	350°F	10–13 lb	160°F*	1½–2¼ hr
Whole, unstuffed	325°F	14–23 lb	160°F*	2–3 hr
Whole, unstuffed	325°F	24–27 lb	160°F*	3–3¼ hr
Whole, unstuffed	325°F	28–30 lb	160°F*	3½–4½ hr
CHICKEN				
Breast halves, boned & skinned	450°F	4–5 oz	No longer pink in center	12–15 min
Whole breast, bone-in	450°F	1 lb	No longer pink in center	15–20 min
Legs & thighs, attached or apart	400°F	10 oz	Not pink at thigh bone	40–45 min
Whole, unstuffed	375°F	3½–5 lb	180°F***	1–1¼ hr
Whole, unstuffed	375°F	5–7 lb	180°F***	1¼–1½ hr
ROCK CORNISH GAME HEN				
Whole, unstuffed	450°F	1–2 lb	Not pink at thigh bone	30–40 min

*Insert meat thermometer through thickest part of breast to bone.
**Insert meat thermometer into center of thickest part of breast.
***Insert meat thermometer through thickest part of thigh to bone.

Lemon Turkey Cutlets

Hands-On Time: 15 minutes ■ Total Time: 15 minutes

For a pretty garnish for these quick turkey cutlets, roll peeled lemon slices in fresh minced herbs such as thyme or mint, and place a slice on each plate or arrange on the serving platter.

- 4 turkey breast cutlets, ¼" thick
- ¼ cup all-purpose flour
- 2 tablespoons vegetable oil
- ½ cup chicken broth
- 1 teaspoon grated lemon zest
- 1 teaspoon chopped fresh thyme
- 1 teaspoon cornstarch mixed with 1 tablespoon cold water

1. Dredge the cutlets in the flour. In a large nonstick skillet, heat the oil over medium-high heat. Add the cutlets and cook, turning once, for about 2 minutes, or until a light golden brown. Transfer the turkey to a warmed plate.
2. Add the broth, lemon zest, and thyme to the pan and bring to a boil. Add the cornstarch mixture. Cook over medium heat, stirring, for 2 minutes, or until the mixture thickens and becomes glossy. Add the turkey and cook for 2 minutes, or until no longer pink.

Makes 4 servings

Accompaniments

Serve this lemony turkey on a bed of plain steamed rice alongside Glazed Carrots (page 263), Minted Peas (page 271), or any other vegetable.

Turkey "Pot Pie" with Buttermilk Biscuits

Hands-On Time: 25 minutes ■ Total Time: 55 minutes

Yes! You can have old-fashioned turkey pot pie in less than an hour. Cooked turkey from the deli and frozen mixed vegetables help streamline the family favorite.

- 1 cup all-purpose flour
- 1 teaspoon baking powder
- ¼ teaspoon baking soda
- Pinch of salt
- 1 tablespoon plus 2 teaspoons chilled unsalted butter, cut into small pieces
- ¼ cup buttermilk
- 3 tablespoons sour cream
- 1¾ cups chicken broth
- ⅓ cup chopped onion
- 2 teaspoons minced garlic
- 2½ tablespoons cornstarch
- ½ teaspoon dried thyme
- ¼ teaspoon dried sage
- 2 cups frozen mixed peas, carrots, and cauliflower, thawed
- 2 cups finely chopped cooked turkey breast

1. Preheat the oven to 425°F.
2. In a medium bowl, mix the flour, baking powder, baking soda, and salt. Cut in the butter with 2 knives or a pastry blender until the mixture resembles fine crumbs. Stir in the buttermilk and sour cream to form a dough. Turn the dough onto a sheet of plastic wrap, flatten into a large disk, and wrap tightly. Refrigerate while you make the turkey mixture.
3. In a large skillet, bring ¼ cup of the broth to a boil over high heat. Add the onion and garlic, reduce the heat to medium-high, and cook for 2 minutes.
4. Meanwhile, in a small bowl, mix the cornstarch, thyme, and sage. Stir in the remaining 1½ cups broth until smooth.
5. Add the cornstarch mixture to the skillet. Cook over medium-high heat until the mixture comes to a boil and thickens. Remove the pan from the heat and stir in the vegetables and turkey. Transfer to an 8" × 8" baking dish.
6. Pat the dough into a 4" × 4" square about ½" thick. Cut the dough into 4 equal pieces. Arrange the dough on top of the filling. Bake for 30 minutes, or until the biscuits are golden brown and the turkey mixture is bubbling.

Makes 4 servings

Cheddar Turkey Burgers

Hands-On Time: 30 minutes ■ Total Time: 30 minutes

Stuffing each burger with Cheddar cheese adds flavor to the mild turkey and gives diners a delightful surprise.

- 1 pound ground turkey breast
- ¼ cup fresh bread crumbs
- 1 tablespoon stone-ground mustard
- ⅛ teaspoon dried thyme
- ⅛ teaspoon dried sage
- ¼ cup shredded extra-sharp Cheddar cheese
- 1 large red onion, sliced crosswise
- 4 hamburger buns, split and toasted
- 1 medium tomato, sliced
- 4 lettuce leaves

1. Preheat the grill or broiler.
2. In a medium bowl, combine the turkey, bread crumbs, mustard, thyme, and sage; mix well. Form into 4 balls. Make an indentation in the center of 1 ball and stuff with one-fourth of the cheese. Close the indentation by pressing the turkey around it to seal in the cheese. Form into a patty. Repeat to make 3 more patties.
3. Coat the onion slices with cooking spray; grill or broil the onion and burgers 4" from the heat, turning the onion slices as needed, for 5 to 7 minutes, or until the onion slices are golden. Place the onion on a plate and cover to keep warm. Turn the burgers and grill for about 5 minutes longer, or until no longer pink near the center.
4. Place the burgers in the buns; top with the onion, tomato, and lettuce; and serve.

Makes 4 servings

Nutri-Note

Just a little bit of sharp Cheddar cheese adds loads of flavor—but little fat—to these healthful burgers. Serve the patties on whole grain buns for an even healthier meal.

Turkey Croquettes

Hands-On Time: 45 minutes ■ Total Time: 1 hour

Here's a time-honored way to use up leftover cooked turkey. You'll need to boil the eggs in advance.

- 4 cups finely chopped cooked turkey
- ½ cup finely chopped onion
- ¼ cup finely chopped celery
- ¼ cup finely chopped fresh parsley
- 2 large hard-boiled eggs, finely chopped
- ⅓ cup mayonnaise
- 2 teaspoons Worcestershire sauce
- ½ teaspoon paprika
- ¼ teaspoon dry mustard
- ¼ teaspoon ground black pepper
- 1 large egg
- 1½ cups fresh bread crumbs
- 1 tablespoon olive oil
- 1½ cups plain yogurt
- 2 tablespoons chopped fresh chives
- 1 teaspoon fresh lemon juice

1. In a large bowl, mix the turkey, onion, celery, parsley, and cooked eggs.
2. In a small bowl, whisk together the mayonnaise, Worcestershire sauce, paprika, mustard, and pepper. Stir into the turkey mixture and blend well. Form into 4 thick patties. Cover and refrigerate for at least 15 minutes to set the mixture.
3. In a shallow bowl, lightly beat the egg with a fork. Place the bread crumbs on a sheet of wax paper. Dip each patty into the egg, then dredge in the bread crumbs to coat well.
4. In a large nonstick skillet, heat the oil over medium-high heat. Add the patties and cook, turning once, for about 10 minutes, or until golden.
5. In a small bowl, whisk together the yogurt, chives, and lemon juice. Serve as a sauce with the patties.

Makes 4 servings

Cincinnati Turkey Chili

Hands-On Time: 35 minutes ■ Total Time: 55 minutes

Cincinnati's famed chili is in a class by itself. Served atop a mound of spaghetti, it may have been the first "have it your way" food: You can order it "three-way" (spaghetti and chili topped with shredded Cheddar),"four-way" (plus chopped raw onions), or "five-way" (crowned with kidney beans). Our five-way turkey chili—here the beans are cooked right in the chili—is served with oyster crackers, a traditional, if surprising, accompaniment.

- 2 tablespoons vegetable oil
- ¾ pound boneless, skinless turkey breast, cut into 1" cubes
- 1 medium yellow onion, finely chopped
- 1 medium green bell pepper, finely chopped
- 3 cloves garlic, minced
- 4 teaspoons chili powder
- 2 teaspoons ground cumin
- 1 teaspoon dried oregano
- ½ teaspoon ground cinnamon
- 1 can (28 ounces) crushed tomatoes
- ¾ cup chicken broth
- 2 cans (15 to 19 ounces each) red kidney beans, rinsed and drained
- 1 teaspoon red wine vinegar
- ½ teaspoon Worcestershire sauce
- 8 ounces spaghetti
- ¼ cup finely chopped red onion
- ½ cup shredded sharp Cheddar cheese
- Oyster crackers (optional)

1. Bring a large covered pot of water to a boil over high heat.
2. Meanwhile, in a large, heavy saucepan, heat the oil over medium-high heat until very hot but not smoking. Add the turkey and cook, stirring, for 2 to 3 minutes, or until browned. Transfer to a plate.
3. Add the yellow onion and bell pepper to the pan. Reduce the heat to medium, cover, and cook, stirring occasionally, for 5 minutes, or until the vegetables are tender. Add the garlic, chili powder, cumin, oregano, and cinnamon and stir for 30 seconds, or until fragrant. Add the tomatoes and broth and bring to a boil. Add the beans, vinegar, and Worcestershire sauce and bring to a boil. Reduce the heat to medium-low, cover, and simmer for 10 minutes. Add the turkey and simmer for 5 minutes longer.
4. While the chili is simmering, add the spaghetti to the boiling water, return to a boil, and cook for 10 to 12 minutes or according to package directions until al dente. Drain in a colander.
5. Divide the spaghetti among 4 bowls. Ladle the chili over the spaghetti and top with the red onion and cheese. Serve with oyster crackers, if desired.

Makes 4 servings

Peppery Turkey Melts with Salsa

Hands-On Time: 30 minutes ■ Total Time: 30 minutes

These grown-up burgers have a bit of heat from the pepper Jack cheese. For younger, more tender palates, use regular Monterey Jack and choose a mild salsa to top the burgers.

- ¾ pound boneless, skinless turkey breast, cut into chunks
- ½ cup prepared salsa
- 1 large egg
- 2 tablespoons unseasoned dried bread crumbs
- 1 tablespoon mayonnaise
- ½ teaspoon coarsely ground black pepper
- 2 tablespoons vegetable oil
- ½ cup shredded pepper Jack cheese
- 2 English muffins, split and toasted
- 1 cup shredded Boston lettuce

1. Place the turkey in a food processor and pulse until coarsely ground. Add 2 tablespoons of the salsa, the egg, bread crumbs, mayonnaise, and pepper and pulse briefly just to combine. Shape the mixture into 4 patties.
2. In a large skillet, heat the oil over medium heat. Add the patties and cook, turning once, for 10 to 12 minutes, or until cooked through. Top the patties with the cheese, cover the skillet, and cook for 1 minute longer, or until the cheese is melted.
3. Place an English muffin half on each of 4 plates and place a turkey burger on each one. Top with some of the remaining salsa and ¼ cup shredded lettuce.

Makes 4 servings

Accompaniment

Serve the sandwiches with pickles (try pickled peppers or tomatoes for a change) and oven-fried potatoes.

Kitchen Tips

To shred lettuce quickly, stack the leaves and roll them loosely into a cylinder. Cut crosswise with a large knife.

Rather then pressing the turkey patties between your palms (which makes for tough burgers), place the mixture on a cutting board covered with wax paper and pat each portion gently into shape.

Chile-Grilled Turkey

Hands-On Time: 30 minutes ■ Total Time: 1 hour (plus marinating)

Quickly sear turkey breast on a grill pan, then bake in the oven atop pickled jalapeño peppers for true Southwest flavor.

Tomatillo Relish

- 1 cup coarsely chopped canned tomatillos
- Juice and grated zest of ½ lime
- 3 tablespoons olive oil
- 1 tablespoon chopped fresh cilantro
- 2 cloves garlic, minced
- ¼ teaspoon salt
- ¼ teaspoon ground black pepper
- Pinch of sugar

Turkey

- ½ cup prepared chipotle salsa
- ⅓ cup fresh lime juice
- 1 teaspoon sugar
- ⅛ teaspoon ground cumin
- Ground black pepper
- 1 pound turkey breast cutlet, lightly pounded to 1" thick
- 1 cup pickled whole jalapeño peppers, drained
- 1 tablespoon cider vinegar
- 2 tablespoons chopped fresh cilantro
- Baked tortilla chips (optional)

1. *To make the relish:* In a food processor, combine the tomatillos, lime juice, lime zest, oil, cilantro, garlic, salt, pepper, and sugar. Pulse until chunky. Transfer to a bowl, cover, and refrigerate until ready to serve.
2. *To make the turkey:* In a small glass bowl, combine the salsa, lime juice, sugar, cumin, and pepper. Spread evenly on the turkey and refrigerate in a zip-top bag for no more than 2 to 3 hours.
3. Preheat the oven to 400°F.
4. Remove the turkey from the marinade (reserve 3 tablespoons) and pat dry. In an ovenproof grill pan set over high heat, cook the turkey, turning once, for 8 minutes. Transfer to a plate and set aside.
5. Spread the jalapeños on the grill pan. Pour the vinegar over the chiles, followed by the reserved marinade. Lay the turkey breast over the chiles. Cover loosely with foil and bake for 15 to 20 minutes. Uncover and bake for 5 minutes longer, or until the turkey is no longer pink. Let rest for about 5 minutes.
6. Slice the turkey against the grain into ¼" strips. Top with the tomatillo relish and cilantro. Serve with the jalapeños and the tortilla chips, if you like.

Makes 4 servings

Tex-Mex Turkey and Black Bean Stew

Hands-On Time: 30 minutes ■ Total Time: 35 minutes

This family-pleasing turkey stew is a lot like chili, but it is served over bulgur—cracked, steamed kernels of wheat that make a satisfying alternative to rice.

- ½ pound boneless, skinless turkey breast, cut into chunks
- 2 tablespoons olive oil
- 1 medium green bell pepper, cut into ½" dice
- 1 medium red bell pepper, cut into ½" dice
- 1 large onion, coarsely chopped
- 2 cloves garlic, minced
- 2 tablespoons chili powder
- 1 tablespoon ground cumin
- ¾ teaspoon ground black pepper
- ½ teaspoon dried oregano, crumbled
- ½ teaspoon salt
- 2 cans (14½ ounces each) stewed tomatoes
- 1 can (16 ounces) black beans, rinsed and drained
- ¾ cup prepared hot or medium salsa
- 2 cups water
- 1 cup medium-coarse bulgur
- ¼ teaspoon hot pepper sauce

1. In a food processor, pulse the turkey until coarsely chopped; set aside.
2. In a Dutch oven, heat 1 tablespoon of the oil over medium-high heat. Add the green and red bell peppers, onion, and garlic and cook, stirring occasionally, for 5 minutes, or until the vegetables are crisp-tender. Stir in the remaining 1 tablespoon oil, then the reserved turkey, chili powder, cumin, black pepper, oregano, and ¼ teaspoon of the salt. Cook, stirring and breaking up any clumps of meat with a spoon, for 1 to 2 minutes, or just until the ingredients are well mixed and the turkey starts to turn white.
3. Add the tomatoes, beans, and salsa and bring to a boil, breaking up the tomatoes with a spoon. Reduce the heat to medium-low, cover, and simmer gently for 20 minutes.
4. Meanwhile, combine the water, bulgur, hot pepper sauce, and remaining ¼ teaspoon salt in a heavy medium saucepan and bring to a boil over high heat. Reduce the heat to low, cover, and simmer for 15 to 20 minutes, or until the bulgur is tender and the liquid has been absorbed.
5. Spoon the bulgur into bowls and ladle the stew on top.

Makes 4 servings

Kitchen Tip

To chill the turkey quickly for easier grinding, cut the meat into chunks and then place it in the freezer for a few minutes.

Cornish Hens with Oranges and Rice

Hands-On Time: 30 minutes ■ Total Time: 1 hour 10 minutes (plus marinating)

Serving fruit with poultry is very popular in many cultures. We like this orange-accented version because the oranges provide a sweet counterpoint to the spicy seasonings.

- 2⁄3 cup apple cider vinegar
- 1 tablespoon Worcestershire sauce
- 1⁄2 teaspoon paprika
- 1⁄4 teaspoon Angostura bitters
- Dash of hot pepper sauce
- 1 dried red chile pepper
- 1 jalapeño pepper
- 2 cloves garlic, minced
- 2 Cornish hens (about 1 pound each), split in half
- 2 cups water
- 1 tablespoon unsalted butter or olive oil
- 1 cup white rice
- 2 tablespoons chopped fresh parsley
- 1 1⁄2 cups orange sections

1. In a large glass baking dish, combine the vinegar, Worcestershire sauce, paprika, bitters, and hot pepper sauce.
2. Wearing rubber gloves to protect your hands, split both the dried chile pepper and the jalapeño pepper in half and remove the seeds. Finely chop both, then transfer to a mortar and pestle. Add the garlic and mash into a paste. Add to the vinegar mixture and stir well.
3. Remove any visible fat from the hens, especially the cavity area. Place in the baking dish, turning the pieces several times to coat with the marinade. Cover and refrigerate overnight or for up to 24 hours.
4. When ready to cook, preheat the broiler. Remove the hens from the marinade, reserving the marinade, and place on a broiler pan. Broil 4" from the heat, turning once, for 20 to 30 minutes, or until no longer pink in the center and the juices at a leg joint run clear. Baste occasionally with the reserved marinade. (If the hens seem to darken too fast, move them farther from the heat.)
5. While the hens are cooking, prepare the rice: In a large saucepan, bring the water and butter to a boil. Add the rice and bring to a simmer. Reduce the heat to low, cover, and cook for 18 to 20 minutes, or until all the liquid is absorbed. Remove from the heat and let stand until the hens are ready.
6. Stir the parsley into the rice. Serve the hens with the rice and orange sections.

Makes 4 servings

Ingredients Note

If you prefer brown rice, start cooking the rice 45 to 60 minutes before serving.

Grilled Cornish Hens with Strawberry Marinade

Hands-On Time: 55 minutes ■ Total Time: 1 hour 15 minutes (plus marinating)

In this summer entrée, fresh ripe strawberries and strawberry vinegar create a distinctive marinade for grilled Cornish hens. If you don't have strawberry vinegar, substitute another mild fruit vinegar.

- 4 Cornish hens (1 to 1½ pounds each), split in half
- 1 cup strawberry vinegar
- ¾ cup puréed fresh or frozen strawberries
- 2 tablespoons finely chopped fresh mint
- 1 tablespoon finely chopped shallot or onion
- Grated zest of 1 lemon
- ⅛ teaspoon ground black pepper
- 2 tablespoons olive oil

1. Place the hens in a shallow glass or ceramic container large enough to hold them in a single layer.
2. In a small bowl, combine the vinegar, strawberries, mint, shallot, lemon zest, and pepper. Whisk in the oil. Pour over the hens. Loosen the skin slightly to place some marinade underneath. Cover and refrigerate for 4 hours.
3. Grease the grill rack. Preheat the grill to medium-hot.
4. Remove the hens from the marinade; reserve the marinade. Place the hens, skin side down, on the rack. Cover the grill and cook for 10 minutes. Turn the hens and cook, basting frequently with the reserved marinade, for 25 to 30 minutes, or until no longer pink in the center and the juices at a leg joint run clear. Discard any remaining marinade.
5. Remove the hens from the grill and let stand for 10 minutes. Remove and discard the skin if you like. Serve hot or at room temperature.

Makes 8 servings

Kitchen Tip

If you have a bounty of ripe berries during strawberry season, you can make your own fruit vinegar: In a stainless-steel or nonstick saucepan, bring 1 quart white wine vinegar and 2 cups cleaned, hulled strawberries to a simmer. Pour into a sterilized crock or jar. Cover and refrigerate for 2 weeks. Strain the mixture through a cheesecloth-lined sieve into a sterilized bottle and store in the refrigerator. Use in salads and marinades, or sprinkle a few drops on grilled fish as an interesting change from lemon.

Meaty Entrées

Pepper-Marinated Flank Steak

Hands-On Time: 20 minutes ■ Total Time: 50 minutes (plus marinating)

This all-in-one broiler dinner pairs pepper-encrusted steak with squash and sweet potatoes. For the most tender steak, be sure to cut the strips on the diagonal against the grain.

- 2 teaspoons dried thyme
- 2 cloves garlic, minced
- ½ teaspoon ground black pepper
- 2 tablespoons olive oil
- 1 pound flank steak, trimmed
- 1 pound sweet potatoes, peeled, halved, and cut into long spears
- 4 small yellow squash, halved lengthwise

1. In a cup, mix the thyme, garlic, and pepper with 1 teaspoon of the oil. Rub three-fourths of the mixture over the steak. Cover and let stand for 30 minutes or refrigerate for up to 1 day.
2. Preheat the broiler. Add the remaining 5 teaspoons oil to the rest of the herb mixture. Brush the sweet potatoes and squash with the herb mixture.
3. Place the vegetables on a broiler pan, leaving room for the steak. Broil the vegetables 6" from the heat for 10 minutes, turning and rearranging them as needed to cook evenly.
4. Add the steak to the broiler pan and cook, turning once, for 12 to 15 minutes for medium-rare to medium. As the meat cooks, continue to turn the vegetables until the sweet potatoes can be easily pierced with a fork. The vegetables will take about 20 minutes total.
5. To serve, cut the meat thinly across the grain on the diagonal. Arrange on a large platter with the vegetables.

Makes 4 servings

Variation

To grill the meat and vegetables: Start the sweet potatoes first because they tend to take longer on a grill. Let them cook for about 10 minutes before adding the squash. Then follow the timetable in the recipe. Be sure to move the vegetables and turn them frequently to compensate for the uneven heat of most grills.

Kitchen Tip

To shorten the cooking time of the sweet potatoes, microwave them for about 5 minutes before broiling.

Round Steak Casserole

Hands-On Time: 25 minutes ■ Total Time: 1 hour 55 minutes

Top round steak is a flavorful cut of beef that takes well to long, moist cooking. Here, it cooks in tomatoes and other vegetables for an easy one-pot dinner.

- 1 tablespoon vegetable oil
- 1 pound top round steak, cut into 1" pieces
- 4 medium potatoes, quartered
- 2 cans (28 ounces each) crushed tomatoes
- 1 can (14½ ounces) green beans, drained
- 1 can (14½ ounces) sliced carrots, drained
- 1 small head cabbage, chopped
- 1 onion, quartered
- 1 teaspoon dried thyme
- 1 teaspoon salt
- ½ teaspoon ground black pepper
- ½ teaspoon garlic powder

1. Preheat the oven to 425°F.
2. In a large Dutch oven, heat the oil over medium heat. Add the steak and cook, stirring occasionally, for about 10 minutes, or until browned. Add the potatoes, tomatoes, green beans, carrots, cabbage, onion, thyme, salt, pepper, and garlic powder.
3. Cover and bake for 1 hour. Reduce the heat to 400°F. Uncover and bake for 30 minutes longer, or until the beef is tender.

Makes 6 servings

Mexican Beef Stew

Hands-On Time: 30 minutes ■ Total Time: 1 hour

Bold flavors from Mexican spices are featured in this beef-and-vegetable stew.

- 1 tablespoon olive oil
- 2 pounds lean, well-trimmed beef chuck blade, cut into ½" cubes
- 1 teaspoon salt
- ¼ teaspoon ground black pepper
- 2 medium onions, coarsely chopped
- 1 red bell pepper, coarsely chopped
- 2 medium zucchini, halved lengthwise and cut into ½"-thick slices
- 2 cloves garlic, minced
- 1 can (28 ounces) crushed tomatoes
- 5 cups water
- 1½ tablespoons chili powder
- 1 tablespoon ground cumin
- 2 cups white rice
- 1 package (10 ounces) frozen corn kernels, thawed
- ¼ cup fresh cilantro, chopped (optional)

1. In a Dutch oven or large, heavy saucepan, heat the oil over medium-high heat. Add the beef and cook, stirring occasionally, for 3 minutes, or until browned on all sides. Stir in ½ teaspoon of the salt and the black pepper.
2. Add the onions, bell pepper, zucchini, and garlic, and cook for 5 minutes, or until the vegetables are softened. Add the tomatoes, 1 cup of the water, the chili powder, and cumin. Cover and bring to a boil; boil for 2 minutes. Reduce the heat to medium, partially cover, and cook for 25 minutes, or until the beef is tender.
3. Meanwhile, in a medium saucepan, combine the rice with the remaining 4 cups water and ½ teaspoon salt. Bring to a boil over medium heat. Cover the pan, reduce the heat to low, and cook for 17 to 20 minutes, or until the rice is tender and the liquid absorbed.
4. When the beef is tender, add the corn to the stew and cook for about 3 minutes, or until heated through. Ladle the stew over the rice and sprinkle with the cilantro, if using.

Makes 8 servings

Make-Ahead

The day before you intend to serve the stew, follow the recipe through step 2. The next day, cook the rice (step 3) while you reheat the stew, then complete step 4 and ladle the stew over the freshly cooked rice.

Chili-Glazed Mini Meat Loaves

Hands-On Time: 20 minutes ■ Total Time: 55 minutes

Your family will love these individual meat loaves. For a healthier option, replace half the beef with skinless chicken breast meat.

- ½ small onion, cut into chunks
- 2 tablespoons fresh parsley
- 1 clove garlic, peeled
- 1 pound trimmed beef top round, cut into chunks
- ¼ cup unseasoned dried bread crumbs
- 4 tablespoons chili sauce
- 1 large egg
- 1 tablespoon milk
- ½ teaspoon dried thyme, crumbled
- ¼ teaspoon ground black pepper
- ⅛ teaspoon salt

1. Preheat the oven to 400°F. Grease a 13" × 9" baking pan.
2. In a food processor, place the onion, parsley, and garlic and process until finely chopped. Add the beef and process until ground. Add the bread crumbs, 2 tablespoons of the chili sauce, the egg, milk, thyme, pepper, and salt and pulse until the mixture is well blended.
3. Divide the mixture into 4 equal portions and shape each into a small oval loaf. Place the meat loaves in the prepared pan, leaving space between them.
4. Bake for 20 minutes. Brush the tops of the loaves with the remaining 2 tablespoons chili sauce and bake for 5 minutes longer, or until browned and a meat thermometer inserted into the center of one of the loaves registers 175°F.

Makes 4 servings

Confetti Meat Loaf

Hands-On Time: 20 minutes ■ Total Time: 1 hour 50 minutes

This pretty meat loaf really does look like it has confetti sprinkled on top. Using brown rice extends the meat loaf mix (which is available at most supermarkets) and keeps the meat loaf moist while adding a nutty flavor. Keep cooked brown rice in the freezer for fast and easy preparation. This makes a nice meal with roasted potatoes and steamed broccoli.

- 1 cup water
- 1½ teaspoons unsalted butter
- ½ cup brown rice
- 1 tablespoon olive oil or vegetable oil
- 1 small onion, chopped
- ½ cup chopped green bell pepper
- ½ cup chopped red bell pepper
- 1 pound prepared meat loaf mix (beef, pork, and veal)
- 1 cup chunky salsa
- ¼ cup seasoned dried bread crumbs
- 1 large egg
- ¾ teaspoon salt
- ½ teaspoon ground black pepper
- ¼ teaspoon celery seed

1. In a large saucepan, bring the water and butter to a boil. Add the rice and bring to a simmer. Reduce the heat to low, cover, and cook for about 45 minutes, or until all the liquid is absorbed. Remove from the heat and let stand, covered, until ready to use.
2. Preheat the oven to 350°F.
3. In a small skillet, heat the oil over medium heat. Add the onion and green and red bell pepper and cook for about 5 minutes, or until softened.
4. In a large bowl, combine the meat loaf mix, salsa, bread crumbs, egg, salt, black pepper, and celery seed. Stir in the rice and sautéed vegetables. Place the mixture in a large round baking dish and shape into an oval loaf about 8" × 5" × 2". Bake for 45 to 50 minutes, or until a meat thermometer inserted into the center registers 160°F and the meat is no longer pink.

Makes 6 servings

Variations

You can use ground chicken or turkey or a combination for this recipe, if you prefer.

Marinated Filet Mignon

Hands-On Time: 15 minutes ■ Total Time: 1 hour 15 minutes

Why not treat yourself to the best when you indulge in steak? Tenderloin fits the bill perfectly. Here, it's enhanced with an herb-mustard vinaigrette.

- 1 beef tenderloin (3 pounds), trimmed
- 1 onion, thinly sliced
- ⅓ cup dry red wine
- ¼ cup chopped fresh basil
- 2 tablespoons olive oil
- 1½ tablespoons ground black pepper
- 1½ tablespoons dried thyme
- 1 tablespoon Dijon mustard
- 2 large cloves garlic, minced

1. Place the beef in a long, shallow casserole or dish. In a medium bowl, combine the onion, wine, basil, oil, pepper, thyme, mustard, and garlic. Pour over the beef. Cover with plastic wrap and refrigerate for at least 3 hours (or up to 24 hours), turning and basting several times.
2. Preheat the oven to 400°F.
3. Remove the beef from the marinade and place in a roasting pan; discard the marinade. Roast, turning and basting the beef in its own juices several times, for 35 minutes, or until the beef reaches an internal temperature of 140°F for rare. If desired, continue roasting to an internal temperature of 160°F for medium. Let stand for 15 minutes before slicing.

Makes 8 servings

Marinated London Broil with Gravy

Hands-On Time: 25 minutes ■ Total Time: 1 hour 5 minutes

While the marinated beef grills, make an oh-so-easy gravy on the stove top.

London Broil and Marinade

- 3 cloves garlic, halved
- 2 pounds beef top round, about 2" thick
- 3 tablespoons balsamic vinegar
- 1 teaspoon dried thyme
- 1 teaspoon ground coriander
- Ground black pepper

Gravy

- 2 tablespoons cornstarch
- ¼ teaspoon dry mustard
- 2 cups beef broth

1. *To marinate the London broil:* Pierce the flat side of each half of the garlic cloves and rub the garlic over the beef. In a large glass baking dish, combine the vinegar, thyme, and coriander. Add the beef and garlic halves. Turn the meat to coat both sides evenly with the marinade. Set aside to marinate, turning once, for 30 minutes. Discard the marinade.
2. Grease the grill rack. Preheat the grill.
3. Place the meat on the rack and grill about 6" from the heat, turning once, for about 15 minutes for rare. (Cook 1 to 2 minutes longer per side for medium doneness.) Remove and let stand for 5 minutes. Carve into thin slices. Season with the pepper.
4. *To make the gravy:* While the London broil is grilling, in a medium saucepan, dissolve the cornstarch and mustard in ¼ cup of the broth. Whisk in the remaining 1¾ cups broth and cook over medium heat until the gravy comes to a boil and thickens. Serve with the London broil.

Makes 8 servings

To make mushroom gravy, heat 1 teaspoon olive oil in a medium saucepan. Add ½ cup chopped shiitake, portobello, or button mushrooms. Cook, stirring, for 5 to 7 minutes, or until the mushrooms begin to release their liquid. Stir in the cornstarch and mustard until dissolved. Add the broth and cook, stirring constantly, until thick.

Home-Run Hamburgers

Hands-On Time: 45 minutes ■ Total Time: 55 minutes

Bulgur adds a little bulk to hamburger patties, while Worcestershire sauce, tomato paste, and garlic contribute piquant flavor. Top the burgers with sautéed sweet onions and mushrooms and you have an incomparable meal. For hotter, smokier flavor, add a couple of drops of liquid smoke and a few dashes of hot pepper sauce to the meat mixture before forming into patties.

- 3 tablespoons bulgur
- ⅓ cup boiling water
- 1 teaspoon olive oil
- 1 medium Vidalia onion, thinly sliced
- 1½ cups sliced shiitake mushroom caps
- 1¼ pounds ground beef
- ⅓ cup fresh bread crumbs
- ¼ cup chopped fresh flat-leaf parsley
- 2 tablespoons Worcestershire sauce
- 2 tablespoons tomato paste
- 2 cloves garlic, minced
- 1 teaspoon black pepper
- ½ teaspoon dry mustard
- 6 leaves red leaf lettuce
- 6 tomato slices
- 6 hamburger buns, split

1. Grease a grill rack or broiler-pan rack. Preheat the grill or broiler.
2. Place the bulgur in a large bowl and add the water. Cover and let stand for 15 minutes, or until soft.
3. Meanwhile, in a large nonstick skillet, heat the oil over medium heat. Add the onion and cook for 10 minutes, or until soft. Add the mushrooms and cook for 5 minutes, or until soft. Set aside.
4. Drain the bulgur and return it to the bowl. Stir in the beef, bread crumbs, parsley, Worcestershire sauce, tomato paste, garlic, pepper, and mustard. Shape the mixture into six 1"-thick patties.
5. Cook the burgers 4" from the heat, turning once, for 8 minutes, or until a thermometer inserted into a burger registers 160°F and the meat is no longer pink.
6. Place the lettuce and tomato on the bottom halves of the buns. Top with the burgers, then divide the onion and mushrooms among the burgers. Top each with the bun tops.

Makes 6 servings

Spicy Beef Burgers

Hands-On Time: 20 minutes ■ Total Time: 25 minutes

Nothing could be faster or easier for a summer weeknight dinner.

1 pound ground beef

2 tablespoons barbecue sauce

1 tablespoon steak sauce

1 tablespoon minced garlic

1 tablespoon seeded and chopped jalapeño pepper (wear plastic gloves when handling)

1 teaspoon chili powder

4 hamburger buns, split

2 tablespoons mayonnaise

1. Grease a grill rack or broiler-pan rack. Preheat the grill or broiler.
2. In a medium bowl, combine the beef, barbecue sauce, steak sauce, garlic, jalapeño pepper, and chili powder. Form into 4 patties.
3. Cook the burgers 4" from the heat, turning once, for 8 minutes, or until a thermometer inserted into a burger registers 160°F and the meat is no longer pink.
4. Toast the buns, spread with the mayonnaise, and top with the patties.

Makes 4 servings

Accompaniments

Serve with Cucumber and Tomato Salad with Sour Cream Dressing (page 65) or Carrot Salad (page 69) and pink lemonade or ice cold mugs of beer.

Sloppy Joes

Hands-On Time: 30 minutes ■ Total Time: 30 minutes

With the advent of fast-food hamburgers, sloppy joes, which were once ubiquitous on the family dinner table, have been more or less forgotten. This dinner is so quick and easy, you'll want to make it often—the kids or grandkids will love it. Italian ciabatta rolls make a nice change from traditional burger buns.

- 4 teaspoons olive oil
- 1 onion, chopped
- 1 green bell pepper, chopped
- 1 stalk celery, chopped
- 2 cloves garlic, minced
- 1 pound lean ground round beef
- 1 bottle (12 ounces) chili sauce
- ½ cup reduced-sodium beef broth
- 2 teaspoons Worcestershire sauce
- 1 teaspoon dried oregano
- 4 ciabatta rolls or sandwich buns, split

1. In a large nonstick skillet, heat the oil over medium heat. Add the onion, pepper, celery, and garlic and cook for 5 to 7 minutes, or until softened. Add the beef and cook, breaking the meat up with a spoon, for about 5 minutes, or until no longer pink.
2. Add the chili sauce, broth, Worcestershire sauce, and oregano. Cook, stirring occasionally, for about 5 minutes, or until hot and bubbly.
3. Spoon the sloppy joe mixture onto the buns and serve.

Makes 4 servings

Variations

You can replace the ground beef with ground turkey breast or ground chicken breast.

Accompaniments

Serve with pickles and a colorful tossed salad or potato salad.

Skillet Goulash

Hands-On Time: 45 minutes ■ Total Time: 1 hour 15 minutes

By using ground beef, the classic Hungarian beef stew can be an easy stove-top dinner. Serve with a green salad and hearty bread.

- 4 teaspoons vegetable oil
- ¾ pound ground beef
- 1 large red onion, finely chopped
- 2 stalks celery, sliced
- 1 large clove garlic, minced
- 1½ cups beef broth
- ⅓ cup dry red wine
- 1 can (15 ounces) tomato sauce
- 2 cups thinly sliced red cabbage
- 2 large carrots, sliced
- 2 teaspoons paprika
- 1 teaspoon dried thyme
- ¼ teaspoon dry mustard
- ¼ teaspoon ground black pepper
- 1 large bay leaf
- 12 ounces thin egg noodles
- ½ to ¾ cup sour cream
- 2 tablespoons chopped fresh parsley

1. In a large nonstick skillet, heat 2 teaspoons of the oil over medium-high heat. Add the beef and cook, breaking up the beef with a spoon, for 7 to 8 minutes, or until no longer pink. Transfer to a plate.
2. Heat the remaining 2 teaspoons oil in the skillet. Add the onion, celery, and garlic, and cook for 6 to 8 minutes, or until the celery is tender. Stir in the broth, wine, and tomato sauce and mix well. Add the cooked beef, cabbage, carrots, paprika, thyme, mustard, pepper, and bay leaf. Bring to a boil. Reduce the heat to medium-low, cover, and simmer for 30 minutes, or until the carrots are tender. Discard the bay leaf.
3. Meanwhile, in a large pot of boiling water, cook the noodles according to package directions. Drain and divide among 6 plates.
4. Reduce the heat under the skillet to the lowest possible setting. Stir in the sour cream to taste and gently heat through; do not boil. Spoon the goulash over the noodles and sprinkle with the parsley.

Makes 6 servings

Variation

Skillet Pork Goulash: Replace the ground beef with ground pork tenderloin.

Deep-Dish Taco Bake

Hands-On Time: 25 minutes ■ Total Time: 55 minutes

Pick up a fork and dig right in: This savory baked dish delivers great taco taste piping hot from the oven.

- 2 teaspoons vegetable oil
- ½ pound ground beef
- ½ cup sour cream
- ½ cup shredded Cheddar cheese
- ⅓ cup mayonnaise
- 1 tablespoon finely chopped onion
- ¼ teaspoon garlic powder
- ⅛ teaspoon ground cumin
- 1 cup buttermilk biscuit mix
- ¼ cup cold water
- 1 or 2 medium tomatoes, thinly sliced
- ½ cup chopped green bell pepper
- Paprika, for sprinkling

1. Preheat the oven to 375°F. Lightly grease an 8" × 8" baking pan and set aside.
2. In a large skillet, heat the oil over medium heat. Add the beef and cook, stirring, until browned. Set aside. In a small bowl, stir together the sour cream, cheese, mayonnaise, onion, garlic powder, and cumin. Set aside.
3. In another small bowl, stir together the biscuit mix and water until a soft dough forms. Using floured fingers, pat the dough into the prepared pan, pressing it ½" up the sides. Spread the beef evenly over the dough. Top with the tomatoes, then the pepper. Spoon the sour cream mixture over the top and sprinkle with the paprika.
4. Bake for 25 to 30 minutes, or until the edges of the dough are golden. Cut into squares and serve.

Makes 4 to 6 servings

Stir-Fried Beef and Broccoli

Hands-On Time: 35 minutes ■ Total Time: 55 minutes

Who needs takeout? It's easy to make the Chinese restaurant favorite at home.

- 1/4 cup chicken broth
- 3 tablespoons dry sherry
- 1 teaspoon grated orange zest
- 1/2 cup orange juice
- 2 tablespoons soy sauce
- 1 tablespoon grated fresh ginger
- 1 tablespoon sugar
- 2 teaspoons cornstarch
- 1 teaspoon toasted sesame oil
- 1/2 teaspoon red pepper flakes
- 1 pound beef sirloin, trimmed and cut into 1/4"-thick strips
- 2/3 cup white rice
- 4 teaspoons vegetable oil
- 1 1/2 pounds broccoli florets
- 1 bunch scallions, cut into 1/4" diagonal slices
- 3 cloves garlic, minced
- 2 tablespoons water

1. In a medium bowl, combine the broth, sherry, orange zest, orange juice, soy sauce, ginger, sugar, cornstarch, sesame oil, and red pepper flakes. Stir to mix. Add the beef, tossing to coat evenly. Allow to marinate for 20 minutes.
2. Meanwhile, prepare the rice according to package directions.
3. In a large skillet, heat 2 teaspoons of the vegetable oil over medium-high heat. Lift the beef from the marinade into the skillet. Reserve the marinade. Cook the beef, stirring constantly, for 2 to 3 minutes, or until browned. Transfer to a plate.
4. Add the remaining 2 teaspoons vegetable oil to the skillet. Add the broccoli, scallions, and garlic and cook, stirring, for 2 minutes. Add the water, cover, and cook for 1 to 2 minutes, or until the broccoli is crisp-tender. Add the reserved marinade. Cook, stirring constantly, for 3 minutes, or until the mixture boils and thickens slightly.
5. Reduce the heat to medium-low. Return the beef to the pan and cook, stirring, for 2 minutes, or until the beef is heated through. Serve over the rice.

Makes 4 servings

Basic Meat Roasting Time & Temperature Chart

CUT	OVEN TEMPERATURE	WEIGHT	DONENESS	ROASTING TIME
BEEF				
Standing rib	350°F	4–6 lb	135°F* (medium-rare) 145°F* (medium-well)	1¾–2¼ hr 2–2½ hr
Standing rib	350°F	8–10 lb	135°F* (medium-rare) 145°F* (medium-well)	2½–3 hr 2¾–3¼ hr
Rib eye, tied	350°F	4–6 lb	135°F* (medium-rare) 145°F* (medium-well)	1¾–2 hr 1¾–2¼ hr
Tenderloin	450°F	4–5 lb	135°F* (medium-rare) 145°F* (medium-well)	35–45 min 45–55 min
VEAL				
Loin	325°F	3–4 lb	155°F* (medium-well)	1¾–2½ hr
Leg, boned & tied	325°F	2–3 lb	155°F* (medium-well)	1¼–1¾ hr
Shoulder, boned & tied	325°F	2½–3 lb	155°F* (medium-well)	1¼–1¾ hr
FRESH PORK				
Loin, bone-in	350°F	3–5 lb	155°F**	1–1½ hr
Loin, boned & tied	400°F	2–4½ lb	150°F*	¾–1¼ hr
Crown, unstuffed	350°F	6–10 lb	155°F**	1¼–1¾ hr
Shoulder (butt)	375°F	3–7 lb	155°F*	1½–3¾ hr
Tenderloin***	450°F	½–1 lb	150°F*	12–20 min
SMOKED PORK				
Ham	325°F	5–7 lb	140°F*	1–¼ hr
Loin	325°F	3–5 lb	140°F*	1–1¼ hr
Picnic shoulder	325°F	5–8 lb	140°F*	1–1½ hr
Shoulder, boned & tied	325°F	2–4 lb	140°F*	¾–1 hr
LAMB				
Leg, whole, bone-in	350°F	5–7 lb	135°F** (medium-rare) 145°F** (medium) 155°F** (medium-well)	1½–2 hr 1¾–2¼ hr 2–2½ hr
Leg, boned & tied	350°F	3½–5 lb	135°F* (medium-rare) 145°F* (medium) 155°F* (medium-well)	1¼–2 hr 1½–2¼ hr 1¾–2½ hr
Crown, unstuffed	450°F	3–5 lb	135°F** (medium-rare) 145°F** (medium) 155°F** (medium-well)	20–30 min 25–35 min 30–40 min
Shoulder, boned & tied	350°F	3½–4 lb	135°F* (medium-rare) 145°F* (medium) 155°F* (medium-well)	1–1¼ hr 1–1½ hr 1¼–1¾ hr
Rib rack***	475°F	1½–2½ lb	135°F* (medium-rare) 145°F* (medium) 155°F* (medium-well)	10–15 min 15–20 min 20–30 min

*Insert meat thermometer into center of thickest part of meat.

**Insert meat thermometer through thickest part of meat to bone.

***Briefly pan-brown before roasting.

Peppery Chili con Carne

Hands-On Time: 35 minutes ■ Total Time: 2 hours 5 minutes

Zesty garnishes can really dress up a "bowl of red." Try a sprinkling of chopped fresh cilantro or parsley leaves, a dollop of sour cream or plain yogurt, chopped scallions, shredded Cheddar cheese, or a squeeze of lime juice.

- 1 tablespoon vegetable oil
- 1½ pounds beef top round, trimmed and cut into ½" cubes
- 2 onions, chopped
- 2 green and/or red bell peppers, chopped
- 3 serrano or jalapeño chile peppers, seeded and chopped (wear plastic gloves when handling)
- 3 cloves garlic, minced
- ¼ cup chili powder
- 5 cups beef broth
- 1 can (28 ounces) diced tomatoes
- 1 can (15 ounces) tomato sauce
- 2 cans (15 ounces each) kidney beans and/or black beans, rinsed and drained

1. In a Dutch oven, heat the oil over high heat. Add the beef and cook, turning, for 3 to 5 minutes, or until browned on all sides. Add the onions, bell peppers, chile peppers, and garlic. Reduce the heat to medium-high and cook, stirring often, for 8 minutes, or until the vegetables are soft. Add the chili powder and cook, stirring constantly, for 2 minutes.
2. Add the broth, tomatoes, and tomato sauce and stir to mix. Bring to a boil, reduce the heat to medium-low, and simmer, stirring occasionally, for 1 hour. Add the beans. Cook for 30 minutes longer, or until the meat is fork-tender.

Makes 8 servings

Accompaniments

Serve steaming bowls of the chili with Chile Cornbread (page 290), using milder peppers if you don't want a chile overload. Finish the meal with refreshing Minted Fruit Salad (page 75).

Beef and Caramelized Onions

Hands-On Time: 40 minutes ■ Total Time: 55 minutes

Caramelizing onions brings out a sweet, mild flavor that complements meaty steak.

Caramelized Onions

- 2 teaspoons vegetable oil
- 2 medium onions, sliced
- ½ cup beef broth
- 1½ teaspoons light brown sugar
- 1 tablespoon balsamic vinegar

Steaks

- 1 tablespoon vegetable oil
- 4 tenderloin or top round steaks (4 to 5 ounces each), trimmed
- ¼ teaspoon cracked black pepper
- 4 shallots, sliced
- 4 cloves garlic, sliced
- ½ cup beef broth
- 1 teaspoon red wine vinegar
- 4 slices sourdough bread, grilled or broiled

1. *To caramelize the onions:* In a large nonstick skillet, heat the oil over medium-high heat. Add the onions and cook, stirring occasionally, for 8 to 10 minutes, or until browned. Add the broth, brown sugar, and vinegar. Cook, stirring occasionally, for 10 to 15 minutes, or until all the liquid evaporates. Transfer to a plate.
2. *To make the steaks:* In the same skillet, heat the oil over medium-high heat. Add the steaks and cook, turning once, for 2 to 4 minutes, or until seared. Season with the pepper. Reduce the heat to medium, add the shallots and garlic, and cook for 2 minutes, or until softened. Add the broth and vinegar, bring to a boil, and cook for 1 to 2 minutes, or until the steaks are medium-rare, or to desired doneness.
3. Serve the steaks and sauce over the bread and topped with the onions.

Makes 4 servings

Osso Buco

Hands-On Time: 35 minutes ■ Total Time: 2 hours

When slowly braised, veal shanks produce a wonderfully rich and flavorful dish. Serve with orzo or steamed rice.

- 1 tablespoon vegetable oil
- 6 pieces veal shank
- ½ cup dry red wine
- ½ cup finely chopped onion
- ½ cup finely chopped carrot
- ½ cup finely chopped celery
- ½ cup finely chopped parsnips
- ¼ teaspoon ground black pepper
- 2 cloves garlic, minced
- 2 cups chicken or beef broth
- 2 tablespoons tomato paste
- ⅓ cup packed fresh parsley
- 1 teaspoon grated lemon zest

1. In a Dutch oven, heat the oil over medium heat. Add the veal and cook, turning once, for about 10 minutes, or until browned. Transfer to a plate and set aside.
2. Add the wine to the pan. Bring to a boil and use a wooden spoon to scrape up any browned bits from the bottom of the pan. Add the onion, carrot, celery, and parsnips. Boil gently for about 5 minutes, or until the wine is reduced by half. Stir in the pepper and half of the garlic. Return the reserved veal and any juices on the plate to the pan, arranging the veal in a single layer.
3. In a medium bowl, whisk together the broth and tomato paste. Pour over the veal. Cover and simmer for about 1¼ hours, or until the veal is very tender. Transfer the veal to a serving platter, cover with foil, and keep warm.
4. Set a strainer over a large bowl. Strain the cooking liquid through it, reserving the liquid and solids. Transfer the solids to a blender. Measure out 1½ cups of the liquid, add to the blender, and purée. (Save any remaining liquid for another use.) Transfer the sauce to a 1-quart saucepan and rewarm over low heat.
5. Finely chop the parsley, lemon zest, and remaining garlic together. Pour the sauce over the veal and sprinkle with the parsley mixture.

Makes 6 servings

Make-Ahead

You may prepare the veal and sauce ahead. Gently reheat in the Dutch oven over low heat.

Lemony Veal Sauté

Hands-On Time: 20 minutes ■ Total Time: 40 minutes

This one-pot meal features tender veal strips, roasted red pepper, and potatoes cloaked in a lemony butter sauce.

- 1 pound potatoes, cut into ¼" slices
- ¾ pound veal scallops, cut into ½" strips
- 2 teaspoons cornstarch
- 1 tablespoon olive oil
- 1 clove garlic, minced
- 2 roasted red peppers, cut into ½" strips
- Salt
- Ground black pepper
- 1 tablespoon finely chopped fresh parsley
- 1 tablespoon snipped chives
- Juice of 1 lemon
- 1 tablespoon unsalted butter

1. Place a steamer basket in a large pot with 1" of water. Bring to a boil over high heat. Place the potatoes in the basket and steam for 10 to 15 minutes, or until tender.
2. Sprinkle the veal with the cornstarch and toss to lightly dust all the pieces. In a large nonstick skillet, heat the oil over medium-high heat. Add the veal and garlic and cook for about 1 minute. Stir in the potatoes and continue to cook for about 1 minute longer, or until the veal is cooked through. Add the red peppers and cook for about 30 seconds. Season with salt and pepper. Transfer the veal and vegetables to a serving plate.
3. Add the parsley, chives, and lemon juice to the pan. Raise the heat to high. Cook, stirring with a rubber spatula to scrape up browned bits from the bottom of the pan, for about 1 minute, or until the sauce is reduced by half. Add the butter and swirl the pan until the butter is melted and incorporated into the sauce. Pour the sauce over the veal and vegetables and toss well.

Makes 4 servings

Stir-Fried Pork with Broccoli and Sesame Seeds

Hands-On Time: 30 minutes ■ Total Time: 30 minutes

Pork tenderloin is not only the leanest pork cut available in the market but also the most convenient. Use a Chinese cleaver or a heavy chef's knife to cut it up for stir-frying.

- 2 cups water
- 1 tablespoon unsalted butter
- 1 cup white rice
- 2 tablespoons sesame seeds
- 2 tablespoons cornstarch
- 1 can (14½ ounces) reduced-sodium chicken broth
- 1 tablespoon reduced-sodium soy sauce
- 1½ tablespoons vegetable oil
- 1 pork tenderloin (1 pound), trimmed of all visible fat and cut into thin, bite-size pieces
- 4 scallions, sliced
- 1 clove garlic, minced
- 1 head broccoli, cut into bite-size pieces
- 1 yellow bell pepper, thinly sliced

1. In a large saucepan, bring the water and butter to a boil over high heat. Add the rice and bring to a simmer. Reduce the heat to low, cover, and cook for 18 to 20 minutes, or until the liquid is absorbed. Remove from the heat and let sit, covered, until ready to use.
2. In a small heavy skillet, toast the sesame seeds over medium heat, tossing frequently, for about 1 minute, or until fragrant and golden. Be careful not to burn. Set aside.
3. In a 2-cup glass measuring cup, whisk the cornstarch with ¼ cup of the broth until smooth. Stir in the soy sauce and remaining broth. Set aside.
4. In a large nonstick skillet or wok, heat the oil over medium-high heat. Add the pork, scallions, and garlic and cook for 3 to 4 minutes, stirring constantly, or until the pork is browned and no pink remains. Transfer to a plate and set aside.
5. Add the broccoli and pepper to the pan and cook, stirring constantly over medium-high heat, for 2 to 3 minutes. Add the broth mixture and cook, tossing occasionally, for 2 to 3 minutes, or until the vegetables are crisp-tender.
6. Return the reserved pork mixture to the pan and cook until heated through. Sprinkle with the reserved sesame seeds just before serving with the rice.

Makes 4 servings

Milanese Pork Stew with Gremolata

Hands-On Time: 35 minutes ■ Total Time: 1 hour 5 minutes

An Italian creation, *gremolata* is a delicious, fresh seasoning mixture made from lemon zest, garlic, and parsley. It's most commonly used on Osso Buco (page 138) but is an equally fine complement to this rich-tasting pork stew. Serve the stew over steamed rice.

Stew

- ¾ pound lean, boneless pork loin, cut into ¾" cubes
- ½ teaspoon salt
- ¼ teaspoon ground black pepper
- 4 teaspoons olive oil
- 1 medium onion, chopped
- 2 medium carrots, chopped
- 2 stalks celery, chopped
- 2 cloves garlic, minced
- ½ teaspoon dried basil
- ½ teaspoon dried thyme
- 1 bay leaf
- ½ cup white wine
- 1 strip (3" long) lemon zest
- 1 can (15 ounces) whole tomatoes in purée
- ½ cup chicken broth
- 8 ounces small white mushrooms, quartered
- 1 cup frozen peas

Gremolata

- ¼ cup chopped fresh flat-leaf parsley
- 1 tablespoon grated lemon zest
- 2 small cloves garlic, minced

1. *To make the stew:* In a medium bowl, toss the pork with ¼ teaspoon of the salt and the pepper. In a large, heavy saucepan, heat 2 teaspoons of the oil over medium-high heat until very hot but not smoking. Add the pork and cook, stirring, for about 2 minutes, or until browned. With a slotted spoon, transfer the pork to a plate.

2. Add the remaining 2 teaspoons oil to the saucepan and heat over medium heat. Stir in the onion, carrots, and celery. Cover and cook, stirring occasionally, for about 5 minutes, or until the vegetables begin to soften. Stir in the garlic, basil, thyme, and bay leaf and cook for 30 seconds. Add the wine and strip of lemon zest and cook for 2 minutes, scraping up any browned bits from the bottom of the pan.
3. Add the tomatoes, broth, and remaining ¼ teaspoon salt. Reduce the heat to medium-low, cover, and simmer for 20 minutes. Stir in the mushrooms and simmer, uncovered, for 5 minutes. Stir in the peas and simmer for 5 minutes, or until the pork is cooked through. Discard the bay leaf and lemon zest strip.
4. *Meanwhile, prepare the gremolata:* In a small bowl, combine the parsley, lemon zest, and garlic.
5. Divide the stew among 4 bowls, sprinkle gremolata over each portion, and serve.

Makes 4 servings

Cherry-Sauced Pork Chops

Hands-On Time: 25 minutes ■ Total Time: 25 minutes

Team this tasty pork dish with hot cooked brown rice. You'll have plenty of the tart-sweet sauce to serve over both the chops and the rice.

- 1 can (14½ ounces) tart red cherries
- ¼ cup packed light brown sugar
- 2 tablespoons cornstarch
- 1 tablespoon vegetable oil
- 6 boneless pork sirloin chops (4 ounces each), trimmed
- ¼ teaspoon salt
- ¼ teaspoon ground black pepper

1. Drain the cherries, reserving the juice. Add enough water to the juice to make 1 cup.
2. In a medium saucepan, stir together the brown sugar and cornstarch. Stir in the cherry juice. Cook over medium heat, stirring, until the mixture begins to thicken and just comes to a boil. Stir in the cherries. Set aside.
3. In a large skillet, heat the oil over medium-high heat. Add the pork and cook, turning once, until browned. Sprinkle with the salt and pepper. Spoon the cherry mixture over the chops and bring to a boil. Reduce the heat to low, cover, and cook for 5 to 6 minutes, or until the pork is only slightly pink in the center when tested with a sharp knife.

Makes 6 servings

Kitchen Tip

When using cornstarch as a thickener, don't cook the sauce too long or at high heat, because the sauce may begin to thin. Cook only long enough to thicken the sauce, then remove from the heat.

Stir-Fry Know-How

One of the fastest cooking methods for meat, poultry, and/or vegetables, stir-frying consists of quickly cooking foods over very high heat, tossing and stirring all the while to prevent sticking or burning. Lest you think stir-fries signify just Asian meals, this technique works equally well for Mediterranean, Mexican, and other dishes. And although a wok is often the pan of choice, a large skillet is just as effective. Here are some stir-fry basics.

Preparing foods for stir-frying: To get the best results for your effort, be sure to cut the food into uniform, bite-size pieces. Thin strips or small cubes are appropriate for a variety of meats as well as for poultry. Vegetables can be sliced, finely chopped, julienned, or shredded.

Stir-frying over an electric burner: Use a flat-bottom wok or a large, flat-bottom skillet. Avoid round-bottom woks or pans, which will result in hot spots and cause food to cook unevenly.

Stir-frying over a gas flame: Use a round-bottom wok. The flames will reach up around the bottom of the wok to heat it evenly. If your gas stove has high, flat grates that prevent the flames from nearing the pan, try removing the grate and setting the wok directly over the flame.

Choosing a stir-fry oil: Use an oil with a high smoke point, such as peanut, canola, or soybean, so that it can withstand the high temperatures of stir-frying without burning.

Testing the pan: Sprinkle a little water into the hot pan. If it evaporates on contact with the pan, you're ready to add the oil to the pan and begin stir-frying.

Thickening a stir-fry sauce: Many recipes call for cornstarch or other thickeners to be mixed right into the sauce. If the cooked sauce is still not thick enough, dissolve 1 teaspoon cornstarch in 1 tablespoon cold broth, soy sauce, or water. Add this mixture to the pan and stir for 30 seconds to 1 minute, or until thickened.

Thinning a stir-fry sauce: Add broth, soy sauce, or water, 1 tablespoon at a time, until the sauce reaches the desired consistency. If you accidentally add too much, cook until the excess liquid evaporates and the sauce thickens again.

Stir-frying tough ingredients: Firm foods such as broccoli stems, cauliflower, potatoes, and turnips will not cook through in the few minutes allotted for most stir-frying. To stir-fry these ingredients, precook them slightly before adding them to the stir-fry, cut them into very thin slices (julienne works well), or plan to cook them in some liquid at some point in the stir-frying. You can also steam-cook tough ingredients in the stir-fry. Sear them first, then add a little broth or water to the pan, cover, and steam-cook just until crisp-tender.

Getting the best flavor: Keep the stir-fry simple. Choose one meat or seafood and just one or two vegetables. For example, chicken or beef with asparagus or green beans is perfect. Rely on other ingredients, such as ginger, garlic, scallions, and sauce, to flavor the stir-fry.

Simmered Sauerkraut and Pork

Hands-On Time: 30 minutes ■ Total Time: 55 minutes

Bring Oktoberfest to your dining room when you serve this authentic German supper. Dark rye bread, chunky cinnamon-flavored applesauce, and mashed potatoes topped with browned onions would complete the meal nicely.

- ½ cup dried apple slices
- 3 strips bacon, finely chopped
- 1 cup finely chopped onions
- 2 cups sauerkraut, rinsed and drained
- 1 cup chicken broth
- ⅛ teaspoon fennel seeds
- ⅛ teaspoon caraway seeds
- 1 tablespoon vegetable oil
- 4 boneless pork sirloin chops (4 ounces each), trimmed

1. Place the apples in a small bowl, cover with hot water, and let stand for 5 minutes. Drain.
2. In a Dutch oven, cook the bacon until crisp. With a slotted spoon, transfer the bacon to a paper towel–lined plate and set aside. Add the onions to the drippings in the pan and cook over medium heat, stirring, for 5 minutes, or until softened. Add the apples, sauerkraut, broth, fennel seeds, and caraway seeds. Cover and simmer for 10 minutes.
3. In a large nonstick skillet, heat the oil over medium heat. Add the pork chops and cook, turning once, for 4 to 5 minutes, or until browned. Transfer the chops to the Dutch oven, cover, and simmer for 10 minutes, or until the chops are only slightly pink when tested with a sharp knife. Sprinkle with the reserved bacon and serve.

Makes 4 servings

Mustardy Ham with Pan Gravy

Hands-On Time: 30 minutes ■ Total Time: 1 hour 30 minutes

Ham steak is a great Southern favorite for Sunday dinner.

- 1 ham steak (1 pound), trimmed
- 2 tablespoons molasses
- 1 tablespoon Dijon mustard
- 2 cloves garlic, minced
- 1 tablespoon vegetable oil
- 1½ cups chicken broth
- 1 tablespoon unsalted butter
- 2 tablespoons all-purpose flour
- ¼ teaspoon ground black pepper

1. In a shallow nonmetal dish, combine the ham, molasses, mustard, and garlic; cover and refrigerate for 1 hour, turning frequently.
2. In a medium nonstick skillet, heat the oil over medium-high heat. Add the ham and marinade and cook for 5 to 7 minutes, or until browned on 1 side. Turn and cook for 5 minutes longer. Transfer the ham to a cutting board and let stand for 5 minutes.
3. Meanwhile, add the broth to the skillet and bring to a boil, scraping to loosen any browned bits. In a small bowl, mash the butter into the flour. Add to the pan and cook, stirring, for about 5 minutes, or until the gravy thickens. Add the pepper. Cut the ham into 4 wedges and serve with the gravy.

Makes 4 servings

Accompaniments

Serve with biscuits and Cucumber and Tomato Salad with Sour Cream Dressing (page 65).

Nutri-Note

If you're watching calories, make this a healthier choice by discarding any fat from the pan before adding the chicken broth in step 3.

Pork Cutlets with Apple Slices

Hands-On Time: 25 minutes ■ Total Time: 30 minutes

This is a delicious dish in the fall when apples are at their best (see Ingredients Note, below). The dish goes well with a side of baked root vegetables, puréed butternut squash, or rice pilaf.

- 1 teaspoon grated lemon zest
- 1 teaspoon fresh thyme leaves or ¼ teaspoon dried
- 1 clove garlic, minced
- 10 ounces pork tenderloin, cut into 8 equal slices (about ½" thick)
- 2 tablespoons olive oil
- 2 or 3 tart baking apples, cut into ½" wedges
- 2 tablespoons fresh lemon juice
- Fresh thyme sprigs, for garnish (optional)

1. On a plate, combine the lemon zest, thyme leaves, and garlic. Lightly rub the pork slices with the mixture.
2. In a large nonstick skillet, heat the oil over medium heat. Add the pork and cook, turning occasionally, for about 6 minutes, or until browned on all sides.
3. Push the pork to 1 side of the pan. Add the apples and 1 tablespoon of the lemon juice. Cook, turning the apples as they brown, for about 5 minutes. Rearrange the pork slices so they are in a single layer under the apples. Cover and cook for about 5 minutes, or until the apples and pork are tender.
4. Transfer the pork and apples to a platter. Add the remaining 1 tablespoon lemon juice to the pan and scrape up any browned bits. Drizzle the juices over the pork and apples, garnish with the thyme sprigs if you like, and serve.

Makes 4 servings

Ingredients Note

Use any type of tart baking apple here; Granny Smith, Northern Spy, and Jonathan all are good choices. Baking apples hold their shape better than do cooking varieties such as McIntosh. If you leave the skin on, the finished dish will be more colorful and have more fiber.

Variations

You can use other boneless cutlets, such as chicken, turkey, or veal.

Orange-Braised Pork Tenderloins

Hands-On Time: 20 minutes ■ Total Time: 30 minutes

Fruit is a natural companion to savory pork. Here, we pair tenderloin with orange sections and red onion for an easy weeknight supper.

- 1 tablespoon vegetable oil
- 1 pound pork tenderloin (cut into 4 pieces), trimmed
- ½ cup thinly sliced red onion
- 1 tablespoon red wine vinegar
- 1 navel orange, peeled and sectioned
- ½ cup orange juice
- ½ cup chicken broth
- Pinch of dried sage, crumbled
- Pinch of dried thyme
- Pinch of salt

1. In a large nonstick skillet, heat the oil over medium-high heat. Add the pork and cook, turning once, for 4 to 6 minutes, or until browned. Remove from the skillet and set aside.
2. Add the onion to the skillet and cook, stirring, for 2 minutes, or until soft. Add the vinegar and toss to coat. Add the orange, orange juice, broth, sage, thyme, and salt.
3. Reduce the heat to medium-low. Return the reserved pork to the skillet, cover, and cook for 8 to 10 minutes, or until the pork is only slightly pink in the center when tested with a sharp knife.
4. Uncover and cook for 1 minute, or until the liquid is slightly reduced. Serve the pork with the orange segments and sauce spooned over it.

Makes 4 servings

Moroccan Lamb and Vegetables with Couscous

Hands-On Time: 25 minutes ■ Total Time: 55 minutes

This easy stew highlights the affinity Moroccan spices have with lamb. Vegetables and couscous are added to the spiced, meaty lamb cubes for a one-dish meal.

- 1 teaspoon ground cumin
- ¾ teaspoon ground coriander
- ¼ teaspoon ground cinnamon
- ¼ teaspoon ground ginger
- ¼ teaspoon salt
- ¾ pound lean lamb, trimmed and cut into 1" cubes
- 1 tablespoon vegetable oil
- 1 green bell pepper, cut into 8 wedges
- 1 large onion, cut into 8 wedges
- 1 large carrot, cut into ½" pieces
- 1 medium tomato, peeled and diced
- 2 cloves garlic, minced
- 2 cups chicken broth
- 1 cup couscous
- 2 tablespoons chopped fresh cilantro
- Hot pepper sauce

1. In a small bowl, combine the cumin, coriander, cinnamon, ginger, and salt. Place the lamb in a large bowl, sprinkle with half of the spice mixture, and toss to coat.
2. In a Dutch oven, heat the oil over medium heat. Add the lamb and cook, stirring occasionally, for 6 to 7 minutes, or until browned.
3. Add the bell pepper, onion, carrot, tomato, garlic, and remaining spice mixture. Pour in the broth and gently stir to combine. Cover and cook over medium heat, gently stirring occasionally, for about 25 minutes, or until the carrots are tender when pierced with a sharp knife.
4. Sprinkle the couscous over the lamb and vegetables, tilting the pan if necessary to moisten all the couscous. Sprinkle with the cilantro. Cover, remove from the heat, and let stand for 5 minutes, or until the couscous is tender and most of the liquid is absorbed. Season to taste with the hot pepper sauce.

Makes 4 servings

Lamb and Eggplant Skillet Dinner in a Pita

Hands-On Time: 1 hour ■ Total Time: 1 hour

Long before you could buy skillet-dinner mixes in a box, cooks were stirring up ground meat, vegetables, and favorite seasonings to feed their families economically and well. Resembling an exotic Greek street snack more than a traditional skillet dinner, these pita sandwiches are stuffed with a delicious lamb-and-eggplant mixture.

- 2 tablespoons vegetable oil
- 1 pound eggplant, cut into ¾" cubes
- ¼ cup reduced-sodium chicken broth
- 1 onion, chopped
- 2 stalks celery, finely chopped
- 3 cloves garlic, minced
- ¾ pound ground leg of lamb or beef top round
- 4 tablespoons chopped fresh mint
- 2 teaspoons ground cumin
- ½ teaspoon dried oregano
- ¼ teaspoon salt
- ¼ teaspoon ground black pepper
- 1 can (14½ ounces) diced tomatoes
- 1 can (15 ounces) chickpeas, rinsed and drained
- 1 cup plain yogurt
- 4 pitas (6" diameter), opened
- 1 cup thinly sliced unpeeled cucumber
- 2 plum tomatoes, thinly sliced
- 4 cups shredded romaine lettuce

1. In a large, heavy skillet, heat 1 tablespoon of the oil over medium-high heat. Add the eggplant and cook, stirring frequently, for 2 to 3 minutes, or until browned. Stir in the broth and bring to a boil. Reduce the heat to medium and cook, stirring occasionally, for about 4 minutes, or until the eggplant is tender and the liquid is absorbed. Transfer the eggplant to a large plate and set aside.
2. In the same large skillet, heat the remaining 1 tablespoon oil over medium-high heat. Add the onion, celery, and garlic and cook, stirring frequently, for 2 to 3 minutes, or until the onion is tender. Crumble in the ground meat and cook, stirring, for about 3 minutes, or until the meat is no longer pink. Stir in 2 tablespoons of the mint, the cumin, oregano, salt, and pepper. Cook, stirring constantly, for 30 seconds.
3. Add the diced tomatoes and bring to a boil. Stir in the chickpeas and reserved eggplant. Reduce the heat to low and simmer, stirring occasionally, for 5 to 7 minutes to blend the flavors. Remove the pan from the heat.
4. In a small bowl, combine the yogurt and remaining 2 tablespoons mint.
5. Line each pita with the cucumber and sliced tomatoes, then spoon one-fourth of the lamb mixture into each. Top with shredded lettuce and serve with the yogurt-mint sauce.

Makes 4 servings

Lamb with Lemon Rice and Mint Sauce

Hands-On Time: 20 minutes ■ Total Time: 50 minutes

There is something special about the combination of lamb and mint jelly. We like to jack up the flavor a bit by adding brown sugar and fresh mint to the jelly to make a sweetish sauce.

Lamb

- 2 teaspoons minced garlic
- 1 teaspoon crushed dried rosemary
- 4 boneless lamb leg center steaks or loin lamb chops (4 ounces each), trimmed
- 1 tablespoon vegetable oil
- Salt
- Ground black pepper

Rice

- 1½ cups chicken broth
- ¾ cup white rice
- 2 teaspoons grated lemon zest
- 1 tablespoon finely chopped fresh mint

Sauce

- ¼ cup packed light brown sugar
- ¼ cup mint jelly
- 2 to 3 teaspoons finely chopped fresh mint

1. *To make the lamb:* In a small bowl, mash the garlic with the rosemary to make a paste. Rub evenly over the lamb. Set aside to marinate for 30 minutes.
2. *To make the rice:* While the lamb is marinating, in a medium saucepan, bring the broth to a boil. Stir in the rice and lemon zest. Reduce the heat to low, cover, and simmer for about 25 minutes, or until the rice is tender and the liquid is absorbed. Stir in the mint. Season with salt and pepper.
3. In a large nonstick skillet, heat the oil over medium heat. Add the lamb and cook, turning once, for about 8 minutes for medium doneness. Transfer to a plate and season with salt and pepper.
4. *To make the sauce:* While the rice is cooking, in a small saucepan, combine the brown sugar and jelly and cook over medium heat until melted. Remove from the heat and stir in the mint.
5. Divide the rice among 4 plates and top with the lamb. Spoon the sauce over the lamb and serve.

Makes 4 servings

Minted Lamb Chops with White Beans

Hands-On Time: 30 minutes ■ Total Time: 50 minutes

Don't be afraid of anchovies! Just a few fillets in the minty marinade here add incomparable flavor—*not* a fishy taste.

- 3 anchovy fillets, rinsed and patted dry
- 1 teaspoon extra-virgin olive oil
- 3 tablespoons chopped fresh mint, plus more for garnish
- ½ teaspoon ground black pepper
- 4 lamb loin chops (5 ounces each), trimmed
- 1 tablespoon vegetable oil
- 1 clove garlic, crushed
- 4 plum tomatoes, coarsely chopped
- 3 cups rinsed and drained canned cannellini beans
- 2 tablespoons beef broth
- ¼ teaspoon salt

1. Grease a broiler-pan rack. Preheat the broiler.
2. On a cutting board, finely chop the anchovies. Sprinkle with the oil, 1 tablespoon of the mint, and ¼ teaspoon of the pepper. Mash to a paste with the flat side of a chef's knife or a fork. Place the chops on the prepared rack and rub the anchovy paste over both sides of each chop. Set aside at room temperature.
3. In a medium nonstick skillet, heat the oil over medium-high heat. Add the garlic and cook for 2 minutes, or until softened. Add the tomatoes and cook, stirring frequently, for 2 minutes, or until they begin to give up their juices. Reduce the heat to medium, cover, and cook for 3 minutes, or until the tomatoes are very soft. Stir in the beans, broth, salt, and the remaining 2 tablespoons mint and ¼ teaspoon pepper. Bring to a boil over high heat. Reduce the heat to low, cover, and simmer, stirring occasionally, for 10 minutes to blend the flavors.
4. While the beans are simmering, broil the lamb chops 4" from the heat, turning once, for 15 minutes, or until a thermometer inserted into the center registers 145°F for medium-rare.
5. To serve, evenly divide the bean mixture among 4 plates and top each with a lamb chop. Garnish with additional chopped mint.

Makes 4 servings

Herb-Crusted Leg of Lamb

Hands-On Time: 30 minutes ■ Total Time: 2 hours 55 minutes (plus marinating)

A paste of sweet roasted garlic and fresh herbs contributes a punch of flavor to roasted leg of lamb.

Marinade and Lamb

- ⅔ cup beef broth
- ½ cup dry vermouth
- ¼ cup balsamic vinegar
- 1 tablespoon chopped fresh rosemary
- 2 cloves garlic, minced
- 1 teaspoon salt
- ¼ teaspoon black pepper
- 1 boneless leg of lamb (4 pounds), butterflied and trimmed

Garlic-Herb Paste

- 1 head garlic
- 1 tablespoon water
- 1 tablespoon olive oil
- ½ teaspoon ground black pepper
- 2 tablespoons each chopped fresh rosemary, oregano, and parsley

1. *To marinate the lamb:* In a 13" × 9" baking dish, combine the broth, vermouth, vinegar, rosemary, garlic, salt, and pepper. Place the lamb in the marinade and turn to coat. Cover, refrigerate, and marinate for at least 4 hours or overnight, turning the lamb occasionally.
2. *To make the garlic-herb paste:* Preheat the oven to 400°F. Slice ¼" off the top of the garlic head. Set the head on a large piece of foil, sprinkle with the water, and wrap loosely. Bake for 25 minutes, or until very soft. Unwrap and let cool. Squeeze the garlic into a small bowl. Using a fork, mash to a paste. Add the oil, pepper, rosemary, oregano, and parsley and mix well. Increase the oven temperature to 450°F.
3. Remove the lamb from the marinade. Roll it up and tie with kitchen string. Refrigerate the marinade until needed. Place the lamb on a rack in a small roasting pan and roast for 15 minutes. Reduce the heat to 350°F and roast for 30 minutes longer.
4. Slather the lamb with the garlic-herb paste. Rotate the pan and roast for 40 to 50 minutes, or until a thermometer inserted into the thickest part registers 145°F for medium-rare. (For medium-well, continue to roast, checking every 5 minutes, until the temperature registers 160°F.) Place the lamb on a cutting board, cover lightly with foil, and let stand for 15 minutes before removing the string and carving.
5. Discard any fat from the pan and add the reserved marinade. Bring to a boil over medium-high heat, scraping the browned bits. Boil gently until reduced by half. Serve the lamb slices with the sauce.

Makes 16 servings

Fisherman's Catch

New England Fish Cakes

Hands-On Time: 30 minutes ■ Total Time: 1 hour 30 minutes

Cod cakes are a New England staple, but you don't have to be a Yankee to enjoy this nutritious dish. Leftover mashed potatoes work beautifully here; use about 1½ cups.

- 1 large baking potato, peeled and cubed
- 2 tablespoons olive oil
- 1 large onion, finely chopped
- ½ pound cod fillets, coarsely chopped
- 1 large egg, lightly beaten
- 2 tablespoons minced scallions
- ½ teaspoon dry mustard
- ½ teaspoon salt
- ¼ teaspoon ground black pepper
- 3 drops hot pepper sauce
- ¾ cup unseasoned dried bread crumbs

1. Cook the potato in boiling water for about 15 minutes, or until soft. Drain. Mash and let cool.
2. In a 10" nonstick skillet, heat 2 teaspoons of the oil over medium-high heat. Add the onion and cook, stirring occasionally, for about 5 minutes, or until softened.
3. In a medium bowl, gently combine the potato, onion, cod, egg, scallions, mustard, salt, black pepper, and hot pepper sauce. Form into 4 patties. Place the bread crumbs in a shallow bowl. Dredge each patty in the bread crumbs to coat both sides. Place on a plate, cover, and refrigerate for 30 minutes.
4. In a 10" nonstick skillet, heat the remaining 4 teaspoons oil over medium-high heat. Add the patties, cover, and cook for 6 minutes. Turn and cook for about 5 minutes longer, or until the patties are firm and golden brown. Serve immediately.

Makes 4 servings

Cajun Catfish

Hands-On Time: 10 minutes ■ Total Time: 15 minutes

We coat farm-raised catfish with a spicy bread-crumb crust, then broil until browned and crunchy in this lightened-up version of the classic Louisiana dish.

- ¼ cup unseasoned dried bread crumbs
- 2 teaspoons olive oil
- 1 teaspoon minced garlic
- ½ teaspoon red pepper flakes
- ½ teaspoon chili powder
- ½ teaspoon ground cumin
- 4 catfish fillets (6 ounces each)

1. Preheat the broiler. Grease the broiler pan.
2. In a small bowl, combine the bread crumbs, oil, garlic, red pepper flakes, chili powder, and cumin. Mix well.
3. Place the catfish on the prepared pan and sprinkle with half of the bread-crumb mixture. Broil 4" from the heat for 5 minutes, or until golden brown. Turn carefully and sprinkle with the remaining bread-crumb mixture. Broil for 2 minutes, or until the fish is opaque in the center when tested with a knife.

Makes 4 servings

Accompaniment

Serve with a tossed green salad, warm crusty bread, and green beans.

Freezing Tip

Arrange the cooled cooked catfish on a tray and place in the freezer for several hours, or until solid. Transfer to a freezer-quality plastic bag. To use, thaw overnight in the refrigerator. Place in a 12" nonstick skillet, cover, and cook over low heat for 8 to 10 minutes, or until heated through.

Spice-Rubbed Cod with Vegetables

Hands-On Time: 25 minutes ■ Total Time: 1 hour 5 minutes

You know how to roast turkey and chicken, beef and pork—now try roasting a thick fish fillet. Here, a cod fillet is rubbed with a cumin-based spice mixture and roasted on a bed of potatoes, carrots, summer squash, and green beans. Because the fish cooks in such a short time, some of the vegetables are briefly parboiled first so that they will be done as quickly as the cod.

- 1½ pounds cod fillet, in 1 piece (1" thick)
- 1 teaspoon ground cumin
- ½ teaspoon ground ginger
- ¼ teaspoon paprika
- Pinch of ground red pepper
- ½ teaspoon salt
- 4 teaspoons extra-virgin olive oil
- 1½ pounds small red potatoes, quartered
- 4 medium carrots, cut diagonally into ¼"-thick slices
- 12 ounces green beans, trimmed
- 12 ounces yellow squash, cut diagonally into ¼"-thick slices
- ¼ teaspoon ground black pepper
- 2 scallions, thinly sliced

1. Preheat the oven to 425°F. Line a baking sheet with foil and place the fish on the foil.
2. In a small bowl, combine the cumin, ginger, paprika, ground red pepper, and ¼ teaspoon of the salt. Stir in 2 teaspoons of the oil. Brush both sides of the fish with the seasoned oil. Cover the fish loosely and refrigerate while you prepare the vegetables.
3. Place the potatoes in a large saucepan and add water to cover. Bring to a boil over high heat. Reduce the heat to medium, cover, and simmer for 5 minutes. Add the carrots, cover, and simmer for 2 minutes. Add the green beans and simmer, uncovered, for 1 minute. Drain the vegetables in a colander.
4. In a large bowl, combine the drained vegetables, squash, black pepper, and remaining 2 teaspoons oil and ¼ teaspoon salt. Toss to combine. Spread the vegetables out in a single layer on a jelly-roll pan. Roast for 15 minutes.
5. Place the fish on top of the vegetables and roast for 10 to 15 minutes longer, or until the fish just flakes when tested with a knife and the vegetables are tender. Transfer whole to a warmed platter or cut into individual servings. Scatter the scallions over the fish and vegetables and serve.

Makes 4 servings

Seafood Jambalaya

Hands-On Time: 30 minutes ■ Total Time: 50 minutes

One of the defining dishes of Louisiana cuisine, jambalaya is delightfully variable, subject to the whims of the person cooking it (although the rice, onions, celery, and bell pepper are unvarying ingredients). The shrimp-scallop-and-ham jambalaya here is just one interpretation of a dish that is frequently made with sausage, crayfish, and/or oysters.

- 1 tablespoon olive oil
- 3 ounces baked ham, diced
- 1 medium green bell pepper, finely chopped
- 1 medium onion, chopped
- 2 stalks celery, chopped
- 3 cloves garlic, minced
- 1 cup white rice
- 1 bay leaf
- ½ teaspoon dried oregano
- ½ teaspoon dried thyme
- ½ teaspoon ground black pepper
- ¼ teaspoon salt
- ⅛ teaspoon ground red pepper
- 1½ cups chicken broth
- 1½ cups water
- ½ pound sea scallops, tough tendons removed
- ½ pound medium shrimp, peeled and deveined, with tails attached
- 1 cup diced tomatoes
- ¼ cup chopped fresh flat-leaf parsley

1. In a large nonstick skillet, heat the oil over medium-high heat. Add the ham, bell pepper, onion, celery, and garlic and cook, stirring occasionally, for 4 to 5 minutes, or until softened.
2. Stir in the rice, bay leaf, oregano, thyme, black pepper, salt, and ground red pepper and cook, stirring, for 1 minute. Add the broth and water and bring to a boil. Reduce the heat to medium-low, cover, and simmer for 15 minutes, or until the rice is just tender.
3. Stir in the scallops, shrimp, and tomatoes. Cover and simmer for 5 minutes, or until the seafood is opaque. Discard the bay leaf. Just before serving, sprinkle the jambalaya with the chopped parsley.

Makes 4 servings

Flounder Dijon

Hands-On Time: 10 minutes ■ Total Time: 20 minutes

The microwave oven makes quick work of cooking carrots and fish fillets topped with a Dijon-honey sauce.

- 4 large carrots, cut into matchsticks
- 2 tablespoons chopped fresh parsley
- 1 tablespoon olive oil
- ⅛ teaspoon salt
- ⅛ teaspoon ground black pepper
- 4 flounder or cod fillets (5 ounces each)
- 2 teaspoons stone-ground Dijon mustard
- 1 teaspoon honey

1. In an 11" × 7" microwaveable dish, combine the carrots, parsley, oil, salt, and pepper. Cover with wax paper. Microwave on high power, stirring once, for 5 minutes.
2. Fold any thin fish fillets to make each an even thickness. Place on top of the carrots in the corners of the dish with the thickest parts toward the outside.
3. In a small bowl, combine the mustard and honey. Spread over the fish. Cover with wax paper and microwave on high for 2 minutes. Rotate the fillets, placing the cooked parts toward the center, and cook for 1 to 3 minutes longer, or just until the fish flakes easily when tested with a fork. Let stand, covered, for 2 minutes.

Makes 4 servings

Accompaniments

Serve with minted peas and buttered red potatoes tossed with chopped chives.

Ingredients Note

Stone-ground mustard, a bit spicier than regular mustard, adds a bit of a kick to these easy fillets. Look for stone-ground Dijon in specialty food shops or the gourmet aisles of larger supermarkets.

Halibut with Nectarine Salsa

Hands-On Time: 20 minutes ■ Total Time: 1 hour 35 minutes

Cilantro and nectarines give distinctive flavor to the fresh salsa that is spooned atop broiled halibut steaks.

Salsa

- 2 nectarines, finely chopped
- ½ cup minced scallions
- ¼ red bell pepper, chopped
- ¼ cup finely chopped fresh chives
- 1½ teaspoons chopped fresh cilantro
- 3 tablespoons fresh lime juice

Halibut

- 1 nectarine, chopped
- 4 halibut steaks (6 ounces each; 1" thick)
- Olive oil, for brushing

1. *To make the salsa:* In a medium bowl, combine the finely chopped nectarines, scallions, red pepper, chives, and cilantro. Stir in the lime juice. Cover and refrigerate for at least 1 hour to blend the flavors.
2. *To prepare the halibut:* Mash the chopped nectarine and spread the pulp over the fish. Place the fish on a plate. Cover and marinate in the refrigerator for 1 hour.
3. Preheat the broiler. Brush the rack of a broiling pan with oil. Scrape the nectarine marinade from the fish and discard it. Brush the fish with oil and place on the rack. Broil 5" to 6" from the heat for 12 to 14 minutes, or until the fish is opaque all the way through when tested with a knife. Serve with the salsa.

Makes 4 servings

Variation

If you're not fond of cilantro, substitute milder-flavored fresh parsley and a bit of grated lime or lemon zest.

Kitchen Tip

If the salsa seems too tangy, stir in 1 or 2 teaspoons sugar.

Tomato and Dill Fish

Hands-On Time: 35 minutes ■ Total Time: 1 hour 5 minutes

Halibut, cooked in an easy sauce of fresh tomatoes and dill, pairs nicely with nutritious brown rice.

- 1 cup brown rice
- 1 teaspoon all-purpose flour
- 1 teaspoon cornmeal
- 4 halibut or whiting fillets or steaks (5 ounces each)
- 1 tablespoon unsalted butter
- 4 medium tomatoes, peeled and chopped
- 1 small onion, chopped
- 6 sprigs fresh dill, chopped
- 4 sprigs fresh parsley, chopped
- 1 lemon, cut into 8 slices

1. Prepare the rice according to package directions.
2. Meanwhile, in a shallow dish or on wax paper, combine the flour and cornmeal. Dredge the fish in the flour mixture to coat both sides.
3. Coat a large skillet with cooking spray and heat over medium heat. Add the butter. When the butter is melted and sizzling, add the fish and cook, turning once, for 4 to 5 minutes, or until browned. Add the tomatoes, onion, and dill. Cook for 5 to 15 minutes, depending on the thickness of the fish, or until the fish flakes easily when tested with a fork.
4. Spoon the rice onto a warm serving platter and top with the fish and sauce. Garnish each serving with the parsley and lemon slices.

Makes 4 servings

Kitchen Tip

Not sure of how long to cook the fish? The "Canadian Rule" offers a simple guideline: For each inch of thickness of the fish (measured at the thickest point), broil or bake it for 10 minutes. So if your fillets are 1" thick, they will probably be done after a total of 10 minutes cooking time. Of course, be sure to start checking for doneness at least 2 minutes before the estimated time. See page 170 for more on timing and cooking temperatures for these and other methods of cooking fish.

Oven-Baked Fish and Chips

Hands-On Time: 15 minutes ■ Total Time: 1 hour

This leaner, oven-baked version of British street fare uses catfish instead of cod. It's a less expensive and more flavorful choice.

- 2 large baking potatoes, cut lengthwise into 1/4"-thick fries
- 1/2 teaspoon paprika
- 1/4 cup unseasoned dried bread crumbs
- 1/2 teaspoon baking powder
- 1/4 teaspoon dried basil
- 1/4 teaspoon ground black pepper
- 1/4 teaspoon dried thyme
- 1/8 teaspoon ground red pepper
- 1/8 teaspoon salt
- 1/4 cup milk
- 1 large egg, lightly beaten
- 4 catfish fillets (4 ounces each)
- 1 lemon, cut into wedges
- Parsley sprigs (optional)

1. Preheat the oven to 350°F. Coat a baking sheet with cooking spray.
2. Arrange the potatoes on the baking sheet and coat lightly with cooking spray. Sprinkle with the paprika and toss to coat. Bake for 30 minutes, or until tender but not browned. Remove the pan from the oven. Arrange the potatoes so they cover just half of the baking sheet.
3. Meanwhile, in a medium bowl, combine the bread crumbs, baking powder, basil, black pepper, thyme, red pepper, and salt. Add the milk and egg and mix well.
4. Pat the catfish dry with paper towels. Dip the fish into the batter and then place next to the potatoes on the baking sheet. Bake for 20 minutes, or until the potatoes are crisp and golden brown and the fish is opaque in the center. Serve with lemon wedges, garnished with parsley, if you like.

Makes 4 servings

Variation

Use Yukon gold potatoes or any type of baking potato you prefer. Sweet potatoes also make delicious "fries," but they won't crisp up.

Grilled Scallop Kebabs

Hands-On Time: 25 minutes ■ Total Time: 1 hour 15 minutes

Marinate meaty sea scallops in a tangy barbecue sauce, then grill for an easy summertime seafood feast. For a main-course salad, remove the scallops from the skewers and serve them on a bed of mixed greens tossed with creamy garlic dressing.

- 2 tablespoons barbecue sauce
- 1 tablespoon fresh lemon juice
- 2 teaspoons olive oil
- 1 teaspoon Worcestershire sauce
- 2 cloves garlic, minced
- 1 pound sea scallops, tough tendons removed

1. In a medium bowl, combine the barbecue sauce, lemon juice, oil, Worcestershire sauce, and garlic. Add the scallops and stir to coat. Cover and marinate in the refrigerator for 40 minutes.
2. Grease the grill rack. Preheat the grill.
3. On 4 (12") skewers, thread the scallops, piercing them through the sides so the round parts face outward. Leave some space between them. Discard any leftover marinade.
4. Place the kebabs on the rack and grill about 5" from the heat, turning once, for 8 to 10 minutes, or until the scallops are opaque and cooked through.

Makes 4 servings

Grilled Shrimp Kebabs: Replace the scallops with 1 pound large shrimp (31 to 40 shrimp per pound), peeled and deveined.

Scallop Sauté

Hands-On Time: 20 minutes ■ Total Time: 20 minutes

This delicious entrée couldn't be easier: Sauté scallops, then make a quick buttery pan sauce of lemon, parsley, and garlic.

- 1 pound sea or bay scallops, tough tendons removed
- 2 teaspoons vegetable oil
- 3 tablespoons fresh lemon juice
- 2 tablespoons unsalted butter
- 1 tablespoon finely chopped fresh parsley
- 1 clove garlic, minced
- ½ teaspoon salt
- ¼ teaspoon paprika
- ⅛ teaspoon ground black pepper

1. If using sea scallops, cut them into thirds or quarters.
2. In a large nonstick skillet, heat the oil over medium-high heat. Add the scallops and cook, stirring frequently, for about 8 minutes, or until golden brown. Transfer to a serving platter and keep warm.
3. In the same skillet, combine the lemon juice, butter, parsley, garlic, salt, paprika, and pepper. Cook, stirring, until the butter is melted. Pour over the scallops and serve.

Makes 4 servings

Kitchen Tip

Scallops, especially the larger sea scallops, sometimes have a creamy-white, tough tendon attached to their sides. Simply pull it off with your fingers and discard.

Accompaniments

Serve with rice, noodles, or crusty bread and a salad of baby spinach tossed with a Dijon vinaigrette.

How Long to Cook Fish

Recipes often direct you to cook a fish fillet "until it flakes easily with a fork" or to cook fish steaks "until just opaque." These are useful doneness tests, but they tell you nothing about the actual time required to cook the fish. To estimate how long it will take, check the thickness.

Thin fillets are no more than ½" thick. These include sole, haddock, some snapper, hake, catfish, and flounder. Thin fillets cook extremely quickly, so keep a watchful eye.

Thick fillets average about 1½" thick. Cod, some snapper, center cuts of salmon, monkfish, orange roughy, and grouper can be considered thick fillets.

Steaks are usually about 1" thick, including swordfish, tuna, mahi mahi, and salmon. The times below vary according to the fat content and density of the fish used.

COOKING METHOD	THIN FILLETS	THICK FILLETS	STEAKS
Poach	5–7 min; medium-low heat or a bare simmer	8–10 min; medium-low heat or a bare simmer	10–12 min; medium-low heat or a bare simmer
Broil	2–6 min, depending on thickness; place 4"–6" from broiler	10 min per 1" of thickness; place 4"–6" from broiler	10 min per 1" thickness; place very close to broiler
Grill	3–5 min; medium-hot fire	5–7 min; medium-hot fire	5–7 min; hot fire
Roast	About 6 min; 450°F	About 10 min per 1" thickness; 450°F	About 10 min per 1" thickness; 450°F
Sauté/sear	4–5 min; medium-high heat	8–10 min; medium-high heat	8–10 min; high heat

Salmon Hash

Hands-On Time: 40 minutes ■ Total Time: 40 minutes

Who needs corned beef? Canned salmon is delicious when given the traditional hash treatment with potatoes, onion, and green pepper. Serve at brunch or as a light dinner.

- 2 large all-purpose potatoes, chopped
- 1 tablespoon vegetable oil
- 1 large onion, finely chopped, with 1 tablespoon set aside for garnish
- 1 green bell pepper, finely chopped
- 1 can (15 ounces) red salmon, drained (do not use fresh)
- ½ teaspoon ground black pepper
- Creole seasoning
- 3 to 4 scallions, minced
- ¼ cup finely chopped fresh parsley, with 2 tablespoons set aside for garnish
- 1 tablespoon grated Parmesan cheese
- 1 teaspoon lemon zest

1. Place the potatoes in a microwaveable bowl. Cover and microwave on high power for 3½ minutes. Let cool while cooking the onion and bell pepper.
2. In a large nonstick skillet, heat the oil over medium heat. Add the onion and bell pepper and cook, stirring frequently, for 5 minutes, or until the onion is soft.
3. Stir in the potatoes, salmon, black pepper, and Creole seasoning to taste. Cook, stirring, for 10 minutes, or until the potatoes are tender and browned.
4. Add the scallions, parsley, and cheese and mix thoroughly. Garnish with the reserved 1 tablespoon onion and 2 tablespoons parsley and the lemon zest.

Makes 4 servings

Ingredients Note

Creole seasoning blends typically include strong, zesty spices and herbs such as garlic powder, onion powder, mustard powder, celery seed, ground red pepper, paprika, and other seasonings. All brands are different, so you might want to experiment to find the one that is the most to your liking. And be sure to use a light hand if you are not familiar with the brand: You can always add more if needed, but it's impossible to remove the seasoning once added!

Five Easy Toppings for Fish

Looking for some new and easy toppings for tasty fish? Here are five quick and delicious suggestions. Each of the following recipes will top off 1 pound of cooked fish.

Lemon-Caper Topping. Combine 2 tablespoons *each* lemon juice and capers, 1 tablespoon olive oil, 8 slivered oil-cured or kalamata olives, and 2 teaspoons chopped fresh oregano or parsley.

Fresh Pepper and Tomato Topping. In a medium nonstick skillet over medium heat, sauté ½ cup chopped green bell pepper and ½ chopped red onion in 1 tablespoon olive oil for 2 minutes. Add 2 chopped tomatoes, 2 tablespoons lemon juice, 1 teaspoon paprika, ½ teaspoon dried thyme, and ⅛ teaspoon hot pepper sauce. Cook for 5 minutes, or until the vegetables are tender.

Ginger-Sesame Sauce. In a small saucepan over medium-low heat, combine 2 teaspoons toasted sesame oil, 1 tablespoon *each* reduced-sodium soy sauce and dry sherry, 1 chopped scallion, 1 teaspoon *each* honey and grated fresh ginger, and a pinch of ground red pepper. Cook just until hot but not boiling.

Tomato-Fennel Sauce. In a small saucepan over medium-low heat, combine ¼ cup white wine, 1 tablespoon olive oil, and ¾ teaspoon crushed fennel seeds. Bring to a simmer. Remove from the heat and let steep for 15 minutes. Stir in 2 chopped plum tomatoes, ¼ cup torn basil leaves, and ¼ teaspoon salt.

Creamy Curry Sauce. Place ½ teaspoon curry powder in a small skillet over medium-low heat. Toast, shaking the pan, until fragrant. Place in a small bowl and stir in ⅓ cup plain yogurt, 3 tablespoons mayonnaise, 2 tablespoons chopped fresh cilantro, and ¼ teaspoon *each* sugar and salt.

Grilled Salmon with Lemon and Herbs

Hands-On Time: 5 minutes ■ Total Time: 35 minutes

Grilled salmon makes such an elegant dinner, and your guests will never guess how easy it was to prepare.

1 salmon fillet (1 pound)
2 tablespoons fresh lemon juice
2 teaspoons olive oil
3 sprigs fresh marjoram
3 sprigs fresh parsley
1 teaspoon grated lemon zest

1. Grease the grill rack. Heat the grill to medium-high. Spray a large piece of foil bigger than the fillet with cooking spray. Score the fish in a few places and place in a large baking dish.
2. In a cup, whisk together the lemon juice and oil; drizzle over the salmon. Place the marjoram and parsley on the salmon and sprinkle with the lemon zest. Let sit for about 10 minutes at room temperature.
3. Place the salmon on the foil and grill, covered, for 10 minutes, or until the fish is opaque and just begins to flake when tested with a fork. Remove and discard the marjoram and parsley.

Makes 4 servings

Kitchen Tip

To remove fish bones, use clean needle-nose pliers, blunt tweezers, a strawberry huller, or a bone puller.

Accompaniments

Serve with rice pilaf and sugar snap peas for a terrific summertime supper.

Shrimp with Parsley Sauce

Hands-On Time: 35 minutes ■ Total Time: 45 minutes

Stop thinking of parsley as a garnish! Its slightly peppery taste adds great flavor to an easy blender sauce that tops sautéed shrimp. Serve the shrimp and sauce with fettuccine, angel hair, or other pasta. If desired, toss the pasta with the parsley sauce, then serve the shrimp on top.

Sauce

- 1 cup tightly packed chopped fresh parsley leaves
- 2 tablespoons chicken broth
- 1 tablespoon olive oil
- 2 teaspoons Dijon mustard
- ½ teaspoon minced garlic
- ½ teaspoon fresh lemon juice

Shrimp

- 1 tablespoon olive oil
- 1 small zucchini, thinly sliced
- 1 small yellow squash, thinly sliced
- 1 carrot, thinly sliced
- 1 pound large shrimp, peeled and deveined
- 2 tablespoons chicken broth
- 2 teaspoons finely chopped fresh parsley
- ½ teaspoon grated lemon zest
- 1 teaspoon fresh lemon juice
- ½ teaspoon minced garlic

1. *To make the sauce:* Drop the parsley into boiling water for 5 seconds. Pour into a strainer and run under cold water for 10 seconds to stop the cooking. Drain well, then shake off the remaining water.
2. In a blender, combine the parsley, broth, oil, mustard, garlic, and lemon juice. Blend until smooth. Set aside.
3. *To make the shrimp:* In a large nonstick skillet, heat the oil over medium heat. Stir in the zucchini, squash, and carrot. Cover and cook, stirring occasionally, for 2 to 3 minutes. Transfer to a platter and set aside.
4. Increase the heat to medium-high. Add the shrimp to the skillet and cook, turning once, for 2 minutes. Add the cooked vegetables, broth, parsley, lemon zest, lemon juice, and garlic. Cook for about 1 minute longer, or until the vegetables are reheated and the shrimp is opaque. Divide among 4 dinner plates and top each portion with parsley sauce.

Makes 4 servings

Kitchen Tips

To prepare the shrimp: First take off the shells, then remove the black vein that runs along the top of each shrimp. To do this, simply run a knife tip down the length of the vein to expose it, then lift it out with the knife or your fingers.

Five-Alarm Shrimp

Hands-On Time: 30 minutes ■ Total Time: 30 minutes

Just one serrano chile provides plenty of heat to quickly sautéed jumbo shrimp. Use less of the chopped chile if you can't take the heat.

- ¼ cup cornstarch
- ½ teaspoon salt
- 1 pound jumbo shrimp, peeled and deveined
- 1 tablespoon vegetable oil
- 4 scallions, coarsely chopped
- 1 small red or yellow bell pepper, cut into slivers
- 2 tablespoons chopped fresh cilantro or parsley
- 2 cloves garlic, minced
- 1 serrano chile pepper, seeded and chopped (wear plastic gloves when handling)
- 3 tablespoons water
- 1 tablespoon fresh lime juice
- 1 teaspoon granulated sugar
- ¾ teaspoon crushed black peppercorns

1. In a shallow bowl, combine the cornstarch and salt. Add the shrimp and toss to coat.
2. In a large nonstick skillet, heat the oil over medium-high heat. Remove the shrimp from the cornstarch mixture and place in the pan. Cook, turning once, for 3 minutes. Add the scallions, bell pepper, cilantro, garlic, and chile pepper. Cook, stirring often, for 1 minute. Add the water, lime juice, sugar, and peppercorns. Cook, stirring constantly, for about 1 minute longer, or until the shrimp are opaque.

Makes 4 servings

Soft Shrimp Tacos: The shrimp make a fantastic filling for soft tacos. Spoon the cooked shrimp mixture down the center of 8 warmed flour or corn tortillas (6" diameter) and sprinkle with shredded Monterey Jack cheese. Makes 4 servings.

Stir-Fried Shrimp with Lemon and Almonds

Hands-On Time: 45 minutes ■ Total Time: 55 minutes

In this hearty shrimp-and-veggie dish, the shrimp is "velveted"—coated with a cornstarch mixture—before stir-frying to give it a silken texture. Serve it with rice, or spoon over cappellini pasta for an Italian take on this Asian recipe.

Shrimp

- 4 teaspoons reduced-sodium soy sauce
- 1 tablespoon dry sherry
- 2 teaspoons cornstarch
- ¾ pound medium shrimp, peeled and deveined, with tails attached
- 1 teaspoon grated lemon zest
- ¼ cup fresh lemon juice
- 2 tablespoons rice wine vinegar
- 4 teaspoons sugar
- ⅛ teaspoon red pepper flakes

Vegetables and Almonds

- 2 tablespoons vegetable oil
- 8 ounces sugar snap peas or snow peas, trimmed
- 1 medium red bell pepper, finely chopped
- 1 medium yellow bell pepper, finely chopped
- 1 small onion, finely chopped
- 2 cloves garlic, minced
- 2 tablespoons water
- ½ cup sliced canned water chestnuts
- 2 tablespoons chopped fresh flat-leaf parsley
- ¼ cup blanched slivered almonds, toasted

1. *To prepare the shrimp:* In a medium bowl, whisk together the soy sauce, sherry, and cornstarch until smooth. Add the shrimp and toss to coat. Refrigerate for 15 minutes.
2. In a small bowl, whisk together the lemon zest, lemon juice, vinegar, sugar, and red pepper flakes until blended; set aside.
3. *To stir-fry:* In a large skillet, heat 1 tablespoon of the oil over medium-high heat. Add the peas, red and yellow bell peppers, onion, and garlic and stir-fry for 1 minute. Add the water, cover, and cook for 2 minutes, or until the vegetables are just tender. Transfer to a plate and keep warm.
4. In the same skillet, heat the remaining 1 tablespoon oil over medium-high heat. Add the shrimp and stir-fry for 5 minutes. Stir in the reserved stir-fry sauce, reduce the heat to medium, and simmer for 1 to 2 minutes longer, or until the shrimp are opaque. Stir in the stir-fried vegetables, water chestnuts, and parsley and heat through. Sprinkle with the toasted almonds and serve.

Makes 4 servings

Chile-Lime Snapper

Hands-On Time: 20 minutes ■ Total Time: 20 minutes

The piquant combination of lime juice and chile peppers is one of the foundations of Thai cooking. It's used here in a spicy fish dish that is quick and easy enough (requiring just a few ingredients) that you can make it on a busy weeknight.

- 2 tablespoons olive oil
- 1 small bunch fresh basil, coarsely chopped
- 1 Thai or serrano chile pepper, finely chopped (wear plastic gloves when handling)
- 1 pound red snapper fillets
- 1 lime
- Salt
- Ground black pepper

1. In a large skillet, heat the oil over medium heat. Add the basil and chile pepper and cook for 1 minute. Remove from the pan and set aside.
2. Add the fish to the pan. Squeeze the juice from the lime over the fish and season with salt and black pepper. Cover and cook for 5 minutes. Turn the fish and season with additional black pepper. Cover and cook for 3 minutes longer, or until the fish flakes easily when tested with a fork.
3. Divide the fish among 4 plates and top each serving with some of the basil mixture.

Makes 4 servings

Ingredients Note

Both Thai and serrano chile peppers can pack quite a bit of heat. If you prefer a milder dish, be sure to remove the seeds from the chile before mincing, or substitute a milder pepper, such as Anaheim or poblano.

Accompaniments

Serve the spicy red snapper over a bed of rice, with a green vegetable on the side.

Steamed Mussels Bistro-Style

Hands-On Time: 20 minutes ■ Total Time: 35 minutes

Tailor this dish to your taste by adding capers or using different fresh herbs, such as tarragon or thyme. No matter how you flavor them, serve the mussels with French bread to soak up the savory broth.

- 2 tablespoons olive oil
- ½ cup julienned leek
- 2 tablespoons minced garlic
- 2 tablespoons chopped shallot or onion
- 2 cups chopped tomatoes
- 2 tablespoons finely chopped fresh basil
- 1½ cups dry white wine
- 1 cup bottled clam juice
- Pinch of salt
- Pinch of ground black pepper
- 72 small mussels in the shell (1" to 2" in diameter), scrubbed and beards removed
- 2 teaspoons unsalted butter

1. In a heavy stockpot or Dutch oven, heat the oil over medium-high heat. Add the leek, garlic, and shallot and cook, stirring, for 1 minute. Stir in the tomatoes and basil and cook, stirring, for 30 seconds.
2. Stir in the wine, clam juice, salt, and pepper. Add the mussels and bring to a boil. Reduce the heat to low. Cover and simmer for 3 minutes, or until the mussels have opened. Simmer for 5 minutes longer. Discard any mussels that fail to open. Stir in the butter until incorporated and serve.

Makes 4 servings

Kitchen Tip

Some mussels have dark threads, known as beards, protruding from between the shells. Before cooking, remove the beards by pulling gently or snipping with scissors.

Baked Stuffed Red Snapper

Hands-On Time: 50 minutes ■ Total Time: 1 hour 50 minutes

A crabmeat stuffing provides an interesting way to prepare a whole fish for a festive occasion.

Stuffing

- 1 tablespoon unsalted butter
- 6 scallions, chopped
- 2 stalks celery, chopped
- 2 tablespoons chopped fresh parsley
- 1 cup toasted bread crumbs
- ½ teaspoon each dried thyme and basil
- Pinch of salt
- Pinch of ground black pepper
- 1 cup lump crabmeat, picked over and flaked
- ¼ cup dry white wine

Red Snapper and Sauce

- 1 whole red snapper (6 pounds), cleaned
- Vegetable oil, for brushing
- ¼ cup chopped onion
- ¼ cup water
- 1 large egg, beaten
- 1 tablespoon unsalted butter, melted and cooled
- 1 teaspoon fresh lemon juice
- 1 teaspoon all-purpose flour
- ½ teaspoon dried basil
- ½ teaspoon sugar
- Pinch of salt and ground black pepper

1. *To make the stuffing:* In a medium saucepan, melt the butter over low heat. Add the scallions, celery, and parsley and cook, stirring occasionally, for about 5 minutes, or until tender. Remove from the heat. Moisten the bread crumbs with a little water and add to the pot along with the thyme, basil, salt, and pepper. Mix in the crabmeat and wine.
2. *To make the snapper:* Preheat the oven to 350°F. Lightly grease a baking pan large enough to hold the fish. Place the fish in the dish and brush lightly with oil. Spoon the stuffing into the fish cavity and fasten the cavity closed with a skewer. Scatter the onion around the fish. Add the water to the dish.
3. Bake the fish for 30 minutes, basting occasionally (add more water if necessary). Using two large spatulas, transfer the fish to a platter. Pour the cooking juices into a small bowl. Return the fish to the baking pan. Reduce the oven temperature to 275°F and bake for 30 minutes, or until the flesh is opaque when tested with a knife. Fillet the fish and serve with the stuffing and sauce.
4. *Meanwhile, make the sauce:* To the juices in the bowl, whisk in the egg, butter, lemon juice, flour, basil, sugar, bay leaf, salt, and pepper. Whisk until smooth. Add water if necessary to make a saucelike consistency. Pour the sauce over the fish.

Makes 8 servings

Sole with Stir-Fried Vegetables

Hands-On Time: 20 minutes ■ Total Time: 35 minutes

Delicate sole fillets are cooked atop stir-fried vegetables in this easy dish. Serve over steamed rice and you have a complete dinner.

- 3 tablespoons soy sauce
- 3 tablespoons dry sherry or chicken broth
- 2 cloves garlic, minced
- 2 teaspoons grated fresh ginger or ½ teaspoon ground ginger
- 2 teaspoons cornstarch
- 1½ teaspoons sugar
- 1 tablespoon vegetable oil
- 4 ounces snow peas
- 4 ounces shiitake or button mushrooms, sliced
- 1 small red bell pepper, cut into strips
- 1 cup mung bean sprouts
- 1 teaspoon toasted sesame oil
- 4 sole fillets (5 ounces each)

1. In a small bowl, combine the soy sauce, sherry, garlic, ginger, cornstarch, and sugar. Stir to blend well and set aside.
2. In a large skillet or wok, heat the vegetable oil over high heat. Add the snow peas, mushrooms, and pepper. Cook, tossing, for 3 to 4 minutes, or until the pepper starts to soften. Add the bean sprouts and sesame oil and toss to combine. Reduce the heat to medium and add the reserved sauce. Cook, stirring, for 2 to 3 minutes, or until thickened.
3. Place the fillets in a single layer over the vegetables. Cover tightly. Cook for 10 to 12 minutes, or until the fish flakes easily when tested with a fork.

Makes 4 servings

Sole in Parchment

Hands-On Time: 25 minutes ■ Total Time: 35 minutes

Parchment packets filled with succulent fish and vegetables emerge from the oven puffed and brown, making for a dramatic presentation.

- 3 tablespoons mayonnaise
- 2 tablespoons finely chopped shallots
- 1 tablespoon Dijon mustard
- 1 tablespoon lemon juice
- 1 clove garlic, minced
- ½ teaspoon dried dillweed
- 4 sole fillets (6 ounces each)
- 4 plum tomatoes, sliced lengthwise
- 1 zucchini, cut into matchsticks
- 1 yellow squash, cut into matchsticks
- 4 tablespoons dry white wine
- ¼ teaspoon salt
- ¼ teaspoon ground black pepper

1. Preheat the oven to 450°F. In a small bowl, combine the mayonnaise, shallots, mustard, lemon juice, garlic, and dillweed.
2. Cut 4 pieces of parchment paper, each 14" long. Lay 1 piece of parchment on a work surface with a long edge facing you, like an open book. Place a fillet on 1 half of the parchment. Spread a generous tablespoon of the sauce over the fillet. Top with overlapping tomato slices, zucchini strips, and yellow squash strips. Pour 1 tablespoon of the wine over the fillet and sprinkle with salt and pepper. Fold the parchment over the fillet so that the short edges come together (as if you were closing a book). Seal the package by tightly rolling and crimping each of the 3 open edges. Repeat to make 3 more packages.
3. Place the packages on a baking sheet and lightly coat with cooking spray. Bake for 10 minutes, or until the packets are puffed and browned. Place on dinner plates and cut an X in the top of each package. Fold back the corners and serve.

Makes 4 servings

Make-Ahead

The fish packets can be assembled and refrigerated for up to 8 hours before baking.

Kitchen Tip

You can remove the fish and vegetables from the parchment before serving, but the presentation will be less dramatic.

Seafood Potpie

Hands-On Time: 30 minutes ■ Total Time: 55 minutes

Superconvenient biscuit dough from your supermarket's dairy case means you can put this savory pie together in minutes.

- 1 tablespoon vegetable oil
- 1 large leek, white part only, sliced
- 4 ounces mushrooms, sliced
- ½ cup dry sherry
- 2 teaspoons dried tarragon
- 2½ tablespoons all-purpose flour
- 1½ cups milk
- 1 cup bottled clam juice
- ½ pound bay scallops
- ¼ pound small shrimp, peeled and deveined
- ¾ cup frozen peas
- 1 jar (2 ounces) pimiento strips, drained
- 1 package (7½ ounces) refrigerated biscuit dough

1. Preheat the oven to 400°F. Grease a medium baking dish.
2. In a Dutch oven, heat the oil over medium heat. Add the leek and mushrooms and cook, stirring occasionally, for 5 to 7 minutes, or until soft. Add the sherry and tarragon and increase the heat to medium-high. Cook for 2 to 3 minutes, or until the liquid has almost evaporated. Sprinkle with the flour and cook, stirring constantly, for 2 minutes to coat the vegetables with the flour. Add the milk and clam juice. Stir, scraping the bottom and side of the pan, for 4 to 5 minutes, or until thickened. Remove from the heat and stir in the scallops, shrimp, peas, and pimientos.
3. Pour the seafood mixture into the prepared baking dish and arrange the biscuits on the top in a single layer. Bake for 25 minutes, or until the filling bubbles and the biscuits are golden brown.

Makes 4 servings

Kitchen Tip

For a quicker preparation, place the biscuits in the mixture in the Dutch oven and bake there.

Mini Seafood Casseroles

Hands-On Time: 20 minutes ■ Total Time: 35 minutes

These superb single-serving casseroles will have guests swooning. If you'd prefer to make a single casserole, use a 1-quart baking dish and bake for about 25 minutes.

- 2 teaspoons vegetable oil
- ⅓ cup chopped onion
- ¼ cup milk
- 3 tablespoons all-purpose flour
- ¾ cup chicken broth
- 2 tablespoons dry sherry
- 1 tablespoon fresh lemon juice
- 1 tablespoon nonfat dry milk
- ½ pound peeled and cooked medium shrimp
- ½ pound king crab or lump crabmeat, picked over and flaked
- 1 can (4 ounces) sliced mushrooms, drained
- 1 cup fresh bread crumbs
- 4 teaspoons grated Parmesan cheese

1. Preheat the oven to 400°F. Lightly grease four 10-ounce casserole dishes and set aside.
2. In a medium saucepan, heat the oil over medium heat. Add the onion and cook, stirring, for 3 minutes, or until tender.
3. In a small bowl, whisk the milk into the flour. Stir the mixture into the onion along with the broth, sherry, lemon juice, and dry milk. Cook, stirring, until the mixture begins to thicken and just comes to a boil. Remove from the heat.
4. Gently stir in the shrimp, crab, and mushrooms. Divide among the prepared casseroles. Top with the bread crumbs and cheese. Bake for 10 minutes, or until heated through. Let stand for 5 minutes before serving.

Makes 4 servings

Kitchen Tips

If you prefer to use fresh mushrooms, use 1 cup sliced mushrooms and cook them with the onion. If necessary, drain off their juices before stirring in the flour-and-milk mixture.

To make 1 cup of fresh bread crumbs, tear 1 to 2 slices of bread into pieces and pulverize in a blender or food processor.

Perfect Pasta

Spaghetti with Turkey Red Sauce

Hands-On Time: 25 minutes ■ Total Time: 50 minutes

Rather than opening a jar, you can spend a worthwhile half hour on a family-pleasing sauce that's homemade, right down to the freshly ground turkey.

- ½ pound skinless turkey breast, cut into 1" chunks
- 1 medium onion, cut into quarters
- 3 cloves garlic, peeled
- ½ teaspoon dried oregano, crumbled
- ½ teaspoon dried basil, crumbled
- ½ teaspoon ground black pepper
- 1½ tablespoons olive oil
- 1 can (28 ounces) crushed tomatoes
- 2 tablespoons tomato paste
- 2 tablespoons dry red wine or beef broth
- ⅛ teaspoon salt
- 12 ounces spaghetti
- 2 tablespoons chopped fresh flat-leaf parsley
- 2 tablespoons grated Parmesan cheese

1. In a food processor, process the turkey until finely chopped. Transfer to a bowl. In the food processor, finely chop the onion and garlic. Return the ground turkey to the processor and add the oregano, basil, and pepper. Pulse just until mixed.
2. In a large, heavy saucepan, heat the oil over high heat until very hot but not smoking. Crumble in the turkey mixture and cook, stirring often, for 4 to 6 minutes, or until the turkey turns white. Stir in the tomatoes, tomato paste, wine, and salt and bring to a boil. Reduce the heat to low, cover, and simmer, stirring occasionally, for 15 minutes.
3. Meanwhile, in a large pot of boiling water, cook the pasta according to package directions until al dente. Drain in a colander and transfer to a warmed serving bowl.
4. Stir the parsley into the sauce. Pour the sauce over the pasta, toss, and sprinkle with the cheese.

Makes 4 servings

The sauce is also good with a sturdy pasta, such as rigatoni or ziti, or any of the thick pasta strands, such as fettuccine, tagliatelle, or perciatelli, which is a hollow version of spaghetti.

Meatball Stroganoff

Hands-On Time: 25 minutes ■ Total Time: 35 minutes

Adding cream of mushroom soup streamlines the preparation of this old family favorite.

- 1 pound ground beef
- ½ cup cracker crumbs
- ¼ cup ketchup
- ¼ cup finely chopped onion
- ½ teaspoon salt
- ½ teaspoon ground black pepper
- 1½ cups evaporated milk
- 3 teaspoons Worcestershire sauce
- 2 tablespoons all-purpose flour
- 1 tablespoon vegetable oil
- 12 ounces egg noodles
- 1 can (10¾ ounces) condensed cream of mushroom soup
- 1 tablespoon vinegar

1. In a medium bowl, combine the beef, cracker crumbs, ketchup, onion, salt, pepper, ½ cup of the milk, and 2 teaspoons of the Worcestershire sauce. Shape the mixture into 18 meatballs. Place the flour in a shallow dish and roll the meatballs in the flour to coat.
2. Coat a large nonstick skillet with cooking spray. Add the oil and place over medium heat. Add the meatballs and cook, turning occasionally, for 10 minutes, or until browned on all sides and cooked through.
3. Meanwhile, in a large pot of boiling water, cook the noodles according to package directions until just tender.
4. In a medium bowl, whisk together the soup, vinegar, and remaining 1 cup milk and 1 teaspoon Worcestershire sauce. Add to the skillet and cook until the sauce is hot; do not boil. Serve the meatballs and sauce over the noodles.

Makes 6 servings

Beef and Noodle Casserole

Hands-On Time: 40 minutes ■ Total Time: 1 hour 35 minutes

This is hot and hearty comfort food for chilly weather. To serve for a weeknight dinner, assemble it ahead and refrigerate, then simply pop it into the oven when you get home from work.

- 1 tablespoon vegetable oil
- 1 cup finely chopped onion
- 1 cup finely chopped red, yellow, or green bell pepper
- 1½ cups finely chopped mushrooms
- ½ pound ground beef
- 3 tablespoons all-purpose flour
- 3 cups milk
- 2 tablespoons finely chopped fresh dill or 1 teaspoon dried
- 1 tablespoon soy sauce
- 1 teaspoon Worcestershire sauce
- ¼ teaspoon ground black pepper
- 6 ounces fine egg noodles
- 10 ounces frozen peas, thawed
- 1½ cups shredded sharp Cheddar cheese
- ¼ cup shelled sunflower seeds

1. Preheat the oven to 350°F. Grease an 11" × 7" baking dish.
2. In a large skillet, heat the oil over medium-high heat. Add the onion, bell pepper, and mushrooms and cook, stirring occasionally, for about 8 minutes, or until the vegetables have softened and all the liquid has evaporated. With a slotted spoon, transfer the vegetables to a large bowl and set aside.
3. Crumble the beef into the skillet. Cook over medium-high heat, breaking up the pieces, until browned. Add to the reserved vegetables and mix well. Set aside.
4. Place the flour in a 2-quart saucepan. Gradually whisk in the milk until smooth. Cook over medium heat, stirring constantly, until the milk comes to a boil and thickens. Stir in the dill, soy sauce, Worcestershire sauce, and black pepper. Stir about half of the sauce into the beef mixture, reserving the remaining sauce.
5. In a large pot of boiling water, cook the noodles according to package directions until just tender. Drain well and return to the pot. Add the peas and the remaining white sauce.
6. Spoon the noodle mixture into the prepared baking dish. Top with the beef mixture and sprinkle with the cheese. Bake for 15 minutes. Sprinkle with the sunflower seeds and bake for 10 minutes longer, or until heated through.

Makes 4 servings

There are a couple of ways you can change up this recipe: Replace the beef with ground turkey or low-fat turkey sausage, or replace the sunflower seeds with pumpkin seeds or chopped nuts.

30-Minute Manicotti

Hands-On Time: 15 minutes ■ Total Time: 30 minutes

Who'd believe real Italian manicotti could be this quick? Part of the secret is cooking the assembled dish in the microwave oven.

- 8 manicotti shells
- 2 cups ricotta cheese
- 1 cup finely chopped spinach
- 1 large egg
- ¼ cup grated Parmesan cheese
- 2 tablespoons finely chopped fresh basil
- ¼ cup chopped fresh parsley
- ¼ teaspoon ground nutmeg
- 2 cups tomato sauce
- 1 cup shredded mozzarella cheese

1. In a large pot of boiling water, cook the manicotti according to package directions until al dente. Drain and transfer to a bowl of cold water.
2. In a medium bowl, mix the ricotta, spinach, egg, Parmesan, basil, parsley, and nutmeg. Drain the manicotti shells and fill each with about ¼ cup of the mixture.
3. Spoon 1 cup of the tomato sauce into an 11" × 7" microwaveable baking dish. Arrange the shells in the pan; spoon the remaining 1 cup sauce on top. Sprinkle with the mozzarella. Cover with vented plastic wrap.
4. Microwave on medium-high (70 percent power) for 15 minutes, or until the sauce is bubbly; rotate the dish every 5 minutes during cooking.

Makes 4 servings

Ingredients Note

If your market has an extensive cheese department, ask for fresh ricotta cheese. It has superior texture and flavor compared to the ricotta found in the dairy case.

New Classic Beef Lasagna

Hands-On Time: 25 minutes ■ Total Time: 1 hour 15 minutes

The old-fashioned goodness of lasagna gets a new flavor twist from smoked mozzarella. If you're not serving an adventurous crowd, you may prefer to use regular mozzarella. No-boil lasagna noodles and prepared pasta sauce make putting the lasagna together a breeze.

- 1 jar (48 ounces) chunky pasta sauce
- 2 large eggs
- 1 container (15 ounces) ricotta cheese
- 2 cups shredded smoked mozzarella cheese or regular mozzarella cheese
- 2 cloves garlic, minced
- ½ teaspoon salt
- ⅛ teaspoon ground black pepper
- ½ pound ground beef
- 10 ounces mushrooms, sliced
- 8 ounces no-boil lasagna noodles
- ¼ cup grated Parmesan cheese
- ½ cup chopped fresh parsley

1. Preheat the oven to 375°F. Coat a 13" × 9" baking dish with cooking spray. Spoon 2 cups of the sauce onto the bottom of the dish.
2. In a medium bowl, combine the eggs, ricotta, 1 cup of the mozzarella, the garlic, ¼ teaspoon of the salt, and the pepper. Set aside.
3. In a large nonstick skillet, combine the beef, mushrooms, and remaining ¼ teaspoon salt. Cook over medium-high heat, stirring occasionally, for about 6 minutes, or until the beef is no longer pink. Drain off any fat. Stir in the remaining sauce and remove the pan from the heat.
4. Place a single layer of the noodles on the bottom of the prepared baking dish. Top with half of the ricotta mixture and a generous 1½ cups of the beef mixture. Repeat the layering.
5. Cover with the remaining noodles, beef mixture, and 1 cup mozzarella. Top with the Parmesan.
6. Cover the baking dish with foil and bake the lasagna for 30 minutes, or until it is hot and bubbly and the noodles are tender. Remove the foil and bake for 10 minutes longer. Let stand for 10 minutes. Sprinkle with the parsley just before serving.

Makes 12 servings

Chicken Lasagna

Hands-On Time: 35 minutes ■ Total Time: 1 hour 40 minutes

Layering sautéed strips of chicken breast with vegetables makes this lasagna decidedly different—and delicious.

- 12 lasagna noodles
- 1 tablespoon vegetable oil
- 1 cup chopped onion
- 2 boneless, skinless chicken breast halves, cut into ¼" strips
- 2 cloves garlic, minced
- 2 cups thinly sliced mushrooms
- 1 cup finely chopped green bell pepper
- 1 cup shredded carrots
- ½ teaspoon salt
- ½ teaspoon ground black pepper
- 1 cup cottage cheese
- ½ cup ricotta cheese
- ¼ cup grated Parmesan cheese
- 2 cans (15 ounces each) tomato sauce
- ¼ cup shredded mozzarella cheese

1. Preheat the oven to 350°F. Grease a 13" × 9" baking dish.
2. In a large pot of boiling water, cook the noodles according to package directions. Drain well and rinse under cold water.
3. Meanwhile, in a medium nonstick skillet, heat the oil over medium-high heat. Add the onion, chicken, and garlic and cook, stirring, for 5 minutes, or until the onion softens. Add the mushrooms, bell pepper, and carrots and cook, stirring, for 2 minutes longer. Remove from the heat and stir in the salt and pepper.
4. In a blender or food processor, combine the cottage cheese, ricotta, and Parmesan and pulse until puréed.
5. Spread one-third of the chicken mixture in the prepared baking dish. Top with 3 noodles and one-third of the cheese mixture and one-third of the tomato sauce. Repeat 2 times. Top with the remaining 3 noodles and the mozzarella.
6. Cover the lasagna and bake for 45 minutes. Uncover and bake for 10 to 15 minutes, or until the lasagna is bubbling and golden brown.

Makes 4 to 6 servings

Pasta with Carrots and Ham

Hands-On Time: 10 minutes ■ Total Time: 40 minutes

This pasta dish cooks all in one pot, saving on cleanup time. It makes a pleasant change when you want to break out of the pasta-with-red-sauce rut.

4 carrots, sliced
1 pound tagliatelle or spaghetti
1 tablespoon unsalted butter
1 cup finely chopped lean ham
3 tablespoons chopped fresh parsley
Pinch of ground black pepper
2 tablespoons grated Parmesan cheese

1. Bring a large pot of water to a boil over high heat. Add the carrots and cook for 8 to 10 minutes, or until tender but still firm. With a slotted spoon, remove the carrots and set aside.
2. Return the water to a boil and add the pasta. Cook according to package directions until al dente. Reserve ½ cup of the cooking water, then drain the pasta.
3. Return the pot to medium heat. Add the butter and melt. Add the ham and cook for 2 minutes. Add the carrots, pasta, parsley, pepper, and enough of the reserved cooking water to moisten the pasta. Heat thoroughly, tossing occasionally.
4. Serve sprinkled with the cheese.

Makes 4 to 6 servings

Ingredients Note

Tagliatelle are long, flat ribbons of pasta from the Emilia-Romagna region of Italy; the name comes from the Italian word meaning "to cut." The ribbons work especially well with the carrot slices and chunks of ham in this recipe, but if you can't find tagliatelle, regular spaghetti is a good substitute.

Mozzarella Chicken with Pasta

Hands-On Time: 30 minutes ■ Total Time: 35 minutes

All this chicken-pasta-and-bean dish needs is a tossed green salad to make a complete meal.

- 6 ounces ditalini pasta or other small macaroni
- ½ teaspoon dried thyme
- ½ teaspoon dried basil
- ⅛ teaspoon salt
- ⅛ teaspoon garlic powder
- ⅛ teaspoon red pepper flakes
- ½ pound thin-sliced chicken breast cutlets, cut into strips
- 1 tablespoon olive oil
- 2½ cups halved cherry tomatoes
- 1 medium zucchini, halved lengthwise and thinly sliced
- 1 cup finely chopped red onion
- ¼ cup chicken broth
- ¼ cup water
- 1 cup canned red kidney beans, rinsed and drained
- ¾ cup shredded mozzarella cheese
- 1 tablespoon chopped fresh flat-leaf parsley (optional)

1. In a large pot of boiling water, cook the pasta according to package directions until al dente. Drain in a colander and keep warm.
2. While the pasta is cooking, in a cup, crumble together ¼ teaspoon of the thyme and ¼ teaspoon of the basil with the salt, garlic powder, and red pepper flakes. Sprinkle the seasonings over both sides of the chicken strips.
3. In a large, heavy nonstick skillet, heat the oil over medium-high heat. Add the chicken and cook, turning the strips, for about 4 minutes, or until lightly browned and cooked through. Transfer to a clean plate.
4. Add the tomatoes, zucchini, onion, broth, water, and remaining ¼ teaspoon thyme and ¼ teaspoon basil to the skillet and toss to blend well. Simmer, tossing frequently, for 4 to 5 minutes, or until the tomatoes have collapsed and the vegetables are tender. Add the beans and simmer for 2 to 3 minutes, or until heated through. Stir in the drained pasta.
5. Place the chicken on top of the pasta and vegetables. Pour any chicken juices that have collected on the plate over the chicken and sprinkle with the cheese. Remove from the heat, cover, and let stand for 3 to 4 minutes, or until the cheese is melted. Sprinkle with the parsley, if desired.

Makes 4 servings

Chicken Parmesan

Hands-On Time: 20 minutes ■ Total Time: 35 minutes

This classic Italian dish is a breeze to make with the help of prepared marinara sauce and quick-cooking boneless chicken breasts.

- 3 tablespoons seasoned dried bread crumbs
- 3 tablespoons grated Parmesan cheese
- 1 tablespoon minced garlic
- ½ teaspoon ground black pepper
- 4 boneless, skinless chicken breast halves
- 1 tablespoon olive oil
- 2 cups prepared marinara sauce
- 8 ounces fettuccine

1. In a shallow bowl, combine the bread crumbs, cheese, garlic, and pepper. Add the chicken breasts, one at a time, and press into the mixture to coat both sides.
2. In a large skillet, heat the oil over medium-high heat. Add the chicken and cook, turning occasionally, for 12 minutes, or until cooked through. Transfer to a plate and keep warm. Add the marinara sauce to the skillet and cook over medium heat for 4 minutes, or until heated through.
3. Meanwhile, in a large pot of boiling water, cook the fettuccine according to package directions until al dente. Drain.
4. Place the fettuccine on a serving plate and top with the chicken and marinara sauce.

Makes 4 servings

Variation

For a change of pace, cut the chicken into thick strips or "fingers"—the kids will love it.

Leftovers

If there is any chicken left over, make a chicken Parmesan sandwich: Split a hero roll and insert a chicken breast. Top with some of the sauce and a thin slice of mozzarella cheese.

Penne with Pepper Chicken

Hands-On Time: 35 minutes ■ Total Time: 35 minutes

There are no fewer than five peppers in this recipe—black pepper; red pepper flakes; and red, green, and yellow bell peppers. Of course, the bell peppers are all the same vegetable, but they differ slightly in flavor: Yellow and red peppers are sweeter than green. If all three colors are not available, feel free to prepare the recipe using whichever bell peppers are at your market.

- 12 ounces penne pasta
- 3 cloves garlic, crushed through a press
- ¾ teaspoon coarsely ground black pepper
- ¼ teaspoon red pepper flakes
- ¼ teaspoon salt
- ¾ pound boneless, skinless chicken breast halves, cut crosswise into thin slices
- 2 tablespoons olive oil, preferably extra-virgin
- 1 medium red bell pepper, cut into thin strips
- 1 medium green bell pepper, cut into thin strips
- 1 medium yellow bell pepper, cut into thin strips
- 1 can (16 ounces) whole tomatoes, drained and coarsely chopped
- ½ cup chicken broth
- Oregano sprigs (optional)

1. In a large pot of boiling water, cook the pasta according to package directions until al dente. Drain in a colander and transfer to a warmed serving bowl.
2. Meanwhile, on a large plate, mix the garlic, black pepper, red pepper flakes, and salt. Add the chicken and toss until well coated.
3. In a large nonstick skillet, heat 1 tablespoon of the oil over high heat. Add the chicken and cook, stirring constantly, for 2 to 3 minutes, or until lightly browned and cooked through. Transfer the chicken to a clean plate.
4. Add the remaining 1 tablespoon oil to the skillet and heat over medium-high heat. Add all of the bell peppers and cook, stirring occasionally, for 3 to 4 minutes, or until they start to soften and brown. Add the tomatoes and broth and bring to a boil. Reduce the heat to low, cover, and simmer, stirring occasionally, for 3 to 4 minutes, or until the peppers are very tender.
5. Return the chicken to the skillet, adding any juices that have collected on the plate. Cover the skillet and simmer for 3 minutes, or until the chicken is heated through and the flavors are blended. Spoon the chicken mixture over the pasta and toss to combine. Garnish with oregano sprigs, if you like, and serve.

Makes 4 serving

10 Ways to Pump Up Pasta

Pasta has become a favorite fast food in many households, and why not? It's delicious and low in fat, and it can often be ready in just 10 minutes. Here are 10 simple ways to increase the nutritional value of any pasta dish. Be sure to use whole wheat pasta for the most nutritious start to any of these dishes.

1. Increase your antioxidant intake by stirring 2 cups broccoli florets into the pasta water during the last 5 minutes of cooking. Drain with the pasta and top with your favorite sauce (see chart, page 203).
2. Pack your favorite tomato sauce (even if it's out of a jar) with calcium. Heat the sauce to a simmer, remove from the heat, and let cool for 1 minute. Stir in plain yogurt, reduced-fat sour cream, or part-skim ricotta cheese.
3. For added fiber, rinse and drain a can of beans (chickpeas or cannellini beans work well with Italian dishes) and add to the simmering sauce just before tossing with the pasta.
4. Bathe your pasta in a flavorful, high-iron sauce. Sauté minced garlic in olive oil until fragrant. Add fresh spinach and sauté just until wilted (be sure to use enough; spinach shrinks to about one-quarter of its volume when wilted). Toss with hot cooked pasta and top with freshly grated Romano cheese.
5. Get more vitamin E by topping your pasta dishes with some toasted almonds or sunflower seeds.
6. Benefit from the vitamin C in red bell peppers by adding them to your favorite sauce. Or make a red pepper sauce. Sauté red bell pepper strips and some shallots in olive oil until browned. Add some vegetable broth and simmer until very tender. Purée in the blender and toss with hot pasta.
7. Add to your soy intake by dicing firm or smoked tofu into bits and adding to a vegetable sauce.
8. Be sure to get your share of omega-3 fatty acids by tossing a light pasta dish with grilled or broiled salmon.
9. Fight disease with the phytochemicals in green tea. Add some tea bags to the pasta water when cooking the pasta. Reserve some of the liquid to add to the sauce.
10. Use pasta as a bed for stir-fried vegetables. Forgo long-cooking brown rice when you're in a rush and top whole wheat spaghetti with stir-fried veggies and fish or chicken.

Penne with Roasted Pepper Sauce

Hands-On Time: 20 minutes ■ Total Time: 20 minutes

Roasted red peppers add a delectable depth to this pasta sauce, which puts leftover cooked chicken to good use. It's an interesting change from tomato sauce.

- 1 tablespoon olive oil
- 1 large onion, chopped
- 1½ cups finely chopped cooked chicken breast
- 1 cup finely chopped green bell pepper
- 1 jar (12 ounces) roasted red peppers, drained and finely chopped
- ¼ cup chopped fresh parsley
- 12 ounces penne
- ¼ cup grated Parmesan cheese

1. Bring a large pot of water to a boil.
2. In a large nonstick skillet, heat the oil over medium-high heat. Add the onion and cook, stirring frequently, for 3 minutes, or until softened slightly. Add the chicken, bell pepper, and roasted peppers. Cook, stirring occasionally, for 5 minutes, or until the peppers soften. Remove from the heat and stir in the parsley.
3. Cook the penne in the boiling water according to package directions until al dente. Drain.
4. Transfer the pasta to a large bowl and top with the sauce. Sprinkle with the cheese and serve.

Makes 4 servings

Ingredients Note

You'll need about ¾ pound raw chicken breasts to make 1½ cups cooked meat. Poach the breasts in simmering water just to cover for 15 to 20 minutes, or until the meat is no longer pink throughout. In a hurry? Pick up a rotisserie chicken and shred the meat into small pieces with your fingers.

Nutri-Note

Peppers are a nutrition powerhouse: Scientists tell us that most peppers are bursting with cancer-fighting vitamin C and heart-healthy beta-carotene. A half-cup of red peppers provides 150 percent of your daily need for vitamin C and one-fifth of your daily supply of beta-carotene.

Tortellini with Tomatoes and Herb Dressing

Hands-On Time: 10 minutes ■ Total Time: 45 minutes

Make an impression at the next potluck: Instead of boring macaroni salad, bring a vibrant tortellini salad seasoned with fresh tomatoes and herbs in Italian dressing.

- 1 package (9 ounces) fresh cheese-filled tortellini
- 1 teaspoon olive oil
- ¼ cup loosely packed fresh basil, torn
- ¼ cup loosely packed fresh parsley leaves
- 3 tablespoons Italian salad dressing
- 1 small clove garlic, minced
- Pinch of ground black pepper
- 2 small tomatoes, seeded and chopped
- 2 tablespoons finely chopped onion

1. In a large pot of boiling water, cook the tortellini according to package directions. Drain, rinse with hot water, and drain again. Transfer to a medium bowl and drizzle with the oil. Toss until evenly coated. Cool to room temperature.
2. In a blender or small food processor, combine the basil, parsley, salad dressing, garlic, and pepper. Pulse until the herbs are very finely chopped and the mixture is well combined, stopping and scraping down the sides of the container if necessary.
3. Add the tomatoes and onion to the tortellini and gently toss until combined. Add the basil mixture and toss until the tortellini mixture is evenly coated. Serve at room temperature.

Makes 4 servings

Kitchen Tip

For the mildest flavor, use minced Vidalia sweet onion or minced shallots instead of the chopped onion.

Make-Ahead

The tortellini and dressing can be made up to 1 day ahead; cover and refrigerate. Combine the pasta, dressing, and vegetables just before serving.

Pairing Pasta with Sauce

Matching pastas to sauces is pretty simple. Strand pastas, such as spaghetti and linguine, work better with smooth sauces. Shaped pastas, such as penne or bow-ties, work best with chunky sauces. Tiny pastas work best in soups and salads. Here's a bit more detail.

BASIC PASTA SHAPES	SPECIFIC PASTA NAMES	BEST SAUCES
STRAND PASTA		
Long and thin	Angel hair, thin spaghetti, vermicelli, capellini	Oil-based sauces and light, thin broth
Long and wide	Fettuccine, spaghetti, linguine, pappardelle, perciatelli	Light cream sauces, Alfredo sauce, and light tomato sauces
SHAPED PASTA		
Short and chunky	Rigatoni, shells, ziti, cut fusilli, penne, farfalle	Chunky sauces, meat sauces, primaveras, pasta casseroles, pasta salads
Tiny	Ditalini, orzo, alphabets, tubetti, pastina, small shells	Soups, stews, salads

Spinach Fettuccine with Shrimp

Hands-On Time: 40 minutes ■ Total Time: 55 minutes

Serve this colorful seafood pasta with warm Italian bread and a tossed salad with creamy Italian dressing.

Sauce

- 2 tablespoons finely chopped fresh parsley
- 2 tablespoons finely chopped fresh basil or 1 teaspoon dried
- 1 tablespoon finely chopped fresh oregano or ½ teaspoon dried
- ½ teaspoon ground black pepper
- ¼ teaspoon red pepper flakes (or to taste)
- ⅓ cup all-purpose flour
- 2½ cups milk
- ½ cup chicken broth
- ¼ cup grated Parmesan cheese

Pasta and Shrimp

- 12 ounces spinach fettuccine
- 8 ounces sugar snap peas, trimmed
- 1 tablespoon olive oil
- ¾ pound large shrimp, peeled, deveined, and halved lengthwise
- 1 clove garlic, minced
- 1 pint cherry tomatoes, each halved or quartered

1. *To make the sauce:* In a small bowl, combine the parsley, basil, oregano, black pepper, and red pepper flakes. Set aside.
2. Place the flour in a 2-quart saucepan. Whisk in about ½ cup of the milk until smooth. Gradually whisk in broth and the remaining 2 cups milk. Cook over medium heat, whisking constantly, for about 5 minutes, or until thickened. Stir in the cheese and half of the herb mixture. Set aside and keep warm.
3. *To make the pasta and shrimp:* In a large pot of boiling water, cook the pasta according to package directions until al dente. Do not overcook. Drain and keep warm.
4. In a vegetable steamer, cook the peas for 5 minutes, or until crisp-tender. Do not overcook. Set aside.
5. In a large nonstick skillet, heat the oil over medium-high heat. Add the shrimp and stir-fry for 1 minute. Add the garlic and stir-fry for 1 minute. Add the tomatoes and reserved peas and stir-fry for 1 minute, or until the shrimp are opaque. Do not overcook. Stir in the remaining herb mixture.
6. Place the fettuccine on a serving platter. Top with the sauce and shrimp mixture and toss to coat.

Makes 4 servings

Pesto Pasta

Hands-On Time: 10 minutes ■ Total Time: 25 minutes

It couldn't be easier to make a flavorful pasta dish; this pesto is positively bursting with the green goodness of fresh basil and parsley.

- 12 ounces linguine
- 3 cups packed fresh basil leaves
- ¾ cup packed fresh parsley leaves
- 3 tablespoons olive oil
- 3 cloves garlic
- 3 tablespoons toasted pine nuts or walnuts
- ¼ cup freshly grated Parmesan cheese
- ¼ cup chicken broth

1. In a large pot of boiling water, cook the pasta according to package directions until al dente.
2. Meanwhile, in a food processor or blender, combine the basil, parsley, oil, garlic, and nuts and pulse to finely chop. Sprinkle with the cheese. With the machine running, add the broth, 1 tablespoon at a time, until the mixture is the consistency of prepared mustard.
3. Toss the pesto with the pasta and serve.

Makes 4 servings

Make-Ahead

You can freeze the pesto for up to 3 months in an airtight container (you'll have about 1 cup). Thaw in the refrigerator, then let it come to room temperature before tossing with linguine, fettuccine, or cheese tortellini.

Ingredients Note

To toast pine nuts: Place the nuts in a medium nonstick skillet and cook over medium heat, shaking the pan frequently, for 3 to 5 minutes, or until lightly browned.

Udon Noodles with Broccoli and Peppers

Hands-On Time: 25 minutes ■ Total Time: 30 minutes

Thick Japanese noodles tossed with crisp-tender vegetables are sure to become a favorite. If you can't find udon noodles, spaghetti works well in this dish.

- 1 package (8 ounces) udon noodles
- 2 teaspoons hot chile oil or toasted sesame oil
- 2 cups broccoli florets
- 2 carrots, julienned
- ½ medium red bell pepper, thinly sliced
- ½ medium green bell pepper, thinly sliced
- 1 can (8 ounces) sliced water chestnuts, drained
- 1 cup vegetable broth
- 2 tablespoons soy sauce
- 1 tablespoon rice vinegar
- 2 cloves garlic, minced
- 1 tablespoon grated fresh ginger
- 1 tablespoon cornstarch

1. In a large pot of boiling water, cook the noodles according to package directions.
2. Meanwhile, in a large skillet, heat the oil over medium-high heat. Add the broccoli, carrots, red and green bell peppers, and water chestnuts. Cook, stirring frequently, for about 3 minutes, or until crisp-tender.
3. In a small bowl, whisk together the broth, soy sauce, vinegar, garlic, ginger, and cornstarch. Add to the skillet and cook, stirring constantly, for about 2 minutes, or until thickened.
4. Drain the noodles and transfer to a warmed serving bowl. Top with the vegetable mixture and toss to coat well.

Makes 4 servings

Pasta with Tender Kale

Hands-On Time: 25 minutes ■ Total Time: 35 minutes

When it's just the two of you for dinner, whip up this easy vegetarian pasta that's bursting with fresh greens and the piquant flavor of sun-dried tomatoes.

- ⅓ cup boiling water
- 6 sun-dried tomato halves, snipped
- 6 ounces fettuccine
- 1 tablespoon olive oil
- 1 large onion, chopped
- 8 ounces mushrooms, sliced
- 2 or 3 cloves garlic, minced
- 8 cups fresh kale, trimmed of ribs
- 1 cup chopped fresh sorrel or spinach
- ½ cup plain yogurt
- 2 tablespoons grated Parmesan cheese

1. In a small bowl, combine the water and sun-dried tomatoes. Let stand for 15 minutes, or until the tomatoes are softened. Drain.
2. In a large pot of boiling water, cook the fettuccine according to package directions until al dente. Drain, rinse with hot water, and drain again.
3. In a large skillet, heat the oil over medium heat. Add the onion and cook, stirring, for 3 minutes, or until tender. Add the mushrooms and garlic and cook, stirring, for 5 minutes. Stir in the sun-dried tomatoes, kale, and sorrel. Cover and cook for 8 minutes, or until the greens are softened.
4. Toss the hot pasta with the kale mixture, yogurt, and cheese.

Makes 2 servings

Nutri-Note

Kale makes this low-fat fettuccine and vegetable combo high in beta-carotene and calcium.

Pasta with Turkey and Fresh Salsa

Hands-On Time: 25 minutes ■ Total Time: 25 minutes

Homemade salsa is a delightful change from cooked pasta sauces: Teamed with fun-to-eat wagon-wheel pasta and turkey strips, it makes a tasty and substantial meal.

Salsa

- 2 large tomatoes, coarsely chopped
- 1 medium green bell pepper, coarsely chopped
- ½ cup coarsely chopped Spanish onion or red onion
- ½ cup cilantro sprigs
- 1 tablespoon fresh lime juice
- 1 tablespoon extra-virgin olive oil
- ⅛ to ¼ teaspoon hot pepper sauce, to taste
- ¼ teaspoon salt
- ¼ teaspoon ground black pepper

Pasta and Turkey

- 12 ounces wagon-wheel pasta
- ½ pound thin-sliced turkey-breast cutlets, cut into 2" × ½" strips
- 1 tablespoon fresh lime juice
- 1½ teaspoons ground cumin
- ¼ teaspoon salt
- ¼ teaspoon ground black pepper
- 1 tablespoon vegetable oil

1. *To make the salsa:* In a food processor, combine the tomatoes, bell pepper, onion, and cilantro and pulse just until finely chopped. Transfer to a large serving bowl. Stir in the lime juice, olive oil, hot sauce, salt, and black pepper. Set aside.
2. In a large pot of boiling water, cook the pasta according to package directions until al dente. Drain in a colander.
3. *To make the pasta and turkey:* Meanwhile, in a shallow bowl, toss the turkey with the lime juice, cumin, salt, and black pepper. In a large skillet, heat the vegetable oil over medium heat. Add the turkey and cook, turning the strips once, for 3 to 4 minutes, or until cooked through.
4. Add the pasta to the bowl of salsa, then add the turkey and any cooking juices from the pan. Toss to coat the pasta and turkey with the sauce and serve.

Makes 4 servings

Baked Macaroni and Cheese

Hands-On Time: 15 minutes ■ Total Time: 45 minutes

Here's a new twist on a classic dinner. And it takes only half an hour to get it on the table.

- 8 ounces elbow macaroni
- 1 tablespoon olive oil
- 1 tablespoon all-purpose flour
- ½ teaspoon dry mustard
- 1¼ cups milk
- 1¼ cups shredded Cheddar cheese
- 2 tablespoons minced scallions, white parts only
- ¼ teaspoon ground black pepper
- ½ cup ricotta cheese
- ¼ cup unseasoned dried bread crumbs

1. Preheat the oven to 375°F. Grease an 11" × 7" baking dish.
2. In a large pot of boiling water, cook the macaroni according to package directions. Drain and place in a large bowl.
3. Meanwhile, in a 2-quart saucepan, whisk together the oil, flour, and mustard. Stir over medium heat for 1 minute. Gradually whisk in the milk. Cook, stirring, for 5 minutes, or until thickened. Stir in the Cheddar, scallions, and pepper. Pour over the macaroni and stir well.
4. In a blender or food processor, process the ricotta until very smooth. Add to the macaroni and mix well.
5. Spoon the macaroni mixture into the prepared dish. Top with the bread crumbs and bake for 20 minutes, or until the top is golden brown.

Makes 4 servings

Meatless Mains

Pasta and White Bean Stew

Hands-On Time: 30 minutes ■ Total Time: 45 minutes

Toss together a green salad and warm some hearty bread to go with this easy vegetarian stew. Orzo pasta is roughly the size and shape of long-grain rice. You could also use conchigliette (tiny shells) or stelline (tiny stars).

- 2 teaspoons olive oil
- 5 medium carrots, finely chopped
- 2 medium onions, chopped
- 4 stalks celery, sliced
- 3 cloves garlic, minced
- 5 cups water
- 2 cups chicken broth
- 1 tablespoon fresh rosemary, chopped
- 1 pound orzo or other small pasta
- 2 cans (15 ounces each) white beans, rinsed and drained
- 1½ pounds kale, stemmed and chopped
- 3 medium tomatoes, chopped
- ½ teaspoon salt
- ½ teaspoon ground black pepper
- ¼ cup plus 2 tablespoons grated Parmesan cheese

1. In a Dutch oven or large, heavy saucepan, heat the oil over medium heat. Add the carrots, onions, celery, and garlic and cook for 3 minutes, or until the onions are softened. Add the water, 1 cup of the broth, and the rosemary. Increase the heat to medium-high and simmer for 2 minutes to blend the flavors.
2. Reduce the heat to medium, add the pasta, and cook according to package directions until al dente.
3. Add the beans, kale, tomatoes, salt, pepper, and remaining 1 cup broth. Cover and cook for 5 minutes longer, or until the kale is wilted. Serve with the cheese sprinkled on top.

Makes 8 servings

Vegetarian Paella

Hands-On Time: 10 minutes ■ Total Time: 30 minutes

The saffron in this meatless version of the classic Spanish rice dish imparts a distinctive flavor and a gorgeous golden hue.

- 1 tablespoon olive oil
- 1 cup chopped onion
- 1 teaspoon minced garlic
- 2 cups water
- ¾ teaspoon salt
- ¼ teaspoon saffron threads
- 1 cup white rice
- 1 cup finely chopped carrots
- 1½ cups frozen peas, thawed
- 1 cup cooked or canned chickpeas, rinsed and drained
- ¼ cup roasted red peppers (from a jar), cut into thin strips
- Salt
- Ground black pepper

1. In a large, heavy saucepan, heat the oil over medium heat. Add the onion and garlic and cook, stirring, for 1 minute. Add the water, salt, and saffron and bring to a boil. Stir in the rice and carrots. Return to a boil and reduce the heat to low. Cover and simmer for about 18 minutes, or just until the rice is tender.
2. Uncover the pan and quickly sprinkle the peas, chickpeas, and red peppers over the rice. Cover and continue to simmer for 2 minutes, or until the rice is cooked and the liquid has been absorbed. Stir gently to fluff up the rice and distribute the vegetables. Season with the salt and black pepper and serve.

Makes 4 servings

Kitchen Tip

Store saffron in the refrigerator to maintain maximum freshness.

Moroccan Vegetable Stew

Hands-On Time: 40 minutes ■ Total Time: 1 hour 5 minutes

The blend of spices in this tasty stew gives it a delicious richness. Serve it over rice or couscous, if you like.

- 2 tablespoons vegetable oil
- 1 cup chopped onion
- 1 cup sliced celery
- 1 medium red bell pepper, sliced
- 4 cloves garlic, minced
- 1 tablespoon all-purpose flour
- 1 teaspoon ground cinnamon
- ½ teaspoon ground cumin
- ½ teaspoon curry powder
- ¼ teaspoon ground red pepper
- ¼ teaspoon ground cloves
- ¼ teaspoon turmeric
- 1 small unpeeled eggplant, cut into ½" cubes
- ½ medium butternut squash, peeled and cut into ½" cubes
- 1 cup vegetable broth
- 1 can (14½ ounces) diced tomatoes, drained
- 1 can (14½ ounces) chickpeas, rinsed and drained
- 8 ounces fresh or thawed frozen whole small okra, stems trimmed (optional)
- ¼ cup blanched whole almonds, toasted (see Kitchen Note, below)
- ¼ cup raisins
- Salt
- Ground black pepper

1. In a large, heavy saucepan or Dutch oven, heat the oil over medium heat. Add the onion, celery, bell pepper, and garlic. Cook, stirring frequently, for about 5 minutes, or until the vegetables are tender.
2. Reduce the heat to medium-low and stir in the flour, cinnamon, cumin, curry powder, red pepper, cloves, and turmeric. Cook, stirring, for 2 minutes.
3. Stir in the eggplant, squash, broth, and tomatoes. Increase the heat to high and bring to a boil. Reduce the heat to low, cover, and simmer for 10 minutes.
4. Stir in the chickpeas, okra (if using), almonds, and raisins. Simmer, covered, for 10 to 15 minutes (if using fresh okra, make sure it is tender). Season to taste with salt and black pepper. Serve in shallow bowls.

Makes 6 servings

Kitchen Note

To toast almonds, place them in a dry nonstick skillet over medium heat. Toast the nuts, shaking the skillet often, for 3 to 5 minutes, or until fragrant.

Chickpea Burgers

Hands-On Time: 20 minutes ■ Total Time: 55 minutes

Mashed chickpeas are a terrific stand-in for ground meat when you want a lighter burger. Serve with all the traditional toppings, such as sliced tomato, sliced onion, ketchup, and mustard.

- 1 can (16 ounces) chickpeas, rinsed, drained, and mashed
- ½ cup finely chopped red onion
- ½ cup finely chopped celery
- 1 cup unseasoned dried bread crumbs
- ½ cup tomato sauce
- ½ cup finely chopped fresh parsley
- 1 large egg white
- 1 tablespoon Dijon mustard
- 1 tablespoon Worcestershire sauce
- 2 teaspoons olive oil
- 1 teaspoon dried thyme
- ½ teaspoon liquid smoke (optional)
- ¼ to ¾ teaspoon salt
- ¼ teaspoon ground black pepper
- 4 hamburger buns, toasted

1. Preheat the oven to 350°F. In a large bowl, combine the chickpeas, onion, celery, bread crumbs, tomato sauce, parsley, egg white, mustard, Worcestershire sauce, oil, thyme, liquid smoke (if using), salt, and pepper. Mix well. Using your hands, shape the mixture into 4 patties.
2. Grease a nonstick baking sheet. Place the patties on the baking sheet and cover with foil. Bake for 30 minutes. Uncover and bake for 5 to 10 minutes longer, or until the patties are lightly browned. Serve in the toasted buns.

Makes 4 servings

Ingredients Note

Traditional Worcestershire sauce contains anchovies, but vegetarian versions can be found in health food stores.

Variation

Instead of baking the burgers, you can sauté them in olive oil in a nonstick pan.

Curried Tofu with Squash and Lima Beans

Hands-On Time: 25 minutes ■ Total Time: 55 minutes

The beauty of tofu is that it readily soaks up the flavors and seasonings of whatever it is cooked in. Here, we simmer tofu cubes and squash in a heady mixture of ginger, garlic, coriander, and cumin.

- 1 pound firm tofu
- 1 tablespoon vegetable oil
- 1½ cups coarsely chopped onions
- 1½ tablespoons minced fresh ginger
- 1 teaspoon minced garlic
- 2½ teaspoons ground coriander
- 1½ teaspoons cumin seeds
- 1½ teaspoons turmeric
- ⅛ teaspoon ground red pepper
- 1 medium butternut squash, peeled, seeded, and cut into ¾" chunks
- 1 cup vegetable broth or water
- ¾ teaspoon salt
- 10 ounces frozen lima beans, thawed
- Ground black pepper
- 2 cups hot cooked basmati rice

1. Set the tofu between 2 plates covered with paper towels and place a heavy pot on top. Let stand for 10 minutes to release excess water. Cut into ¾" cubes and set aside.
2. In a large saucepan, heat the oil over medium-high heat. Add the onions, ginger, garlic, coriander, cumin seeds, turmeric, and red pepper. Cook, stirring, for 2 minutes. Add the reserved tofu, squash, broth, and salt and bring to a boil. Reduce the heat to medium-low, cover, and cook, stirring occasionally, for 15 to 20 minutes, or until the squash is tender.
3. Mash some of the squash against the sides of the pan to create a thick sauce. Add the beans and stir well. Cover and simmer for 2 to 3 minutes, or until the beans are tender and heated through. Season with the black pepper and serve over the rice.

Makes 4 servings

A Crash Course on Tofu

The process of making tofu, also known as bean curd, is similar to that of making cheese. Soy milk is curdled, drained, and pressed into blocks. Depending upon how much whey has been pressed out, tofu can be soft, firm, or extra-firm. Tofu has a very mild flavor that readily takes on the flavors of other foods, particularly marinades and sauces. It is usually sold packed in tubs of water. The custardlike "silken" tofu is sold in small, aseptic boxes.

Choosing tofu: There are two basic types of tofu: regular and silken. If a recipe doesn't specify silken tofu, use the regular type. Regular tofu has a firmer texture than silken tofu and is best when marinated and grilled, broiled, baked, browned, sautéed, or stir-fried. You can also mash regular tofu with seasonings and use it in casseroles like you would use ricotta cheese. The custardlike texture of silken tofu works best when cubed and served in broth or when puréed to use in creamy soups, dips, sauces, and dressings. Puréed silken tofu makes a good substitute for sour cream or yogurt in baking as well. More processed forms of tofu are also available. Premarinated and baked or smoked tofu can be eaten right out of the package or used in recipes.

Storing tofu: Once opened, submerge tofu (regular or silken) in water in an airtight container and refrigerate for up to 5 days, changing the water once or twice. Tofu spoils easily, so handle it as you would a fresh meat product. Marinate it in the refrigerator and keep it cold or bring it to room temperature just before cooking.

Freezing tofu: When frozen, tofu becomes slightly darker in color and chewier in texture. It also has a more spongelike appearance, with many small holes throughout, which allows it to absorb more liquid flavorings. Regular tofu works best when frozen, then thawed, crumbled, and browned like ground beef. Simply remove regular tofu from the packaging, drain the liquid, wrap the tofu in plastic, and freeze it until solid. Thaw and press out excess liquid before using. To thaw tofu quickly, wrap it in foil and submerge it in hot tap water for 15 minutes, adding more hot water if the water gets too cool. Freezing silken tofu is not recommended.

Pressing tofu: Some recipes call for tofu to be drained and pressed. Pressing out excess liquid gives the tofu a firmer texture and allows it to absorb more flavors. Drain the packing liquid, then place the block of tofu on a plate lined with paper towels. Cover the tofu with more paper towels and top with a weight, such as a cast-iron skillet, a water-filled saucepan, or an unopened heavy can. Let it sit for 10 to 15 minutes or up to overnight for a very firm texture. When pressing tofu for more than 30 minutes, do so in the refrigerator.

Quick-pressing tofu: When tofu will be crumbled in a recipe, skip the step of pressing out the water. Instead, place the tofu in a clean, nonterry dish towel; twist the ends; and firmly wring out the moisture. The tofu will be pressed and crumbled in one step.

Tofu Stir-Fry with Vegetables

Hands-On Time: 25 minutes ■ Total Time: 45 minutes

This quick and easy stir-fry takes mere minutes to cook, so be sure to have all the ingredients prepped and ready to go before you heat up the wok.

- 1 pound firm tofu
- 2 tablespoons soy sauce, plus more to taste
- 2 tablespoons peanut or canola oil
- 2 tablespoons minced fresh ginger
- 1 tablespoon minced garlic
- 6 ounces mushrooms, sliced
- 1 large red bell pepper, cut into thin strips
- ½ teaspoon red pepper flakes
- 6 scallions, cut into 1½" diagonal slices
- 1 pound bok choy, coarsely chopped
- 1 can (15 ounces) baby corn, drained
- 1½ teaspoons toasted sesame oil
- 3 cups hot cooked white or brown rice

1. Set the tofu between 2 plates covered with paper towels and place a heavy pot on top. Let stand for 10 minutes to release excess water. Cut into ½" cubes and place in an airtight container or plastic bag. Add the 2 tablespoons soy sauce and seal. Marinate, shaking occasionally, for 10 minutes.
2. Heat a wok or large skillet over medium-high heat. Add the peanut oil and tilt the pan in all directions to coat the pan. Add the ginger and garlic and stir-fry for 10 seconds. Add the mushrooms, bell pepper, and red pepper flakes and stir-fry for 2 to 3 minutes, or until the mushrooms release their liquid and the liquid has evaporated.
3. Stir in the tofu and its marinade, the scallions, and bok choy. Cover and cook for 1 to 2 minutes, or until the bok choy is crisp-tender.
4. Stir in the baby corn, sesame oil, and additional soy sauce to taste and heat through. Serve over the rice.

Makes 4 servings

Vegetable Pizza with Goat Cheese

Hands-On Time: 20 minutes ■ Total Time: 35 minutes

Here's a homemade pie that's in the oven in 10 minutes. The secret is prepared pizza dough and store-bought pesto. Pat the veggies dry to keep the pizza topping from becoming soggy.

- 1 teaspoon cornmeal
- 1 pound fresh pizza dough
- 2 tablespoons prepared pesto
- 1 large tomato, sliced
- 1 red onion, thinly sliced
- 1 jar (7 ounces) roasted red peppers, drained and cut into ¼"-wide pieces
- 1 cup small broccoli florets
- ⅓ cup crumbled goat cheese
- 2 tablespoons grated Parmesan cheese

1. Preheat the oven to 500°F.
2. Sprinkle the cornmeal on a 12" pizza pan or large baking sheet. Pat out the dough to a 12" round and place on the pan or baking sheet.
3. Spread the pesto on the dough; top with the tomato and then the onion. Sprinkle with the peppers, broccoli, goat cheese, and Parmesan.
4. Bake for 10 to 15 minutes, or until the crust is browned.

Makes 4 servings

Ingredients Notes

You can find fresh pizza dough in the refrigerated section of most supermarkets. Many small, family-run pizzerias also offer dough to their customers.

You can also use homemade pesto. See Pesto Pasta, page 205, for a recipe.

Bahamian Bean and Corn Stew with Sweet Potatoes

Hands-On Time: 30 minutes ■ Total Time: 2 hours 15 minutes (plus bean soaking)

Bold spices of the Caribbean are featured in this hearty stew that is finished with the sweetness of pineapple. Habaneros and Scotch bonnet chile peppers are extremely hot, so use them only if you enjoy the heat.

- 1 cup dried appaloosa, calypso, pinto, or cranberry beans, sorted and rinsed
- ½ teaspoon dried thyme, crushed
- 2 tablespoons vegetable oil
- 1 large onion, chopped
- 1 large red bell pepper, chopped
- 5 cloves garlic, minced
- 1 habanero or Scotch bonnet chile pepper or 2 jalapeño chile peppers, seeded and chopped (wear plastic gloves when handling)
- 3 cups chicken or vegetable broth
- 1 large sweet potato, peeled and cut into 1" chunks
- 1 tablespoon minced fresh ginger
- 2 teaspoons turmeric
- 1 teaspoon paprika
- 1 teaspoon ground coriander
- ¼ teaspoon salt
- 2 cups fresh or frozen corn kernels
- 1 can (4 ounces) pineapple tidbits packed in juice
- Lime wedges (optional)

1. In a bowl, place the beans and add water to cover by 2". Cover and let stand overnight. Drain and rinse.
2. In a medium saucepan, place the soaked beans and add water to cover by 2". Bring to a boil over high heat. Skim off the foam and stir in the thyme. Reduce the heat to low and cover. Simmer, stirring occasionally, for 1¼ hours, or until tender. Drain the beans, return to the pot, and set aside.
3. In a Dutch oven, heat the oil over medium-high heat. Add the onion, bell pepper, garlic, and chile pepper (if using) and cook, stirring occasionally, for 6 minutes, or until the vegetables are tender. Stir in the reserved beans, broth, sweet potato, ginger, turmeric, paprika, coriander, and salt. Bring to a boil over high heat. Reduce the heat to low, partially cover, and simmer for 25 minutes, or until the sweet potato is tender.
4. Stir in the corn, cover, and simmer for 5 minutes longer, or until tender. Remove from the heat and stir in the pineapple (with juice). Ladle the stew into bowls and serve with lime wedges, if using.

Makes 4 servings

Make-Ahead

The beans can be soaked and cooked 1 to 3 days ahead of time.
Store in the refrigerator until ready to use.

Fast Tempeh Stir-Fry

Hands-On Time: 15 minutes ■ Total Time: 45 minutes

Quick-cooking tempeh makes for an easy dinner when stir-fried with frozen vegetables.

- 1 cup brown rice
- 2 tablespoons olive oil
- ½ pound tempeh, cut into cubes
- 2 cloves garlic, minced
- 8 ounces favorite frozen Asian vegetable mix
- 3 tablespoons soy sauce or tamari
- 3 tablespoons apple juice or orange juice
- 1 tablespoon cornstarch

1. Prepare the rice according to package directions.
2. Meanwhile, in a large nonstick skillet, heat the oil over medium-high heat. Add the tempeh and cook, stirring occasionally, for 5 minutes, or until cooked through. Add the garlic and vegetables and cook, stirring frequently, for 5 minutes, or until the vegetables are crisp-tender. Add the soy sauce, apple juice, and cornstarch. Cook, stirring, until the sauce thickens. Serve over the rice.

Makes 4 servings

Kitchen Tip

We like to use a vegetable mix that includes broccoli, carrots, soybeans, bok choy, and snow peas.

Ingredients Note

Tempeh is a nutty, yeasty meat substitute made from fermented soybeans. You can find it near the tofu in the refrigerated section of natural food stores and larger grocery stores.

Cilantro Crêpes with Corn and Black Bean Relish

Hands-On Time: 45 minutes ■ Total Time: 45 minutes

Build a brunch around these zippy crêpes that creatively blend French and Mexican cooking influences. Serve them with pineapple wedges and corn muffins.

Filling

- 8 ounces cream cheese, softened
- 8 ounces sour cream
- ¼ cup mild chopped canned green chile peppers
- ½ teaspoon ground cumin

Relish

- 1 can (15 ounces) black beans, rinsed and drained
- 1 can (11 ounces) corn, drained
- 1 red bell pepper, finely chopped
- 2 tablespoons chopped fresh cilantro
- 2 tablespoons lime juice
- 2 teaspoons olive oil
- 1 teaspoon chili powder

Crêpes

- 1½ cups milk
- 1 cup all-purpose flour
- ½ cup water
- 4 large eggs
- ¼ cup unsalted butter, melted, plus additional for brushing
- ½ cup chopped fresh cilantro
- ¼ cup chopped scallions, white and green parts

1. *To make the filling:* In a medium bowl, mix the cream cheese, sour cream, peppers, and cumin. Set aside.
2. *To make the relish:* In a medium bowl, mix the beans, corn, bell pepper, cilantro, lime juice, oil, and chili powder. Set aside.
3. *To make the crêpes:* In a medium bowl, mix the milk, flour, water, eggs, butter, cilantro, and scallions. The batter should be the consistency of heavy cream; if necessary, thin with a little more water.
4. Brush a medium nonstick skillet with butter and heat over medium heat. Add about ¼ cup of the batter and swirl to coat the bottom of the pan. Cook the crêpe for 1 minute, or until it easily comes loose from the pan. Turn and cook on the other side for 30 seconds. Transfer to a plate.
5. Repeat to use all the batter.
6. Place a spoonful of the filling down the middle of each crêpe and roll up. Top with the relish and serve.

Makes 4 to 6 servings

Tofu Marinades

Use any of these marinades to flavor 1 pound of tofu. Press the tofu to remove excess liquid, then cut through the side to make two ½"-thick slabs. Marinate for 15 minutes or up to 5 days in the refrigerator. Then bake at 350°F for 30 minutes, turning halfway through. These marinades can also be used with 1 pound of chicken, beef, or pork.

French Herb Marinade. Mix ¼ cup lemon juice, 3 tablespoons *each* olive oil and white wine vinegar, 2 teaspoons *each* honey and Dijon mustard, 1 crushed garlic clove, and 1½ teaspoons herbes de Provence.

Sesame-Soy Marinade. Mix ¼ cup *each* rice vinegar, soy sauce, and vegetable broth; 3 tablespoons lime juice; 1 tablespoon sesame oil; and 1 teaspoon ground coriander.

Sweet-and-Sour Marinade. Mix ½ cup *each* ketchup and crushed pineapple, ⅓ cup *each* white vinegar and brown sugar, 2 minced garlic cloves, and 3 sliced scallions.

Barbecue Marinade. In a small saucepan, combine 1 cup ketchup, ⅓ cup *each* molasses and sherry, ¼ cup soy sauce, and 2 tablespoons brown mustard. Bring to a simmer, partially cover, and cook for 10 minutes.

Vegetarian Moussaka

Hands-On Time: 45 minutes ■ Total Time: 2 hours 5 minutes

Traditional Greek moussaka contains ground lamb or beef. In this vegetarian version, barley helps create a hearty, flavorful dish.

Filling

- 1 large eggplant, sliced ½" thick
- 2 teaspoons olive oil, plus additional for brushing
- 3 cups cubed unpeeled potatoes
- 2 cups chopped onions
- 2 cups chopped carrots
- 3 cloves garlic, minced
- ¾ cup vegetable broth
- 1 teaspoon ground cinnamon
- 1 teaspoon dried oregano
- 1 teaspoon dried mint
- 1 can (14½ ounces) diced tomatoes with roasted garlic
- 1 can (8 ounces) tomato sauce
- 2 cups sliced mushrooms
- 2 cups cooked barley
- Salt
- Ground black pepper

Topping

- 5½ tablespoons unsalted butter
- ½ cup all-purpose flour
- 3 cups milk
- 1 large egg
- 2 large egg whites
- ¼ teaspoon salt
- ⅛ teaspoon ground black pepper
- Pinch of ground nutmeg

1. *To make the filling:* Preheat the oven to 400°F. Line a nonstick jelly-roll pan with foil and grease the foil. Grease a 13" × 9" nonstick baking dish.
2. Arrange the eggplant slices on the prepared jelly-roll pan and brush the tops with oil. Bake for 20 minutes, or until the eggplant is tender. Arrange the eggplant slices in the bottom of the prepared dish and set aside. Reduce the oven temperature to 350°F.
3. Meanwhile, in a large nonstick skillet, heat the 2 teaspoons oil over medium heat. Add the potatoes, onions, carrots, and garlic. Cover and cook for 5 minutes. Add the broth, cinnamon, oregano, and mint and bring to a boil over high heat. Reduce the heat to low and simmer, uncovered, for 5 minutes.

Add the tomatoes, tomato sauce, mushrooms, and barley. Cook, stirring occasionally, for 10 minutes, or until the mixture is thick. Season to taste with salt and pepper. Spoon the mixture evenly over the eggplant.

4. *To make the topping:* In a large saucepan over medium-low heat, melt the butter. Stir in the flour and cook, stirring constantly, for 2 to 3 minutes. Stir in the milk and bring to a boil. Cook and stir until thickened. In a small bowl, whisk together the egg and egg whites. Whisk 1 cup of the milk mixture into the eggs. Whisk back into the milk mixture in the saucepan. Cook over low heat for 2 minutes, or until thickened. Stir in the salt and black pepper.
5. Pour the topping over the vegetable mixture and sprinkle with the nutmeg. Bake for 45 minutes, or until bubbly and browned on top. Cool for 5 minutes before cutting and serving.

Makes 8 servings

Variations

Mixed-Grain Moussaka: Replace 1 cup of the barley with 1 cup cooked brown rice.

Squash Moussaka: Replace the potatoes with 3 cups peeled and cubed butternut squash. Replace the carrots with 2 cups chopped yellow squash.

Tofu Moussaka: Replace 1 cup of the barley with 1 cup crumbled firm tofu.

Winter Moussaka: Replace 1½ cups of the potatoes with 1½ cups chopped parsnips or rutabagas. Replace 1 cup of the carrots with 1 cup halved brussels sprouts. Replace the cinnamon and mint with 1 teaspoon dried basil and 1 teaspoon dried savory.

Broccoli and Cheese Frittata

Hands-On Time: 20 minutes ■ Total Time: 20 minutes

This frittata makes a great breakfast served with whole grain toast and fruit. Or have it for a light lunch with rolls and a simple vegetable salad.

- 6 large eggs
- 1 tablespoon finely chopped fresh basil or ½ teaspoon dried
- ½ teaspoon soy sauce
- ⅛ teaspoon ground black pepper
- 1 teaspoon olive oil
- ½ cup finely chopped cooked red potato
- 1 cup cooked broccoli florets
- ¼ cup sliced drained roasted red peppers (from a jar)
- 1 tablespoon sliced scallion
- ⅓ cup shredded Cheddar cheese

1. Preheat the broiler.
2. In a large bowl, whisk together the eggs, basil, soy sauce, and black pepper.
3. In an ovenproof 10" skillet, heat the oil over medium-high heat. Add the egg mixture and cook, gently pushing the outer edges toward the center with a spatula, until the eggs are about half set. Do not stir. Sprinkle with the potato, broccoli, red pepper, and scallion.
4. Place the pan under the broiler, 5" to 6" from the heat, and broil for 3 minutes, or until the eggs are set.
5. Sprinkle with the cheese, slice into wedges, and serve immediately.

Makes 4 servings

This recipe calls for cooked potatoes and broccoli, which you need to prepare in advance. You'll need about ½ pound small red potatoes and one-third of a bunch of broccoli. Steam the broccoli florets and whole potatoes together for about 5 minutes, or until just tender when pierced with a sharp knife or skewer. If the broccoli is done first, remove it with tongs and cook the potatoes a few minutes longer. You can also prepare the entire frittata ahead. Serve it cold, at room temperature, or reheated.

Feel free to use other vegetables, such as zucchini, mushrooms, bell peppers, or carrots.

Rotini with Roasted Vegetable Sauce

Hands-On Time: 30 minutes ■ Total Time: 1 hour 25 minutes

A bounty of autumn vegetables is roasted, then made into a hearty tomato sauce for rotini pasta.

- 1 red bell pepper, cut into 1" pieces
- 1 medium sweet potato, peeled and cut into ½" pieces
- ½ medium butternut squash, peeled and cut into ½" pieces
- ½ medium eggplant, cut into 1" pieces
- 3 portobello mushrooms, thickly sliced
- 2 tablespoons olive oil, plus additional for brushing
- Salt
- Ground black pepper
- 1 head garlic
- 2 pounds plum tomatoes, halved lengthwise
- 1 can (15 ounces) tomato sauce
- 12 ounces tricolor rotini
- ¼ cup finely chopped fresh basil
- 2 tablespoons toasted pine nuts

1. Preheat the oven to 400°F. Grease 2 baking sheets.
2. Place the bell pepper, sweet potato, squash, eggplant, and mushrooms on 1 of the baking sheets and drizzle with the 2 tablespoons oil. Sprinkle lightly with salt and black pepper.
3. Slice ¼" off the top of the garlic head and discard. Set the bulb on a piece of foil, lightly brush the top with oil, and wrap loosely. Place on the second baking sheet.
4. Squeeze each tomato half to remove the seeds and excess juice. Place the tomatoes, cut side up, on the sheet with the garlic. Brush with oil and sprinkle lightly with salt and black pepper. Place both sheets in the oven and bake for 25 minutes. Remove the tomatoes and garlic from the oven. Bake the vegetables for 10 to 15 minutes longer, or until lightly browned and softened.
5. Place the tomatoes and other vegetables in a large saucepan. Stir in the tomato sauce. Squeeze the garlic flesh from their skins into a small bowl and mash into a paste. Stir into the sauce and simmer for 15 minutes.
6. Meanwhile, in a large pot of boiling water, cook the pasta according to package directions until al dente.
7. Add the pasta to the saucepan and toss to coat. Serve sprinkled with the basil and pine nuts.

Makes 4 servings

Vegetarian Enchiladas

Hands-On Time: 15 minutes ■ Total Time: 40 minutes

Tofu replaces the ground beef in this meatless entrée.

- ¼ pound extra-firm tofu
- ½ cup prepared medium-hot salsa
- ⅓ cup shredded Monterey Jack cheese
- ¼ cup chopped mild green chile peppers, such as Anaheim
- ¼ cup shredded carrot
- 2 scallions, minced
- 4 flour tortillas (8" diameter)
- 1½ cups tomato purée
- 1 teaspoon chili powder
- ¼ teaspoon ground cumin
- ¼ cup shredded mozzarella cheese
- ¼ cup sour cream
- ½ cup chopped fresh cilantro

1. Preheat the oven to 425°F. Grease a 13" × 9" baking dish.
2. In a medium bowl, mash together the tofu and salsa. Add the Monterey Jack, chile peppers, carrot, and scallions. Spoon onto the tortillas and roll up. Place seam side down in the prepared baking dish.
3. In a small bowl, combine the tomato purée, chili powder, and cumin. Spoon over the enchiladas. Top with the mozzarella and sour cream.
4. Bake for 20 to 25 minutes, or until browned and bubbly. Top with the cilantro and serve.

Makes 4 servings

Accompaniments

Serve with Spanish rice and a green salad enriched with sliced avocado.

Sweet Potato Gnocchi with Sage Sauce

Hands-On Time: 35 minutes ■ Total Time: 1 hour

If you're a fan of gnocchi, you'll enjoy this new twist on the Italian classic. Be sure to use fresh sage in the sauce for maximum flavor. The addition of Parmesan just before serving takes this dish over the top.

- ½ cup semolina flour
- 1 pound sweet potatoes, peeled and cut into ½" cubes
- 1 large egg
- 1 tablespoon chopped fresh thyme
- ¼ teaspoon ground nutmeg
- ¼ teaspoon salt
- 1 cup all-purpose flour
- ¼ cup plus 2 tablespoons grated Parmesan cheese, plus additional for topping
- 1 cup chicken broth
- 3 fresh sage leaves, chopped, plus whole leaves for garnish (optional)
- ⅔ cup heavy cream
- Ground black pepper

1. Evenly dust 2 baking sheets with 2 tablespoons of the semolina flour.
2. In a large saucepan, place the sweet potatoes and cover with cold water. Bring to a boil over high heat. Reduce the heat to medium and cook for about 12 minutes, or until tender. Drain, place in a large bowl, and mash until smooth. Let cool for 10 minutes.
3. Meanwhile, bring a large pot of water to a boil over high heat.
4. When the potatoes have cooled, stir in the egg, thyme, nutmeg, and salt. Add the all-purpose flour, ¼ cup of the grated Parmesan, and the remaining 6 tablespoons semolina flour. Mix well. Shape the dough into a ball and divide into 8 portions.
5. On a lightly floured surface, roll out 1 portion of the dough at a time into a 16" rope. Cut the rope into 1" pieces and place on the prepared baking sheets.
6. In a medium saucepan, bring the broth and chopped sage to a boil over high heat. Boil for about 3 minutes, or until reduced by one-third. Reduce the heat to medium. Whisk in the cream and cook, stirring constantly, for about 3 minutes, or until the mixture is slightly thickened. Add the remaining 2 tablespoons grated Parmesan and cook, stirring constantly, for about 2 minutes, or until thickened. Season to taste with the pepper. Keep warm over low heat.
7. Cook the gnocchi in the boiling water for about 45 seconds, or until they float to the surface. With a slotted spoon, transfer the gnocchi to the pan with the sauce. Stir gently until well coated. Sprinkle each serving with additional Parmesan and garnish with whole sage leaves, if you like.

Makes 4 servings

Spaghetti Squash with Veggie Gratin

Hands-On Time: 30 minutes ■ Total Time: 1 hour 40 minutes

The long, thin strands of baked spaghetti squash are a great stand-in for pasta. We like to toss them with vegetables, tomato sauce, and mozzarella for a terrific meatless gratin.

- 1 spaghetti squash (about 3 pounds)
- 1 tablespoon olive oil
- 2 medium zucchini, finely chopped
- 1 cup sliced mushrooms
- ¼ cup chopped scallions
- 2 cloves garlic, minced
- 1 can (14½ ounces) diced tomatoes with Italian seasonings
- ¾ cup shredded mozzarella cheese
- ¼ cup chopped fresh parsley
- ½ teaspoon salt
- ½ teaspoon ground black pepper

1. Preheat the oven to 350°F.
2. Slice the squash in half lengthwise and scoop out the seeds. Place the squash, cut sides down, in a 13" × 9" × 3" baking dish. Add water to the dish to a depth of ½". Bake for 50 minutes, or until fork-tender. Remove from the oven. Increase the oven temperature to 450°F.
3. When the squash is cool enough to handle, scrape with a fork to remove the spaghetti-like strands. Grease the baking dish and return the pulp to the dish.
4. Meanwhile, in a large nonstick skillet, heat the oil over medium-high heat. Add the zucchini, mushrooms, scallions, and garlic and cook, stirring frequently, for 10 minutes, or until tender. Remove from the heat and stir in the tomatoes, cheese, parsley, salt, and pepper.
5. Add the vegetable mixture to the baking dish with the squash, toss to combine, and spread evenly. Bake for 15 minutes, or until hot and bubbly.

Makes 6 servings

Best-Ever Rice, Beans & Grains

Brown Rice with Peppers and Zucchini

Hands-On Time: 10 minutes ■ Total Time: 25 minutes

Vary this filling side by using different vegetables—whatever is in your crisper drawer. For a main dish, add chicken strips or peeled shrimp.

- 1 cup quick-cooking brown rice
- 1 packet or cube (1 teaspoon) beef or chicken bouillon
- 1½ tablespoons olive oil
- 1 medium red bell pepper, thinly sliced
- 1 medium yellow bell pepper, thinly sliced
- 1 medium zucchini, thinly sliced
- 1 tablespoon dried cilantro
- ½ teaspoon dried basil
- ½ teaspoon salt

1. Prepare the rice according to package directions, adding the bouillon to the water instead of salt.
2. Meanwhile, in a large skillet, heat the oil over low heat. Add the red and yellow bell peppers, zucchini, cilantro, basil, and salt. Increase the heat to medium and cook, stirring, for 3 minutes, or until crisp-tender.
3. Spoon the vegetables over the rice and serve.

Makes 4 servings

Nutri-Note

Brown rice retains each grain's bran coating, unlike white rice, which has had the bran and hull removed. This means brown rice has more fiber—up to four times as much as white rice—and greater concentrations of nutrients such as magnesium and potassium.

Cilantro and Tomato Rice

Hands-On Time: 20 minutes ■ Total Time: 50 minutes

Add chickpeas and a homemade salsa to brown rice for a nutrition-packed accompaniment to simple roasted chicken or grilled steak.

- 1 cup short-grain brown rice
- 2 cups water
- ½ teaspoon salt
- 1 pound tomatoes, coarsely chopped
- ⅓ cup chopped fresh cilantro
- 1 tablespoon extra-virgin olive oil
- 1 tablespoon fresh lime juice or lemon juice
- 1 clove garlic, minced
- 1 teaspoon ground cumin
- ¼ teaspoon ground black pepper
- 1 can (14 to 19 ounces) chickpeas, rinsed and drained
- ¼ cup slivered almonds, toasted

1. In a medium saucepan, combine the rice, water, and ¼ teaspoon of the salt. Bring to a boil over high heat. Reduce the heat to low, cover, and simmer for 40 to 50 minutes, or until the rice is tender and the liquid is absorbed.
2. Meanwhile, in a medium bowl, combine the tomatoes, cilantro, oil, lime juice, garlic, cumin, pepper, and remaining ¼ teaspoon salt. Cover and let stand at room temperature.
3. Stir the rice and chickpeas into the tomato mixture, top with the almonds, and serve.

Makes 4 servings

Kitchen Tip

To toast slivered almonds: Cook in a dry skillet over medium-high heat, tossing occasionally, for about 5 minutes, or until lightly browned. Or spread out in a jelly-roll pan and bake in a 375°F oven, turning the almonds once or twice, for 10 to 15 minutes, or until lightly browned.

Make Your Own Quick-Cooking Grains

Most supermarkets carry quick-cooking grains, which are parboiled and then dried to halve the amount of stove time. You pay up to double the cost, though.

By planning ahead, you can cook extra of any grain. Simply place the uncooked grain in a medium saucepan with water or Chicken Stock (page 40); see below for amounts. Bring to a boil, then reduce the heat to low. Cover and cook for the time indicated. Let cool completely, then pack into freezer-weight containers or plastic bags and freeze for up to 6 months.

Add cooked grains to salads, soups, stews, and chili. Serve them with spaghetti sauce or pesto. Dress them up with stir-fried vegetables. No matter how you use them, you get extra protein and fiber in your meals.

Enjoy quick-cooking grains in the time that it takes to thaw and reheat them in your microwave—all for a huge savings.

GRAIN (1 CUP DRY)	WATER	COOKING TIME	YIELD
Basmati rice	2 c	20 min	3 c
Brown rice	2 c	60 min	3 c
Bulgur	2 c	20 min	2½ c
Long-grain white rice	2 c	20 min	3 c
Millet	3 c	45 min	3½ c
Pearl barley	3 c	75 min	3½ c
Quinoa	2 c	30 min	3 c
Wild rice	3 c	60 min	4 c

Rice and Lentil Pilaf

Hands-On Time: 15 minutes ■ Total Time: 35 minutes

This easy pilaf is perfect served with marinated and grilled chicken or fish. Chill any leftovers and serve the next day as a salad with a light vinaigrette.

- 2 teaspoons olive oil
- 1 cup finely chopped carrots
- 1 cup finely chopped red bell pepper
- ¼ cup finely chopped onion
- ¾ cup white rice
- ¼ cup lentils
- 2 cups chicken broth
- 1 bay leaf
- ½ teaspoon ground cumin
- 1 cup peas

1. In a 2-quart saucepan, heat the oil over medium-high heat. Add the carrots, pepper, and onion and cook, stirring, for 1 to 2 minutes. Add the rice and lentils. Continue to cook, stirring, for about 2 minutes, or until the grains are coated.
2. Add the broth, bay leaf, and cumin. Bring to a boil. Stir once, cover with a tight lid, and reduce the heat. Simmer for about 12 minutes. Add the peas. Cover and cook for 5 to 7 minutes longer, or until the rice is tender and the liquid has been absorbed. Discard the bay leaf before serving.

Makes 4 servings

Kitchen Tips

Before using the lentils, pick through them to remove any small stones or other foreign objects.

If using fresh peas, you'll need about 1 pound to get 1 cup of shelled peas.

Variation

For a Mexican flavor, add oregano, replace the lentils with kidney beans, and use corn instead of peas.

El Paso Pilaf–Stuffed Tomatoes

Hands-On Time: 25 minutes ■ Total Time: 45 minutes

Beautiful ripe tomatoes are filled with a savory combination of rice, beans, and corn to make a lovely luncheon dish. Serve with toast points and a small green salad.

- 1 tablespoon olive oil
- ½ cup chopped onion
- 1¾ cups chicken broth
- 1 can (15 ounces) red kidney beans, rinsed and drained
- 1 cup long-grain white rice
- 1 cup canned or frozen corn
- 1 cup prepared chunky salsa
- ¼ cup lentils
- ¼ cup chopped red bell pepper
- ½ teaspoon chili powder
- Pinch of garlic powder
- 4 large tomatoes, hollowed out (see Kitchen Note, below)
- Cilantro sprigs (optional)

1. In a large saucepan, heat the oil over medium heat. Add the onion and cook, stirring, for about 5 minutes, or until softened but not browned.
2. Add the broth, beans, rice, corn, salsa, lentils, pepper, chili powder, and garlic powder and bring to a boil. Reduce the heat to low and cover. Simmer for 20 to 25 minutes, or until the rice and lentils are tender and the liquid has been absorbed.
3. Spoon the pilaf into the tomatoes. Garnish with cilantro, if you like, and serve any extra pilaf on the side.

Makes 4 servings

Kitchen Note

The easiest way to hollow out tomatoes is to slice off the tops, then use a spoon to scoop out the interiors. Turn the tomatoes over and let drain for a few minutes before filling. We used yellow tomatoes here, but you can use red if you prefer.

Variations

You can serve the pilaf over tomato slices, or use it as a filling for tortillas.

Baked Rice and Vegetables

Hands-On Time: 20 minutes ■ Total Time: 1 hour 30 minutes

This savory rice is a fine companion to roasted chicken, pork tenderloin, or grilled fish.

- 1½ tablespoons unsalted butter
- 2 medium onions, chopped
- 1 cup finely chopped celery
- 1 medium green bell pepper, finely chopped
- 1 cup white rice
- 2 cups chopped tomatoes
- 2 tablespoons sliced green olives
- 1 teaspoon ground black pepper
- ½ teaspoon salt
- 2½ cups boiling water

1. Preheat the oven to 350°F. Grease a 1½-quart casserole.
2. In a large skillet, melt the butter over medium heat. Add the onions, celery, and bell pepper. Cook, stirring occasionally, for 10 minutes, or until the vegetables are almost tender. Add the rice and cook, stirring frequently, for 2 minutes. Remove the skillet from the heat and stir in the tomatoes, olives, black pepper, and salt. Add the water.
3. Transfer to the prepared casserole and bake for 1 hour, or until the rice is tender and the liquid is absorbed.

Makes 4 servings

Ingredients Note

For 2 cups chopped tomatoes, you'll need approximately 1 pound, which is about 3 medium tomatoes or 8 plum tomatoes.

Risotto with Shrimp, Peas, and Fennel

Hands-On Time: 1 hour ■ Total Time: 1 hour

Rich and creamy risotto is comfort food, Italian style.

- 4 cans (14½ ounces each) chicken broth
- 2 cups water
- ½ cup dry white wine
- ½ teaspoon salt
- 1 tablespoon olive oil
- 1 large leek, white part only, sliced
- 1 bulb fennel, trimmed, cored, quartered, and thinly sliced
- 2 cups Arborio rice
- ¾ pound medium shrimp, peeled and deveined
- 2 cups fresh or frozen peas
- ½ cup grated Parmesan cheese

1. In a medium saucepan, combine the broth, water, wine, and salt. Bring to a boil over high heat. Reduce the heat to low.
2. Meanwhile, in a Dutch oven, heat the oil over medium heat. Add the leek and fennel and cook, stirring occasionally, for 3 to 4 minutes, or until the fennel starts to soften. Add the rice and cook, stirring, for 1 minute to coat the grains.
3. Add about 1 cup of the hot broth mixture. Cook, stirring constantly, for 5 minutes, or until all the broth is absorbed. Cook, stirring frequently and adding ½ cup of the broth at a time, for 20 minutes, or until the rice is almost tender.
4. Add the shrimp and peas. Cook, stirring constantly, for 5 minutes, or until the shrimp is opaque and the rice is tender. Remove from the heat and top with the cheese.

Makes 4 servings

Kitchen Tip

Arborio rice, a short-grained high-starch rice appropriate for risotto, is sold in many supermarkets and Italian food stores.

Dirty Rice

Hands-On Time: 10 minutes ■ Total Time: 1 hour

Traditional Cajun dirty rice includes minced chicken liver or giblets. Our vegetarian version substitutes mushrooms for the liver for a healthier dish. And this one-pot wonder couldn't be easier to put together: Put in just a few minutes of prep, then relax while it bakes in the oven.

- ¾ cup white rice
- 1 can (10¾ ounces) beef broth
- 1 can (8 ounces) sliced mushrooms, drained
- ½ small onion, finely chopped
- 3 tablespoons unsalted butter, melted

1. Preheat the oven to 400°F.
2. In a 2-quart baking dish, combine the rice, broth, mushrooms, onion, and butter. Bake for 55 minutes, or until the rice is tender.

Makes 4 servings

Kitchen Tip

Melt the butter in a small bowl on high in the microwave oven for 1 to 2 minutes. Or to save cleanup of another bowl, put the butter in the baking dish and place in the oven while it is preheating; it should take 4 to 5 minutes for the butter to melt completely.

Black Bean Pie

Hands-On Time: 20 minutes ■ Total Time: 1 hour 15 minutes

Enjoy the bold flavors of the Southwest by combining beans, onions, chiles, and other seasonings in a savory pie. Serve with a green salad and whole grain bread.

- 1 can (15 ounces) black beans, rinsed and drained
- ¼ cup vegetable broth
- 2 teaspoons olive oil
- 1 cup finely chopped red onions
- 3 cloves garlic, minced
- 2 teaspoons ground cumin
- 1 teaspoon chopped canned green chile pepper
- ¼ teaspoon chili powder
- 2 or 3 drops hot pepper sauce
- 2 large eggs
- 1 partially baked 9" pie crust (follow package directions)
- ½ cup prepared salsa
- ½ cup shredded Monterey Jack cheese

1. Preheat the oven to 400°F.
2. In a food processor, purée ½ cup of the beans and the broth until smooth.
3. In a medium nonstick skillet, heat the oil over medium heat. Add the onions and cook, stirring occasionally, for 4 minutes, or until soft. Add the puréed beans, garlic, cumin, chile pepper, chili powder, and hot pepper sauce and bring to a simmer. Stir in the remaining beans, cover, and simmer for 5 minutes, or until heated through. Remove from the heat and set aside to cool. Stir in the eggs.
4. Pour the bean mixture into the pie crust and bake for 10 minutes. Spread the salsa evenly over the bean mixture. Sprinkle with the cheese. Reduce the oven temperature to 325°F and bake for 15 minutes longer, or until the cheese is bubbly. Remove from the oven and cool for 5 minutes. Cut into wedges and serve.

Makes 6 servings

Mediterranean Baked Beans

Hands-On Time: 5 minutes ■ Total Time: 1 hour 50 minutes (plus bean soaking)

Garlic, sage, and olive oil flavor these creamy beans—what could be more Mediterranean?

- 1 cup dried great Northern beans, picked over and rinsed
- 1 cup dried red kidney beans, picked over and rinsed
- 2 cups chicken broth
- 1½ cups water
- 6 cloves garlic, minced
- 2 tablespoons extra-virgin olive oil
- 1 large sprig fresh sage or ½ teaspoon dried, crushed
- ½ teaspoon ground black pepper

1. In a bowl, combine the great Northern and kidney beans with cold water to cover by 2". Cover and let stand overnight.
2. Preheat the oven to 325°F.
3. Drain the beans and place in a Dutch oven. Stir in the broth, water, garlic, oil, sage, and pepper. Cover and bake for 1 hour 45 minutes, or until the beans are very creamy and tender. (Add a little more water during baking, if needed.)

Makes 4 servings

Kitchen Tip

To make peeling garlic easier, place a clove on your cutting board and smack it with the side of a chef's knife. This loosens the skin, which should then easily slip off.

Accompaniment

Serve with braised lamb shanks or Herb-Crusted Leg of Lamb (page 156).

Fennel and White Beans au Gratin

Hands-On Time: 15 minutes ■ Total Time: 40 minutes

Just a little bit of Asiago, a sharp-flavored cheese, goes a long way in these substantial individual gratins. If Asiago is unavailable, use provolone cheese.

- 2 tablespoons unsalted butter
- 1½ tablespoons all-purpose flour
- 1 cup fat-free milk
- ¼ cup chicken broth
- 3 tablespoons grated Asiago cheese
- 1 teaspoon dried thyme
- ¼ teaspoon paprika
- ⅛ teaspoon ground white pepper
- 4 cups coarsely chopped fennel bulb
- ½ can (15 ounces) white beans, rinsed and drained
- ½ cup chopped red onion

1. Preheat the oven to 350°F. Grease 4 individual au gratin or shallow baking dishes.
2. In a small saucepan, melt the butter over medium heat. Using a wire whisk, stir in the flour. Cook, stirring, for 1 minute. Add the milk and broth and cook, stirring, for 3 to 4 minutes, or until the sauce thickens. Remove from the heat and stir in the cheese, thyme, paprika, and pepper.
3. Place equal amounts of the fennel, beans, and onion in each of the au gratin or baking dishes. Pour the sauce over each. Bake for 20 to 25 minutes, or until the fennel is tender.

Makes 4 servings

Ingredients Note

You'll need 4 small fennel bulbs to make 4 cups of chopped fennel. Look for clean, crisp bulbs with brightly colored greens. Cut off the stems, cut each bulb in half, and then cut out the tough cores before coarsely chopping.

Mixed-Grain and Chickpea Tabbouleh

Hands-On Time: 35 minutes ■ Total Time: 1 hour 15 minutes

Middle Eastern tabbouleh is traditionally a one-grain salad, made solely from bulgur (a form of cracked wheat), along with tomatoes, fresh herbs, olive oil, and lemon juice. This "tabbouleh extraordinaire" includes other favorite Middle Eastern ingredients—couscous, barley, chickpeas, and apricots—as well as a sprinkling of feta cheese. Serve the salad with pita wedges or strips of seeded crackerbread.

- 5¾ cups water
- ½ cup barley
- 1¼ teaspoons salt
- ½ cup couscous
- ½ cup bulgur
- ⅓ cup fresh orange juice
- 3 tablespoons red wine vinegar
- 1 tablespoon plus 1 teaspoon extra-virgin olive oil
- 2 cloves garlic, minced
- 1 teaspoon honey
- ½ teaspoon ground black pepper
- ½ cup slivered dried apricots
- ½ cup canned chickpeas, rinsed and drained
- 1 medium yellow bell pepper, finely chopped
- 1 cup finely chopped kirby or English cucumber
- 1 cup halved cherry tomatoes
- ½ cup chopped fresh flat-leaf parsley
- 4 scallions, white parts only, thinly sliced
- ¼ cup chopped fresh mint
- 8 Boston lettuce leaves
- 3 ounces feta cheese, crumbled
- Pitas cut into wedges (optional)

1. In a medium saucepan, combine 4 cups of the water, the barley, and ½ teaspoon of the salt. Bring to a boil over high heat. Reduce the heat to medium-low, cover, and simmer for 35 minutes, or until the barley is tender. Transfer to a colander, rinse under cold running water, and drain.
2. While the barley is cooking, in another medium saucepan, bring the remaining 1¾ cups water and ½ teaspoon of the salt to a boil over high heat. Stir in the couscous and bulgur and remove from the heat. Cover and let stand for 10 minutes, or until the grains have absorbed the liquid. Fluff with a fork, transfer to a jelly-roll pan, and place in the freezer for 10 minutes to chill.
3. While the grains are chilling, make the dressing: In a large bowl, whisk together the orange juice, vinegar, oil, garlic, honey, black pepper, and remaining ¼ teaspoon salt. Stir in the apricots.
4. Add the barley, chilled couscous and bulgur, chickpeas, bell pepper, cucumber, tomatoes, parsley, scallions, and mint to the dressing and toss well.
5. Divide the lettuce among 4 plates. Spoon the grain mixture on top and sprinkle with the cheese. Serve with pita wedges, if desired.

Makes 4 servings

Millet with Broccoli and Garlic

Hands-On Time: 15 minutes ■ Total Time: 40 minutes

Expand your side-dish repertoire with millet, an oft-neglected grain with a mild taste that takes well to seasoning. Look for millet in larger supermarkets and natural foods stores.

- 2 cups chicken or beef broth
- 1 cup millet
- 2 to 3 cups small broccoli florets
- 1 tablespoon olive oil
- 1 medium onion, halved and cut into thin wedges
- 1 or 2 cloves garlic, thinly sliced
- ⅛ to ½ teaspoon red pepper flakes
- 2 tablespoons red wine vinegar
- ¼ teaspoon ground black pepper
- 2 tablespoons grated Parmesan cheese

1. In a 2-quart saucepan, bring the broth to a boil over high heat. Stir in the millet. Reduce the heat to medium-low and cover. Cook for 25 minutes, or until the millet is tender and all the liquid has been absorbed. Remove from the heat, uncover, and let stand for 10 minutes. Fluff with a fork.
2. Meanwhile, place a steamer basket in a large pot with 1" of water. Bring to a boil over high heat. Place the broccoli in the basket and steam for 5 minutes, or until just tender.
3. In a large nonstick skillet, heat the oil over medium-low heat. Add the onion, garlic, and red pepper flakes and cook, stirring occasionally, for 10 to 20 minutes, or until the onion is the color of pale straw; do not let the onion brown.
4. Stir in the millet, broccoli, vinegar, and black pepper and toss well to combine. Transfer to a serving dish and sprinkle with the cheese.

Makes 8 servings

Accompaniment

Serve with grilled chicken, roasted turkey breast, or kebabs.

Variations

Replace the broccoli with julienned zucchini, finely chopped carrots, sliced red peppers, peas, or corn.

A Crash Course on Polenta

The Italian word for cornmeal, *polenta* also refers to a dish made by cooking cornmeal in boiling water until it forms a soft mass. Polenta is served either soft or cooled and cut into slices, which are then baked, grilled or broiled, fried, or sautéed. Here are some preparation basics.

Choosing cornmeal: Polenta may be made from white or yellow cornmeal, though yellow is more common. Choose a coarse-grained cornmeal for polenta with a more robust texture. Fine-grained cornmeal will make polenta with a smoother, creamier texture.

Avoiding lumps: Classic Italian recipes instruct you to very slowly sprinkle the cornmeal into boiling water as you stir constantly. This assures that the grains are separate and constantly moving. An easier way to avoid lumps is to add the cornmeal all at once to the cold water in the saucepan, whisk vigorously, then bring it to a boil.

Evaluating when polenta is done: When the polenta forms a mass that pulls cleanly away from the sides of the pot, remove it from the heat.

Serving soft polenta: Pour the cooked polenta into a bowl moistened with cold water. Let it stand for about 10 minutes, then unmold the polenta onto a platter and serve hot.

Making firm polenta for grilling or frying: Spread the cooked polenta onto a baking sheet and let it cool until firm.

Storing firm polenta: Cover with plastic wrap and refrigerate for up to 3 days before using.

Cutting firm polenta into squares: Use a pizza cutter or a knife dipped in hot water.

Baking polenta: Arrange ½"-thick slices of firm polenta in a single layer on an oiled baking sheet. Bake at 350°F until heated through.

Grilling polenta: Cut squares of firm polenta about ¼" thick. Brush the squares with olive oil and grill over a medium-hot fire until browned on both sides.

Saucing and broiling: Slice firm polenta into squares or rounds ½" thick and sauté in butter or olive oil to lightly brown. Top with tomato sauce and Parmesan cheese, then run under the broiler or bake in the top of a hot oven. Hot, soft polenta can also be spooned into a gratin dish, then topped with sauce and cheese and baked until golden.

Cleaning the polenta pot: Don't bother to scrub the dried polenta from the sides of the pot. Instead, fill it with cold water and let it stand overnight. In the morning, the dried polenta will easily pull away from the pot.

Red Lentil Burritos

Hands-On Time: 25 minutes ■ Total Time: 1 hour 15 minutes

Quick-cooking lentils are low in fat and high in fiber and protein. Mixed with dried tomatoes and vegetables, they make a tasty vegetarian filling for burritos.

- 10 sun-dried tomatoes
- 1 cup boiling water
- 2½ cups water
- 1 cup red lentils, picked over and rinsed
- 1 tablespoon olive oil
- ½ cup chopped onion
- ½ cup chopped broccoli florets
- ½ cup chopped cauliflower florets
- ½ cup thinly sliced carrots
- 1½ cups tomato sauce
- 1 teaspoon curry powder
- ½ teaspoon ground cinnamon
- 4 whole wheat tortillas (8" diameter), warmed

1. Place the tomatoes in a small bowl and cover with the boiling water. Let soak for 10 minutes, or until the tomatoes are soft. Drain, reserving ½ cup of the soaking liquid. Chop the tomatoes and set aside.
2. In a medium saucepan, combine the soaking liquid, 2½ cups water, and lentils. Bring to a boil over medium-high heat. Reduce the heat to low and simmer for 6 to 10 minutes, or just until the lentils are tender. Drain.
3. In a large nonstick skillet, heat the oil over medium heat. Add the onion, broccoli, cauliflower, and carrots and cook, stirring, for 4 to 5 minutes, or until the vegetables are tender. Stir in the tomato sauce, curry powder, and cinnamon. Add the dried tomatoes and lentils and simmer for15 to 20 minutes, or until slightly thickened.
4. Divide the lentil mixture evenly among the tortillas. Roll up each to enclose the filling.

Makes 4 servings

Polenta with Mushroom-Tomato Sauce

Hands-On Time: 25 minutes ■ Total Time: 55 minutes

Instant polenta makes this dish fast to prepare.

- 3½ cups vegetable broth
- 1 cup instant polenta
- 1 tablespoon olive oil
- 2 shallots, finely chopped
- 2 teaspoons chopped fresh rosemary
- 4 cups thinly sliced mushrooms
- 1 cup canned crushed tomatoes
- ¼ cup dry white wine or tomato juice
- 1 tablespoon balsamic vinegar
- 2 tablespoons grated Parmesan cheese
- 2 tablespoons chopped fresh parsley
- Salt
- Ground black pepper

1. In a 2-quart saucepan, bring the broth to a boil over high heat. Reduce the heat to low and slowly whisk in the polenta. Cook, stirring occasionally, for 10 minutes, or until very thick.
2. In a large nonstick skillet, heat the oil over medium heat. Add the shallots and rosemary and cook, stirring, for 2 minutes. Stir in the mushrooms, tomatoes, wine, and vinegar. Bring to a boil. Cover, reduce the heat, and simmer for 5 minutes.
3. Uncover and cook for 15 to 20 minutes, or until the sauce thickens. Stir in the cheese and parsley and season with salt and pepper to taste. Serve over the polenta.

Makes 4 servings

To serve the polenta as slices: Pour the cooked polenta into a loaf pan. Cover and refrigerate until firm. Cut into 2" slices and place on a baking sheet. Bake at 400°F for 10 minutes, or until golden brown. Reheat the sauce and serve over the polenta slices.

Polenta with Italian Sausage, Onion, and White Beans

Hands-On Time: 20 minutes ■ Total Time: 30 minutes

This is a hearty, homey dish for a cold winter night. Use whatever type of mild or spicy Italian sausages you like.

- 3½ cups chicken broth
- 1 cup instant polenta
- ½ teaspoon salt
- 3 small Italian sausages (6 ounces)
- 1 small onion, thinly sliced
- 2 tablespoons orange juice
- 1 can (19 ounces) cannellini beans, rinsed and drained
- 1 teaspoon fennel seeds
- 1 teaspoon orange zest
- 1 teaspoon dried oregano
- 2 tablespoons chopped fresh parsley

1. In a large saucepan, bring the broth to a boil over high heat. Reduce the heat to low and slowly whisk in the polenta and salt. Cook, stirring occasionally, for about 10 minutes, or until very thick. Set aside.
2. Meanwhile, in a large nonstick skillet over medium-high heat, brown the sausages on all sides for about 3 minutes. Cover and cook for 2 to 3 minutes longer, or until the sausages are no longer pink when tested with a knife. Transfer to a cutting board and cut into ½"-thick slices.
3. Wipe any fat from the pan with a paper towel. Return the pan to the heat, add the onion, and cook, stirring frequently, for 2 minutes. Add the orange juice, cover, and cook for 3 to 4 minutes, or until the onion is very soft. Stir in the sausages, beans, fennel seeds, orange zest, and oregano.
4. Spoon the reserved polenta onto individual plates, top with the sausage mixture, and sprinkle with the parsley.

Makes 4 servings

Ingredients Note

To appeal to the busy cook, this recipe uses instant polenta rather than the long-cooking kind. If you have the time, you can use regular polenta and adapt the amount of broth accordingly per the package directions.

Couscous with Chickpeas and Tomatoes

Hands-On Time: 20 minutes ■ Total Time: 30 minutes

Serve this slightly spicy entrée with pitas and a dish of cooling yogurt on the side.

- 2 teaspoons olive oil
- 1 onion, thinly sliced
- 2 carrots, diagonally sliced
- 1 cup chopped canned tomatoes (with juice)
- 1 cup frozen peas
- 2 tablespoons raisins
- ¾ teaspoon curry powder
- ¼ teaspoon ground cinnamon
- 2 cups canned chickpeas
- 2 cups couscous
- 2 scallions, white parts only, sliced
- 1 teaspoon chopped seeded jalapeño pepper (wear plastic gloves when handling)
- 3 cups chicken broth
- ¼ cup chopped fresh parsley
- ½ teaspoon salt
- ½ teaspoon ground black pepper

1. In a 10" nonstick skillet, heat the oil over medium-high heat. Add the onion, carrots, and tomatoes and cook, stirring, for 5 minutes. Add the peas, raisins, curry powder, and cinnamon. Cook, stirring, for 1 minute. Add the chickpeas, couscous, scallions, and jalapeño peppers. Cook, stirring, for 1 minute. Add the broth and bring to a boil.
2. Remove the skillet from the heat and cover. Let stand for 5 minutes, or until the liquid has been absorbed. Add the parsley, salt, and pepper. Toss with a fork to combine.

Makes 4 servings

Vegetables on the Side

Roasted Beets with Herbs and Garlic

Hands-On Time: 10 minutes ■ Total Time: 1 hour 10 minutes

These tender jewel-like beets require just a few minutes of prep, then you can fix the rest of the dinner while they roast in the oven (see Accompaniments, below).

- 2 pounds small beets, scrubbed
- 2 tablespoons chicken or vegetable broth
- 1 tablespoon extra-virgin olive oil
- 2 cloves garlic, minced
- 1 large shallot, finely chopped
- ½ teaspoon dried sage, crushed
- ⅛ teaspoon salt
- ⅛ teaspoon ground black pepper
- Pinch of ground allspice

1. Preheat the oven to 400°F.
2. Cut each beet into 8 wedges. In an 11" × 7" baking dish, combine the beets, broth, oil, garlic, shallot, sage, salt, pepper, and allspice and toss to coat well.
3. Cover tightly with foil and bake, stirring occasionally, for 1 hour, or until the beets are very tender.

Makes 4 servings

Accompaniments

Roast the beets alongside chicken or pork tenderloin, then serve with sautéed new potatoes.

Ingredients Note

Look for small, tender beets with smooth, blemish-free skin and crisp, brightly colored greens. Don't throw out those greens—you can cook them as you would spinach or kale.

Leftovers

Any leftover beets are delicious the next day drizzled with a little lemon juice and olive oil.

Broccoli-Cauliflower Casserole

Hands-On Time: 20 minutes ■ Total Time: 50 minutes

Here's a comforting old-fashioned dish that pairs nicely with a roast or broiled chops.

- ½ cup fresh bread crumbs
- 1 teaspoon olive oil
- 2 cups broccoli florets
- 2 cups cauliflower florets
- 1 tablespoon unsalted butter
- 1 large onion, chopped
- 1 can (5 ounces) evaporated milk
- 1 can (10¾ ounces) condensed cream of chicken soup
- ¼ cup grated Parmesan cheese
- ½ teaspoon ground black pepper

1. Preheat the oven to 350°F. Grease a 2-quart casserole dish. In a small bowl, combine the bread crumbs and oil. Set aside.
2. In a large pot of boiling water, cook the broccoli and cauliflower for 5 minutes, or until tender but still crisp. Drain and set aside.
3. Meanwhile, in a medium saucepan, melt the butter over medium heat. Add the onion and cook, stirring, for 5 minutes, or until tender. Remove from the heat and add the milk, soup, cheese, and pepper. Stir well.
4. Layer the reserved broccoli and cauliflower in the prepared casserole. Pour the soup mixture over the vegetables. Top with the reserved bread-crumb mixture. Bake for 25 minutes, or until the mixture is bubbly.

Makes 6 to 8 servings

Ingredients Note

To make fresh bread crumbs, tear 1 large slice fresh bread into pieces and briefly process in a food processor or blender.

Kitchen Tips

If desired, substitute frozen broccoli and cauliflower for the fresh. Two 10-ounce packages total will be sufficient. Thaw before using.

Variation

For a lower-calorie version, use reduced-fat soup and evaporated fat-free milk.

Autumn Stir-Fry

Hands-On Time: 25 minutes ■ Total Time: 25 minutes

This colorful medley of fall vegetables is ready in less than half an hour.

- 1 tablespoon vegetable oil
- 2 cloves garlic, minced
- 1 teaspoon minced fresh ginger
- 2 cups broccoli florets
- 1 medium red or yellow bell pepper, cut into 1" pieces
- 1 medium sweet potato, peeled and shredded
- 2 cups shredded cabbage
- 2 tablespoons chopped roasted peanuts

1. In a wok or large skillet, heat the oil over medium-high heat. Add the garlic and ginger and cook, stirring constantly, for 2 minutes. Add the broccoli and stir-fry for 2 minutes.
2. Add the pepper, sweet potato, and cabbage. Stir-fry for 5 minutes, or until the broccoli is crisp-tender and the sweet potatoes are cooked through. Sprinkle with the peanuts and serve.

Makes 6 servings

Accompaniments

The stir-fry is best with a simple entrée: teriyaki pork tenderloin, Oven-Fried Chicken (page 90), or Lemon Turkey Cutlets (page 107).

Ingredients Note

To shred cabbage, remove the tough outer leaves and the core, then cut into thin strips with a thin knife. You'll need about half of a 1-pound head for this recipe. Use the leftover cabbage to make coleslaw: Mix shredded cabbage with some grated carrot and toss with mayonnaise, a little vinegar and sugar, and a pinch of salt.

Variation

The stir-fry can be a nutritious vegetarian entrée: Simply spoon over cooked brown rice and serve with a green salad on the side.

Sweet-and-Sour Red Cabbage and Apples

Hands-On Time: 25 minutes ■ Total Time: 40 minutes

Apples and cabbage are both natural companions to pork, so this is the perfect accompaniment to meaty pork chops.

- 1 tablespoon unsalted butter
- 1 tablespoon vegetable oil
- 1 large onion, chopped
- ½ medium head red cabbage, cored and shredded
- ½ teaspoon salt
- ¼ teaspoon ground black pepper
- ¼ teaspoon ground allspice
- 3 medium sweet-tart apples, peeled, cored, and cut into thin wedges
- ¼ cup frozen apple juice concentrate
- 2 tablespoons red wine vinegar

1. In a large saucepot or Dutch oven, heat the butter and oil over medium heat until the butter melts. Add the onion and cook, stirring frequently, for 6 minutes, or until soft.
2. Add the cabbage, salt, pepper, and allspice. Cook, stirring frequently, for 4 minutes, or until the cabbage begins to wilt and color.
3. Add the apples, apple juice concentrate, and vinegar and bring to a boil. Reduce the heat to low and cover. Simmer, stirring frequently, for 15 minutes, or until the cabbage is very tender.

Makes 6 servings

Ingredients Notes

Any firm sweet-tart apple works well here, especially Golden Delicious.

When buying cabbage, look for heads with crisp-looking leaves and no blemishes. You can store cabbage, tightly wrapped, in the crisper for up to 1 week.

Creole Cabbage

Hands-On Time: 20 minutes ■ Total Time: 1 hour

Good-quality canned tomatoes are almost always a better choice than fresh tomatoes during the winter months. In this dish, canned tomatoes, combined with green pepper and onion, enliven a dish of braised cabbage wedges topped with Cheddar.

- ½ medium head green cabbage, cored and cut into 6 wedges
- 1 tablespoon unsalted butter
- 1 medium onion, thinly sliced and separated into rings
- 1 medium green bell pepper, thinly sliced into rings
- 1 can (28 ounces) plum tomatoes, drained and quartered
- 1 teaspoon sugar
- ½ teaspoon salt
- ¼ teaspoon ground black pepper
- ½ cup shredded Cheddar cheese

1. Preheat the oven to 350°F. Grease a 2-quart shallow baking dish.
2. In a large pot, bring 2" of water to a boil. Place the cabbage in the pot, cover, and cook for 10 minutes, or until softened. Drain, transfer to the prepared dish, and set aside.
3. In a large skillet over medium heat, melt the butter. Add the onion and bell pepper and cook, stirring, for 5 minutes, or until tender. Add the tomatoes, sugar, salt, and black pepper and simmer for 3 minutes.
4. Scrape the vegetables over the cabbage. Bake for 20 minutes. Sprinkle with the cheese and bake for 2 minutes longer, or until the cheese is melted.

Makes 6 servings

Kitchen Tip

Box graters can be difficult to clean after grating a semi-soft cheese such as Cheddar. For easy cleanup, spray the grater with cooking spray before grating.

Glazed Carrots

Hands-On Time: 10 minutes ■ Total Time: 20 minutes

This colorful dish—a big hit with kids who love carrots—couldn't be easier to put together on a busy weeknight. Look for sliced carrots at your supermarket's salad bar for an even quicker prep time.

- 2 cups sliced carrots
- ¾ cup apple juice
- 1 tablespoon honey
- 1 teaspoon unsalted butter
- 1 teaspoon grated orange zest
- 1 teaspoon grated lemon zest

1. In a medium saucepan, combine the carrots and apple juice. Cover and cook over medium-high heat for 10 minutes, or until the carrots are soft.
2. Add the honey, butter, orange zest, and lemon zest and cook, stirring, for 3 to 5 minutes, or until the sauce is thick.

Makes 4 servings

Accompaniments

Beautiful glazed carrots are perfect with roasted turkey, of course. But you can also serve them with hamburgers and sloppy joes.

To zest citrus, wash the fruit thoroughly and run a fine grater or rasp diagonally across the peel to remove thin shreds of the peel. Use a light hand, and don't grate any of the white pith below the colored part—it can be bitter.

Carrots with Garlic and Basil

Hands-On Time: 15 minutes ■ Total Time: 25 minutes

Fresh basil is a great way to bring out the natural sweetness of carrots. If you like, substitute 1 tablespoon of fresh thyme for a slightly different taste. Serve alongside grilled chicken or fish.

1 pound carrots
1 teaspoon olive oil
¼ cup minced fresh basil
1 or 2 cloves garlic, minced
1 teaspoon fresh lemon juice
Ground black pepper

1. Peel the carrots and cut as you wish: into sticks, coins, or diagonal slices.
2. Place a steamer basket in a large pot with 1" of water. Bring to a boil over high heat. Place the carrots in the basket and steam for 4 to 5 minutes, or until tender. Remove the carrots from the basket and pat dry.
3. In a large nonstick skillet, heat the oil over medium-high heat. Add the carrots, basil, garlic, and lemon juice and cook, stirring, for about 3 minutes, or until cooked through and fragrant. Season with pepper and serve at room temperature or very slightly chilled.

Makes 4 servings

Kitchen Tip

Instead of steaming, you can microwave sliced carrots. Place in a 9" glass pie plate with 2 tablespoons of water. Cover with vented plastic wrap and microwave on full power for about 3 minutes.

Ingredients Note

Look for brightly colored basil with no sign of brown spots. Chopped or minced basil can discolor quickly, so mince the leaves just before tossing with the carrots.

Cauliflower and Red Pepper with Garlic

Hands-On Time: 15 minutes ■ Total Time: 25 minutes

Minced garlic is only briefly cooked—just enough to remove its bite—in this colorful, flavor-packed side dish.

- 1 large head cauliflower, cut into small florets
- 1 large red bell pepper, cut into 1" squares
- 2 tablespoons extra-virgin olive oil
- 4 cloves garlic, minced
- 1 tablespoon red wine vinegar
- 2 teaspoons chopped fresh thyme or ¼ teaspoon dried, crushed
- ¾ teaspoon paprika
- ½ teaspoon salt

1. Place a steamer basket in a large pot with ½" of water. Bring to a boil over high heat. Place the cauliflower and pepper in the basket and steam for 4 minutes, or until crisp-tender. Place in a serving bowl.
2. In a small skillet, heat the oil over medium heat. Remove from the heat and stir in the garlic. When the sizzling stops, stir in the vinegar, thyme, paprika, and salt. Add to the vegetables, toss to coat well, and serve.

Makes 4 servings

Make-Ahead

You can prep the cauliflower and red pepper well in advance. Place the cut-up vegetables in a zip-top bag and refrigerate for up to a day. You can also steam the vegetables up to 2 hours ahead of time. However, the garlic and thyme should be chopped just before cooking.

Kitchen Tip

While chopping the garlic, add a pinch or two of salt—it will help keep the garlic bits from sticking to your knife blade.

Corn and Spinach Fritters

Hands-On Time: 25 minutes ■ Total Time: 25 minutes

These corn fritters are such a snap to prepare that you can serve them often. Their appealing color comes from a combination of corn, spinach, and carrots, giving them a nutritional edge over standard fried fritters. Serve with grilled lamb, roasted chicken, or sautéed fish.

- 1 cup packed spinach leaves, chopped into ½" pieces (see Ingredients Notes, below)
- 1 cup fresh, frozen, or canned corn (see Ingredients Notes, below)
- ¼ cup finely shredded carrot
- ¼ cup shredded mozzarella cheese
- 2 large egg whites
- 1 tablespoon cornstarch
- ¼ teaspoon minced garlic (optional)
- ¼ teaspoon salt
- 1 tablespoon olive oil, plus additional if needed
- Sour cream and snipped chives (optional)

1. Place the spinach in a strainer and plunge into a pot of boiling water. Blanch for about 1½ minutes, or until soft. Drain well and pat dry.
2. In a medium bowl, combine the spinach, corn, carrot, mozzarella, egg whites, cornstarch, garlic (if using), and salt and stir well.
3. In a large nonstick skillet, heat the oil over medium-high heat. Use a tablespoon to measure out well-rounded scoops of the batter and form into patties. They'll be a bit loose. As they're formed, place the patties in the skillet (in batches, if necessary) and flatten them gently with a spatula. Sizzle the fritters, turning once, for about 6 minutes, or until lightly browned. (If cooking in batches, you may need to add a little more oil.) Serve warm with sour cream and chives, if you like.

Makes 4 servings

To easily chop fresh spinach, stack the leaves, roll them up, and slice. You can also use frozen chopped spinach; just thaw and squeeze dry—no need to blanch. You'll need half of a 10-ounce box; reserve the rest for another use.

If using fresh corn, cut the kernels from the cob with a serrated knife.

Use other greens in place of the spinach, such as kale, lettuce, or even dandelion leaves.

Cooking Vegetables

Cold-weather vegetables typically require long cooking times to get even remotely tender, whereas spring and summer vegetables are more obliging. They cook quickly and can be made crunchy-tender in just a few minutes. Here are guidelines for the more common cooking techniques. For tips on stir-frying, see page 145.

Steaming

Steaming is often considered the best cooking method for tender, lightweight vegetables such as peas and summer squash. Steam cooks quickly and evenly, helping to retain important nutrients.

- Putting fresh herbs, flavored liquids such as herbal vinegars, or other aromatic ingredients in the cooking water lends a delicate nuance to steamed foods.
- Steamed food continues to cook even after you turn off the heat. Make it a point to slightly undercook food. By the time it reaches the table, it should be just right.

Boiling

Boiling is really too vigorous for many of the more delicate spring and summer vegetables. For heavier vegetables such as corn on the cob, however, boiling is a good choice.

- For all but the toughest vegetables, it's best not to cut them into pieces smaller than an inch or two. Otherwise, you'll expose too great a surface to the rolling action of the water, leaching out nutrients.
- As with steaming, boiled vegetables can be embellished by putting aromatic herbs, spices, or flavorful liquids into the water.

Baking and Roasting

Cooking vegetables in the oven caramelizes their sugars, bringing out all their richness. Baking and roasting are often recommended for firm-fleshed vegetables, such as peppers and corn on the cob, which take on a slightly smoky flavor. For more on roasting vegetables, see page 277.

Grilling

As with roasting, grilling enhances a vegetable's natural sweetness and distinctive flavors. Because grilling is a dry heat, vegetables will quickly toughen if left on too long. Cut them into slices no more than ½" thick and turn them as soon as they become just slightly brown.

Blanching

Blanching is used when preparing summer vegetables, such as green beans, for the freezer. To blanch a vegetable, plunge it briefly into boiling water, then immediately into very cold water. The process kills certain enzymes that would hasten the spoilage of vegetables during freezer storage.

The technique is also helpful for intensifying the color of green vegetables that you want to serve raw. Green beans, snow peas, snap peas, and asparagus turn beautifully bright when blanched for a minute.

Stuffed Eggplant

Hands-On Time: 25 minutes ■ Total Time: 1 hour 10 minutes

A savory stuffing of onion, mushrooms, red pepper, and herbs fills eggplant shells—so good alongside roasted chicken.

- 2 eggplants (about 1 pound each), halved
- 2 tablespoons olive oil
- Salt
- Ground black pepper
- 1½ cups fresh bread crumbs
- 2 teaspoons minced garlic
- 1 cup finely chopped onion
- 4 ounces mushrooms, finely chopped
- 1 cup finely chopped red bell pepper
- ½ teaspoon dried oregano
- ½ teaspoon dried rosemary
- ½ teaspoon fennel seeds
- ¾ cup tomato sauce
- 2 tablespoons minced fresh parsley

1. Preheat the oven to 375°F.
2. Using a paring knife, carefully cut away the flesh of each eggplant half, leaving about ½" of flesh adhering to the skin. Discard any large clumps of seeds and finely chop the remaining flesh. Set aside. (If there are no seeds, discard about one-third of the flesh anyway.)
3. Lightly brush the insides of each eggplant half with a small amount of the oil. Sprinkle with the salt and black pepper to taste. Set aside.
4. In a large bowl, combine the eggplant flesh with the bread crumbs, garlic, onion, mushrooms, bell pepper, oregano, rosemary, fennel seeds, 2 tablespoons of the tomato sauce, and the remaining oil. Stir in additional salt to taste.
5. Divide the filling equally among the reserved eggplant halves. Spoon 2 heaping tablespoons tomato sauce over each half.
6. Arrange the eggplant halves in a 13" × 9" baking dish. Add ¼" water to the bottom of the dish. Cover tightly with foil and bake for 30 minutes. Uncover and add more water to the bottom of the dish, if necessary. Bake, uncovered, for 15 minutes, or until the eggplant is tender. Sprinkle with the parsley before serving.

Makes 4 servings

Kitchen Tips

You can also bake the stuffed eggplant halves in two 10" pie plates.

For a tasty flavor boost, sprinkle the stuffed halves with grated Parmesan cheese before baking.

Baked Fennel with Cheese

Hands-On Time: 20 minutes ■ Total Time: 1 hour

The savory tang of fresh Parmesan cheese is a nice partner to the almost sweet, licorice-like flavor of fennel.

- 2 medium fennel bulbs, trimmed, peeled, and julienned
- 3 cloves garlic, thinly sliced
- ½ teaspoon dried thyme
- 1 cup chicken broth
- 1 tablespoon olive oil
- 2 teaspoons Dijon mustard
- ½ teaspoon ground nutmeg
- 1 cup toasted fine bread crumbs
- 2 tablespoons grated Parmesan cheese

1. Preheat the oven to 400°F. Grease a 1½-quart shallow casserole dish. Spread the fennel and garlic in the dish and sprinkle with the thyme.
2. In a small bowl, combine the broth, oil, mustard, and nutmeg and pour over the fennel. Top with the bread crumbs and cheese.
3. Cover and bake for 20 minutes. Uncover and bake for 20 minutes longer, or until golden brown.

Makes 4 servings

Ingredients Notes

Fennel is easy to grow in the garden and is often a bargain at farm stands during the summer months. Its delicious licorice flavor sweetens as it bakes.

Trim the fennel bulb by peeling away any tough outer layer and cutting off the feathery tips, which can be saved to add to soup broth or chopped for salads.

Minted Peas

Hands-On Time: 10 minutes ■ Total Time: 10 minutes

Mint really perks up the flavor of peas. And with frozen peas and dried mint, this super-simple side just couldn't be any easier.

- ½ cup water
- 1 teaspoon dried mint
- ⅛ teaspoon salt
- ⅛ teaspoon ground black pepper
- Pinch of sugar
- 1 package (10 ounces) frozen tiny peas
- 1 teaspoon unsalted butter

In a small saucepan, combine the water, mint, salt, pepper, and sugar. Bring to a boil. Add the peas and cook for 2 to 3 minutes, or until tender. Drain. Add the butter and toss until melted.

Makes 3 servings

Kitchen Tip

There's no need to defrost the peas before cooking. They're so small that they thaw and cook very quickly.

Variations

Substitute fresh peas in the pod, if you're lucky enough to get hold of some. You'll need about 2 pounds of pods to yield the 2 cups of shelled peas used here. Shell the peas just before using.

For an even fresher flavor, use 1 tablespoon minced fresh mint instead of the dried.

Accompaniments

Peas go with just about any dinner, but they are especially good with roasted chicken and mashed potatoes. They're also good with any kind of lamb and grilled seafood.

Mediterranean Stuffed Peppers

Hands-On Time: 5 minutes ■ Total Time: 30 minutes

In this recipe, colorful bell peppers are stuffed with a mixture of Mediterranean-style vegetables. The vegetable stuffing makes a good side dish all by itself, and it's also an easy topping for pasta and polenta. Using a mix of bell peppers makes a prettier presentation.

- 4 large green, red, yellow, and/or orange bell peppers, halved vertically, seeded, and cored (stems left on, if desired)
- ½ cup orange juice
- 1 cup finely chopped onion
- 1 medium red bell pepper, finely chopped
- 1 medium zucchini, finely chopped
- 3 cups cubed eggplant
- 3 cups chopped tomatoes
- 3 cloves garlic, minced
- 1 teaspoon dried Italian seasoning
- ½ cup shredded mozzarella cheese

1. Preheat the broiler.
2. Place the pepper halves on a broiler pan and coat with cooking spray. Broil about 4" from the heat, turning several times, for 10 minutes, or until crisp-tender; do not let the skin blacken. Set aside on the broiler pan.
3. In a large nonstick skillet, bring the orange juice to a boil over medium-high heat. Add the onion, chopped red pepper, zucchini, and eggplant. Cook, stirring, for about 5 minutes, or until softened. Add the tomatoes, garlic, and Italian seasoning. Cover, reduce the heat to medium, and cook for 10 minutes, or until the vegetables thicken.
4. Spoon the vegetable mixture into the reserved pepper halves and sprinkle with the cheese. Broil for 3 minutes, or until the cheese melts.

Makes 8 servings

Kitchen Tip

There's no need to peel the eggplant or zucchini for this recipe.

Pepperonata

Hands-On Time: 15 minutes ■ Total Time: 35 minutes

This colorful side goes well with simple baked chicken or fish. Play with the herbs, if you like: Rosemary or herbes de Provence would both be tasty alternatives to oregano.

- 1 tablespoon olive oil
- 1 medium onion, sliced
- 1 clove garlic, minced
- 1 large potato, peeled and cut into ½" cubes
- ¼ cup water
- 2 large green, yellow, or red bell peppers, cut into strips
- 1 large tomato, peeled and cut into large chunks
- ½ teaspoon dried oregano
- ¼ teaspoon dried thyme
- ¼ teaspoon salt

1. In a large nonstick skillet, heat the oil over medium heat. Add the onion and garlic and cook, stirring, for 5 minutes, or until the onion is crisp-tender.
2. Stir in the potato and water. Cover and cook over low heat, stirring occasionally, for 10 minutes. Stir in the peppers, tomato, oregano, thyme, and salt. Cover and cook for 10 minutes, or until the peppers are crisp-tender and the potato is cooked through.

Makes 6 servings

Ingredients Note

To easily peel a tomato, place in enough boiling water to cover. Carefully remove with a slotted spoon after 30 seconds and place under cold running water. When cool enough to handle, use a sharp paring knife to peel off the skin.

Grilled Summer Peppers

Hands-On Time: 15 minutes ■ Total Time: 25 minutes

When the garden or farmers' market is overflowing with colorful peppers, fire up the grill. Grilling brings out the sweetness of peppers like no other cooking method.

- ¼ cup red wine vinegar
- 2 tablespoons olive oil
- 2 tablespoons finely chopped onion
- 1 tablespoon Dijon mustard
- 4 cloves garlic, minced
- ¼ teaspoon ground black pepper
- 1 large red bell pepper, quartered
- 1 large yellow bell pepper, quartered
- 2 large green bell peppers, quartered

1. Grease a grill rack. Preheat the grill to medium.
2. In a small bowl, combine the vinegar, oil, onion, mustard, garlic, and black pepper. Place the bell peppers on the grill and lightly brush with the vinegar mixture. Grill for 3 minutes, or until the peppers are lightly browned. Turn, brush the other side, and cook for 2 minutes longer, or until the peppers are softened and browned.
3. Drizzle with the remaining vinegar mixture and serve.

Makes 4 servings

During the colder months or if you are without a backyard grill, the peppers can be broiled. Place about 3" from the heat and broil, turning two or three times, for 8 to 10 minutes.

Grilled Portobellos, Peppers, and Onions

Hands-On Time: 30 minutes ■ Total Time: 30 minutes

This trio of grilled veggies is sure to be a hit at your next barbecue. They're delicious both hot off the grill and at room temperature.

- 1/4 cup chopped fresh flat-leaf parsley
- 3 tablespoons fresh lemon juice
- 2 tablespoons extra-virgin olive oil
- 3 cloves garlic, minced
- 1 teaspoon dried Italian seasoning, crushed
- 1/2 teaspoon ground black pepper
- 1/4 teaspoon salt
- 2 large red bell peppers, cut into strips
- 6 ounces portobello mushrooms, gills scraped, sliced
- 1 large sweet white onion, halved and cut into 1"-thick slices

1. Preheat the grill to medium-hot.
2. In a large bowl, combine the parsley, lemon juice, oil, garlic, Italian seasoning, black pepper, and salt. Add the bell peppers, mushrooms, and onion and toss to coat well.
3. Place a vegetable basket or grill screen on the grill rack and place the vegetables in the basket or on the screen. Grill, turning often, for 15 minutes, or until very tender and lightly charred.

Makes 4 servings

Kitchen Tip

To cook this dish indoors, coat a broiler-pan rack with cooking spray and preheat the broiler. Place the vegetables on the rack and broil, turning often, for 10 minutes, or until browned.

Make-Ahead

The vegetables can be tossed with the marinade, covered, and refrigerated for up to 2 days.

Vegetable Roasting Times

Almost any vegetable can be roasted, even greens. Winter squash takes on a wonderful flavor because the high heat enhances the vegetable's natural sugar. To roast any of the following vegetables, prepare them as necessary and roast on a lightly oiled, rimmed baking sheet in the lower third of a 450°F oven for the specified time. Toss any cut-up vegetables with 1 teaspoon olive or canola oil. The amounts are calculated for about 4 servings.

VEGETABLE	AMOUNT	PREPARATION	ROASTING TIME
Acorn squash	1 or 2	Halve and seed; place, cut side up, on pan.	50 min
Asparagus	1 lb	Trim.	10–15 min
Beets	2 lb	Leave whole; scrub well.	60–90 min (when cool enough to handle, slip off skins)
Bell peppers	3	Cut into thin strips.	12 min (stir halfway through cooking)
Buttercup squash	1	Peel and cut into 1" chunks; cover pan with foil.	10–12 min
Carrots	1 lb	Cut into ½" sticks.	18–20 min
Corn	4 whole ears	Soak in water for 1 hour; place directly on oven rack.	8–10 min
Eggplant	1 medium	Cut into ½"-thick slices; brush with 1 Tbsp oil.	20 min (turn slices over halfway through cooking)
Green beans	1 lb	Trim.	12 min (stir halfway through cooking)
Potatoes	2 lb	Cut into ½"-thick slices.	30–35 min (turn halfway through cooking)
Red onions	2	Leave unpeeled; halve; place, cut side down, on pan; cover with foil.	25–30 min
Shallots	1 lb	Peel; leave whole.	20 min (stir every 5 min)
Sweet potatoes	2	Peel; cut into ¼"-thick slices; cover with foil.	20 min (uncover and roast 10 min more)
Tomatoes	2 lb	Use whole plum tomatoes.	20–25 min (turn halfway through cooking)
Zucchini	2 lb	Halve lengthwise and cut into 1½" chunks.	20 min (stir halfway through cooking)

Twice-Baked Potatoes

Hands-On Time: 10 minutes ■ Total Time: 30 minutes

Sweet-tasting Yukon gold potatoes are a particularly delicious choice for twice-baked spuds, but you could also use red-skinned or other potatoes. To save time, a microwave oven is used to bake the potatoes.

4 medium Yukon gold potatoes

2 tablespoons snipped chives

3 tablespoons sour cream

1 tablespoon finely shredded Cheddar cheese

Pinch of ground black pepper

1. Preheat the oven to 475°F.
2. Pierce the potatoes in several places with a fork. Microwave on high power, turning once, for 7 to 10 minutes, or until tender. Let stand for 5 minutes, or until cool enough to handle.
3. Cut the potatoes in half lengthwise and scoop out the flesh with a spoon, leaving ¼"-thick shells. Place the flesh in a medium bowl and stir in 1 tablespoon of the chives, the sour cream, cheese, and pepper until well combined.
4. Spoon the mixture into the potato shells and place on a large baking sheet. Bake for 3 to 5 minutes, or until the filling is hot. Sprinkle with the remaining 1 tablespoon chives just before serving.

Makes 4 servings

Variation

If you'd like to prebake the potatoes in the oven instead of microwaving, prick them with a fork, then bake directly on the oven rack at 400°F for about 1 hour.

Kitchen Tip

To snip fresh chives, grab a bunch with one hand, then use very clean, sharp kitchen scissors to cut them into ¼" to ½" pieces.

Garlic Mashed Potatoes

Hands-On Time: 10 minutes ■ Total Time: 30 minutes

Garlic softens and mellows when boiled with potatoes, making for creamy mashed potatoes enhanced with the sweet flavor of garlic.

- 4 medium all-purpose potatoes, peeled and cut into cubes
- 6 cloves garlic, peeled
- ⅓ cup milk
- ¼ cup sour cream

1. In a 3-quart saucepan, place the potatoes and garlic and add cold water to cover. Bring to a boil over high heat. Reduce the heat to medium and cook for 15 minutes, or until the potatoes are tender.
2. Drain well and return to the pan. Off the heat, mash with a potato masher until smooth. Add the milk and stir over medium heat for 1 minute. Stir in the sour cream and serve.

Makes 4 servings

Variation

For a lower-calorie version, use fat-free milk and reduced-fat sour cream.

Leftovers

Use leftovers to make potato cakes: Form the mashed potatoes into 3" cakes. Dip in beaten egg and then dredge in dried bread crumbs. If you have time, cover and refrigerate for up to ½ hour; this helps prevent the cakes from falling apart when cooking. Cook in a nonstick skillet in vegetable oil over medium heat, turning once, for 10 to 12 minutes, or until browned.

Orange Sweet Potatoes

Hands-On Time: 10 minutes ■ Total Time: 1 hour 10 minutes

Sweet potatoes braised in orange juice are a great alternative to traditional candied sweet potatoes for the holidays. In the summer, top them with fresh cilantro and pair with grilled fish.

- 1 tablespoon unsalted butter
- 3 large sweet potatoes or yams, peeled, halved, and cut into ½"-thick slices
- 1 cup orange juice
- 1 teaspoon grated orange zest
- ¾ teaspoon salt
- ½ teaspoon ground nutmeg
- ¼ teaspoon ground black pepper
- ¼ cup packed brown sugar

1. Preheat the oven to 375°F. Grease a 9" × 9" baking dish.
2. In a small skillet, cook the butter over medium heat, swirling the skillet, until it turns a nutty color. Remove from the heat and set aside.
3. Place the potatoes in the prepared baking dish and pour over the orange juice. Sprinkle with the orange zest, salt, nutmeg, and pepper. Top with the brown sugar and browned butter.
4. Cover and bake for 40 to 45 minutes, or until the sweet potatoes are crisp-tender. Uncover and bake for 12 to 15 minutes longer, or until the juices are almost absorbed.

Makes 4 servings

Make-Ahead

You can peel and slice the sweet potatoes ahead of time. To prevent browning, soak the slices in acidulated water (2 tablespoons lemon juice added to 4 cups water).

Ingredients Note

You can use either light or dark brown sugar in this recipe. Dark brown sugar will impart a slightly more intense sweetness.

Baked Sweet Potatoes and Apples

Hands-On Time: 10 minutes ■ Total Time: 1 hour 40 minutes

These cinnamony apples and sweet potatoes will become a new staple at your holiday table.

- 4 medium sweet potatoes, peeled and cut into ½"-thick slices
- ½ cup plus ⅓ cup water
- 1 apple, cored and thinly sliced
- ⅓ cup packed light brown sugar
- ¾ teaspoon ground cinnamon
- 1 tablespoon unsalted butter

1. In a large saucepan, combine the sweet potatoes and ½ cup of the water. Bring to a boil over high heat. Reduce the heat to medium, cover, and simmer for 30 minutes, or until tender. Arrange in a 13" × 9" baking pan and top with the apple.
2. Preheat the oven to 350°F.
3. In a small bowl, stir together the brown sugar and cinnamon. Sprinkle over the apples. Dot with the butter. Pour on the remaining ⅓ cup water.
4. Cover and bake for 40 minutes, or until the apples are tender. Uncover and bake for 5 minutes longer to crisp the topping slightly.

Makes 4 servings

Kitchen Tip

If fresh sweet potatoes are unavailable, you can use 4 cups vacuum-packed canned sweet potatoes instead. There is no need to cook the canned sweet potatoes; simply arrange in the pan, top with the apples and butter, add the water, and bake.

Ingredients Note

Braeburn and Gala apples are good choices here, but you can use any firm apple that will hold its shape when cooked.

Maple Squash with Cardamom

Hands-On Time: 10 minutes ■ Total Time: 1 hour 10 minutes

The warm, spicy flavor of cardamom and the sweetness of maple syrup bring out the best in butternut squash.

- 1 large butternut squash (3¼ pounds)
- 1 tablespoon unsalted butter, melted
- 1 tablespoon maple syrup
- 1 teaspoon ground cardamom
- ¼ teaspoon salt

1. Preheat the oven to 400°F. Grease a 13" × 9" baking pan.
2. Pierce the squash in several places with a fork. Place in the microwave oven and cook on high power for 4 minutes, or until slightly softened. When cool enough to handle, peel and seed, then cut into 1" chunks.
3. In a large bowl, combine the butter, maple syrup, cardamom, and salt. Add the squash and toss to coat well. Transfer to the prepared baking pan.
4. Bake the squash, tossing occasionally, for 45 minutes, or until browned and tender.

Makes 4 servings

Ingredients Note

Microwaving the whole squash for a few minutes makes it easier to peel, but it still can be difficult. Use a sharp, heavy knife to cut the squash in half, then a vegetable peeler or sharp knife to peel away the tough skin. Use an ice cream scoop to remove the seeds from the cavities.

Kitchen Tip

It can be messy to measure maple syrup and other sticky liquids. For quick cleanup, spray the measuring spoon with cooking spray. Or use the spoon to measure out the oil before measuring the syrup.

Root-Vegetable Medley

Hands-On Time: 25 minutes ■ Total Time: 40 minutes

Quick cooking on the grill or under the broiler allows root vegetables to stay tender inside and golden brown on the outside. Don't bother peeling the vegetables—just scrub them well.

- 1 large peeled sweet potato, thickly sliced
- 1 large peeled turnip, halved and thickly sliced
- 2 large red potatoes, thickly sliced
- 1 large carrot, halved and sliced into thick strips
- Juice of 1 lemon
- 2 cloves garlic, minced
- 2 tablespoons olive oil, plus additional if needed
- ½ teaspoon ground black pepper
- ¼ teaspoon salt

1. Preheat the grill or broiler.
2. In a shallow nonmetal dish, combine the sweet potato, turnip, red potatoes, carrot, lemon juice, garlic, and oil; toss well. Let stand for 15 minutes at room temperature, stirring occasionally.
3. Place the vegetables in a grill basket or on a broiler pan; reserve any marinade remaining in the dish. Grill or broil 4" from the heat, turning frequently and basting with the marinade (or with additional oil), for 15 minutes, or until the vegetables are crisp-tender and golden brown. Check by inserting the tip of a sharp knife into 1 piece. Sprinkle with the pepper and salt and serve.

Makes 4 servings

Accompaniments

These hearty vegetables are good alongside other substantial fare such as grilled lamb chops.

Breads, Muffins & More

Lemon Bread

Hands-On Time: 20 minutes ■ Total Time: 1 hour 20 minutes (plus standing)

This lovely quick bread, enhanced with pecans and a sweet-tart lemon topping, is delightful with a cup of tea. Or toast a slice for breakfast or a snack.

Bread

- 1 cup sugar
- ¼ cup fresh lemon juice
- 3 tablespoons unsalted butter, melted
- 3 tablespoons unsweetened applesauce
- 1 teaspoon lemon extract
- 4 large egg whites
- 1½ cups all-purpose flour
- 1 teaspoon baking powder
- ¼ teaspoon salt
- ¼ cup chopped pecans, toasted
- 1½ teaspoons grated lemon zest

Topping

- ¼ cup confectioners' sugar
- 2 tablespoons lemon juice

1. *To make the bread:* Preheat the oven to 350°F. Lightly grease an 8" × 4" loaf pan.
2. In a large bowl, stir together the granulated sugar, lemon juice, butter, applesauce, and lemon extract. One at a time, whisk in the egg whites.
3. In a small bowl, stir together the flour, baking powder, and salt. Stir into the egg-white mixture. Stir in the pecans and lemon zest.
4. Spread the batter evenly in the prepared pan. Bake for 45 minutes, or until a wooden pick inserted into the center comes out clean; do not overbake. Cool in the pan on a wire rack for 15 minutes, then remove from the pan.
5. *To make the topping:* In a small saucepan, stir together the confectioners' sugar and lemon juice. Cook over medium heat, stirring, for 1 to 2 minutes, or until the sugar dissolves.
6. Set a wire rack on a piece of foil; place the bread on the rack. Pierce the top of the bread in several places with a thin-bladed knife or the tines of a fork. Pour the topping over the bread. Cool completely. Wrap the bread in foil and let stand at room temperature for 24 hours before slicing.

Makes 1 loaf (16 slices)

Kitchen Tip

To toast the pecans, preheat the oven to 350°F. Place the pecans in a single layer in a shallow baking pan. Bake, stirring occasionally, for 5 minutes, or until lightly browned.

Spiced Pumpkin Bread

Hands-On Time: 15 minutes ■ Total Time: 1 hour 10 minutes

A mixture of spices gives this quick bread real pumpkin pie flavor.

- 1½ cups all-purpose flour
- 2 tablespoons cornstarch
- ¾ teaspoon baking powder
- ½ teaspoon baking soda
- ¼ teaspoon ground cinnamon
- ¼ teaspoon ground nutmeg
- ⅛ teaspoon ground cloves
- ⅛ teaspoon ground allspice
- ¼ teaspoon salt
- 1 large egg
- 1 large egg white
- ⅓ cup granulated sugar
- ¼ cup packed light brown sugar
- 1 cup canned pumpkin
- 6 tablespoons buttermilk
- 1½ tablespoons vegetable oil
- ½ teaspoon vanilla extract

1. Preheat the oven to 350°F. Grease a 9" × 5" loaf pan.
2. In a large bowl, whisk together the flour, cornstarch, baking powder, baking soda, cinnamon, nutmeg, cloves, allspice, and salt.
3. In a medium bowl, whisk together the egg, egg white, granulated sugar, and brown sugar until smooth. Whisk in the pumpkin, buttermilk, oil, and vanilla extract. Pour over the flour mixture and stir just until combined; do not overmix.
4. Spoon the batter into the prepared pan. Bake for 45 minutes, or until a wooden pick inserted into the center comes out clean. Cool on a wire rack for 10 minutes. Remove from the pan and cool completely.

Makes 1 loaf (18 slices)

Zucchini Bread

Hands-On Time: 10 minutes ■ Total Time: 1 hour 20 minutes (plus standing)

Don't be alarmed if a crack forms in the top of this cinnamon-spiced, zucchini-flecked bread. That's typical of quick bread loaves.

- 1 cup sugar
- 3 large egg whites, lightly beaten
- ¼ cup vegetable oil
- ¼ cup unsweetened applesauce
- 1 teaspoon vanilla extract
- 1 cup finely shredded zucchini
- 1½ cups all-purpose flour
- ½ teaspoon baking powder
- ½ teaspoon ground cinnamon
- ⅛ teaspoon salt

1. Preheat the oven to 350°F. Grease an 8" × 4" loaf pan.
2. In a large bowl, stir together the sugar, egg whites, oil, applesauce, and vanilla extract. Stir in the zucchini.
3. In a small bowl, stir together the flour, baking powder, cinnamon, and salt. Stir into the zucchini mixture.
4. Spread the batter in the prepared pan. Bake for 1 hour, or until a wooden pick inserted into the center comes out clean. Cool the bread in the pan on a wire rack for 10 minutes, then remove from the pan and cool completely. Wrap the bread in foil and let stand overnight before slicing.

Makes 1 loaf (16 slices)

Applesauce Gingerbread

Hands-On Time: 15 minutes ■ Total Time: 1 hour

No fewer than five distinct spices give this glossy-topped gingerbread a pleasing pungency you won't find in any packaged mix. In addition, chopped apples are added to the batter, which contains applesauce, and when the cake comes out of the oven, the top is glazed with apple juice concentrate for a triple hit of apple flavor. This bread is lighter than most because the applesauce in the batter replaces some of the oil of standard gingerbread recipes.

- 2 cups all-purpose flour
- 1¼ teaspoons baking powder
- ¼ teaspoon baking soda
- 1½ teaspoons ground cinnamon
- 1 teaspoon ground nutmeg
- ¾ teaspoon ground ginger
- ⅛ teaspoon ground cloves
- Pinch of ground cardamom (optional)
- ⅛ teaspoon salt
- ¼ cup packed dark brown sugar
- ¼ cup dark molasses
- 1 large egg
- 1 tablespoon vegetable oil
- 1 cup unsweetened applesauce
- 1 teaspoon vanilla extract
- ½ cup chopped Golden Delicious apple
- 1 tablespoon frozen apple juice concentrate, thawed

1. Preheat the oven to 375°F. Grease an 8" round cake pan.
2. In a large bowl, stir together the flour, baking powder, baking soda, cinnamon, nutmeg, ginger, cloves, cardamom (if using), and salt.
3. In a medium bowl, whisk together the brown sugar, molasses, egg, and oil until smooth. Stir in the applesauce and vanilla extract.
4. Scrape the applesauce mixture into the flour mixture and stir until well blended. Fold in the apple.
5. Pour the batter into the prepared pan and smooth the top. Bake for 30 to 35 minutes, or until the top of the cake is springy to the touch and a wooden pick inserted just off center comes out clean. Transfer the pan to a wire rack and cool for 10 minutes.
6. Run a knife around the edge of the cake to loosen it, then turn the cake out onto a rack; immediately invert it onto a serving plate so it is right-side up. Brush the top of the cake with the apple juice concentrate. To serve, cut into wedges.

Makes 8 wedges

Chile Cornbread

Hands-On Time: 15 minutes ■ Total Time: 40 minutes

Cornbread makes a delicious accompaniment to enchiladas, chicken and rice, and tomato-based soups. You can also serve it warm with chili, such as our Cincinnati Turkey Chili (page 112) or Peppery Chili con Carne (page 136).

- ⅔ cup yellow cornmeal
- ⅔ cup all-purpose flour
- 1 tablespoon baking powder
- 1 teaspoon chili powder
- ½ teaspoon salt
- 1 cup fresh, canned, or frozen thawed corn
- 2 mild or hot green chile peppers, seeded and chopped (wear plastic gloves when handling)
- 2 scallions, minced
- 3 large egg whites
- ½ cup milk
- 2 tablespoons honey
- 1 tablespoon vegetable oil

1. Preheat the oven to 350°F. Grease a 9" glass pie plate.
2. In a large bowl, combine the cornmeal, flour, baking powder, chili powder, and salt. Stir in the corn, peppers, and scallions.
3. In a medium bowl, whisk together the egg whites, milk, honey, and oil. Add to the dry ingredients and stir to combine; do not overmix.
4. Spoon the batter into the prepared pie plate and level the top. Bake for about 25 minutes, or until a wooden pick inserted into the center comes out clean. Cut into 8 wedges and serve warm.

Makes 8 servings

The bread will keep at room temperature, covered loosely with wax paper, for several days. To reheat, wrap in foil and bake at 350°F for 5 minutes, or until warm. Or heat individual pieces in a toaster oven. If desired, serve drizzled with honey.

Substitute cooked pinto beans for the corn.

Spicy Garlic Bread

Hands-On Time: 15 minutes ■ Total Time: 15 minutes

Ground red pepper adds zip to this flavorful bread that is always a crowd-pleaser.

- ¼ cup olive oil
- 3 cloves garlic, minced
- 1 loaf French bread, cut in half lengthwise
- ¼ cup grated Parmesan cheese
- ¼ teaspoon ground red pepper

1. Preheat the broiler.
2. In a small bowl, mix together the oil and garlic. Spread onto the cut sides of the bread. Sprinkle with the cheese and pepper.
3. Place the bread, cut sides up, on a baking sheet. Broil about 4" from the heat for 3 to 4 minutes, or until lightly browned. Cut into 16 slices.

Makes 1 loaf (16 slices)

Nutri-Note

This garlic bread uses olive oil instead of butter so the amount of saturated fat is kept to a minimum, making the tasty slices a heart-healthy choice.

Ingredients Note

Using the best-quality ingredients will make a difference here. Be sure to use freshly grated Parmesan cheese and plump cloves of fresh garlic.

Braided French Bread with Herb Spread

Hands-On Time: 25 minutes ■ Total Time: 1 hour 15 minutes (plus time for yogurt cheese and rising)

This hearty whole grain bread is a satisfying source of fiber and complex carbohydrates.

- ½ cup fat-free milk
- 1 cup boiling water
- 1 package (¾ ounce) active dry yeast
- ¼ cup warm water (about 115°F)
- 1½ tablespoons olive oil
- 1 tablespoon honey
- ½ teaspoon salt
- 2 cups sifted whole wheat flour
- 1¾ cups all-purpose flour or bread flour
- 1 large egg white
- 1 teaspoon water
- 1 tablespoon poppy seeds or sesame seeds
- ¼ cup yogurt cheese (see Ingredients Note)
- ¼ cup (4 tablespoons or ½ stick) unsalted butter, softened
- ¼ cup mayonnaise
- 1 tablespoon minced fresh basil
- 1 tablespoon minced fresh dill
- ¼ teaspoon minced garlic

1. In a 1-quart saucepan, scald the milk. Add the boiling water. Set aside until lukewarm. In a large bowl, dissolve the yeast in the warm water. Stir in the oil, honey, and salt. Let stand until foamy.
2. Add the milk mixture to the yeast mixture and whisk thoroughly. Add the flour 1 cup at a time, stirring until a soft dough forms. Form the dough into a ball. Leave the dough in the bowl and cover with a damp cloth. Let stand in a warm, draft-free place for about 2 hours, or until doubled in bulk.
3. Punch down the dough. Place on a lightly floured board and roll into a 10" × 14" rectangle. Cut lengthwise into 6 strips. Using 3 strips at a time, braid the dough into 2 loaves.
4. Grease a baking sheet. Place the dough on the sheet and let stand in a warm place for about 45 minutes, or until doubled in bulk.
5. Preheat the oven to 400°F. In a cup, whisk together the egg white and water. Brush over the top of each loaf. Sprinkle with the poppy seeds.
6. Bake the loaves for 10 minutes. Reduce the temperature to 350°F and bake for 10 minutes longer, or until golden brown. Let cool for at least 20 minutes.
7. In a small bowl, whisk together the yogurt cheese, butter, and mayonnaise. Stir in the basil, dill, and garlic. Serve with the bread.

Makes 2 loaves (16 slices each)

Ingredients Note

To make yogurt cheese, spoon yogurt into a cheesecloth-lined strainer and let drain for at least 2 hours.

Troubleshooting Yeast Breads

Even for the experienced home baker, bread holds a certain mystique. Here is how to come ever closer to the perfect loaf.

PROBLEM	POSSIBLE CAUSES	SOLUTIONS/SUGGESTIONS
Dough is not rising.	Yeast is old. Yeast was dissolved in too-hot or too-cold water. Dough was kneaded too stiff; gluten was overdeveloped. Rising location was too cold.	Try proofing new yeast and kneading it into the dough; additional flour might be necessary.
Dough is bloated and blistering.	Dough has overrisen. Rising place is too warm.	Punch down, reshape, and let rise again.
Bread rises and bakes unevenly.	Dough was shaped unevenly. Dough was not scored or was scored unevenly. Oven heats unevenly.	Try rotating the loaf; there is little more you can do at this point.
Bread browns unevenly on top.	Loaf is or was too close to the oven top. Oven heats unevenly.	Rotate loaf if browning unevenly. Lower the rack on which the bread sits if browning too quickly.
Bread is too brown on bottom.	Baking stone or oven is too hot.	Place a rack or wire cake stand between loaf and stone; check that oven is calibrated correctly.
Bread is too brown all over.	Oven is too hot.	Lower heat; check that oven is calibrated correctly.
Bread interior has gaping holes.	Too much yeast was used in dough. Too little flour was used. Too little kneading was done. Dough overrose. Oven was too cool.	Use the bread for toast; the uneven texture is desirable in certain breads such as sourdough and French bread.
Bread didn't rise high enough.	Water was too hot for yeast. Too little flour was used. Too little kneading was done. Dough was underrisen. Pan was too large.	Slice thin and serve small pieces.
Bread is heavy and dense.	Too much flour was used. Too little kneading was done. Dough was underrisen.	Slice thin and serve small pieces.
Bread has a yeasty taste.	Dough overrose. Temperature was too high during rise.	Let the bread dry 1 day and use to make bread crumbs.

Apricot-Pecan Scones

Hands-On Time: 25 minutes ■ Total Time: 45 minutes

Dried fruit and nuts are a winning combination in these easy, versatile treats. See Variations, below, for other winning fruit-and-nut pairings.

- 2 cups all-purpose flour
- 3 tablespoons plus 2 teaspoons sugar
- 2 teaspoons baking powder
- ½ teaspoon baking soda
- ¼ teaspoon salt
- 2 tablespoons cold unsalted butter, cut into small pieces
- 1¼ cups chopped dried apricots
- ¼ cup chopped pecans, toasted
- ¾ cup buttermilk or low-fat plain yogurt
- 1 large egg white
- ¼ teaspoon ground cinnamon

1. Preheat the oven to 400°F. Grease a baking sheet.
2. In a large bowl, combine the flour, 3 tablespoons of the sugar, the baking powder, baking soda, and salt. Using a pastry blender or a fork, cut the butter into the flour mixture until evenly dispersed. Add the apricots and pecans and stir to mix.
3. In a medium bowl, combine the buttermilk and egg white. Beat with a fork to mix. Add to the flour mixture and stir with a fork until the dough comes together.
4. Spoon the dough onto the prepared baking sheet in 12 equal portions. In a small bowl, combine the cinnamon and remaining 2 teaspoons sugar. Sprinkle over the scones.
5. Bake the scones for 15 minutes, or until lightly browned. Transfer to a rack to cool for 5 minutes.

Makes 12 scones

Variations

Using the same proportions of dried fruits and nuts, try these variations.

- Dried peaches and almonds, plus ¼ cup chopped candied ginger
- Dried cranberries and walnuts, plus 2 teaspoons grated orange peel
- Dried sour cherries, substituting semisweet chocolate chips for the nuts
- Dried pineapple or papaya, substituting toasted coconut for the nuts

Orange Popovers with Honey Butter

Hands-On Time: 10 minutes ■ Total Time: 55 minutes

Smooth, creamy honey butter brings out the best in crispy yet delicate popovers. Serve them with soup or salad for an elegant luncheon.

Popovers

- 2 large egg whites
- 1 large egg
- 1 cup fat-free milk
- 1 cup all-purpose flour
- 1/8 teaspoon salt
- 1½ teaspoons grated orange zest

Honey Butter

- 2 tablespoons honey
- 1 tablespoon unsalted butter, softened

1. *To make the popovers:* Position 1 oven rack at the lowest level. Preheat the oven to 450°F. Generously grease five 6-ounce custard cups.
2. In a small bowl, whisk together the egg whites, egg, and milk until smooth.
3. In a medium bowl, stir together the flour and salt; make a well in the center and pour the egg mixture into it. Add the orange zest and beat with a wire whisk until well mixed.
4. Divide the batter among the cups, filling them about two-thirds full. Place on a baking sheet and bake on the lowest oven rack for 20 minutes. Reduce the heat to 350°F and bake for 25 minutes longer, or until the popovers are very brown and crusty. Do not open the oven during baking, or the popovers won't rise properly. Remove from the oven and insert a sharp knife into each popover to release steam.
5. *To make the honey butter:* In a small bowl, stir together the honey and butter. Serve with the hot popovers.

Makes 5 popovers

Kitchen Tips

Make sure the popovers are very brown and crusty before removing them from the oven or they may collapse. To bake in a popover pan: Place the pan in the oven until very hot. Remove and grease 5 of the cups. Add the batter and proceed as above.

New Life for Old Bread

There's no need to toss stale bread. Here are three great solutions for reviving yesterday's loaf.

Bread Salad. Tear ½ pound stale Italian bread into 1" pieces and combine in a large serving bowl with 4 seeded and chopped tomatoes; 1 peeled, seeded, and chopped cucumber; 1 chopped red onion; and ½ cup torn basil leaves. In a small bowl, whisk together ½ cup extra-virgin olive oil, ¼ cup red wine vinegar, 1 teaspoon salt, and ¼ teaspoon ground black pepper. Pour onto the salad and toss well. Let stand for about 20 minutes before serving. *Makes 4 servings.*

Parmesan Croutons. Cut 1 old baguette diagonally into ¼"-thick slices. Brush each slice with melted butter and sprinkle with grated Parmesan cheese. Toast under the broiler until the cheese is melted and golden. Serve alongside salads and soups. *Makes 6 servings.*

French Toast. Day-old brioche and white bread are ideal for making French toast. Beat 4 eggs with 2 cups milk, 1 tablespoon sugar, and ¼ teaspoon *each* vanilla extract and ground nutmeg. Melt 2 tablespoons butter in a large skillet over medium heat. Dip 1"-thick slices cut from 1-pound bread into the egg mixture and fry in hot butter for 5 minutes on each side, or until golden brown. *Makes 4 servings.*

Golden Grain and Herb Loaves

Hands-On Time: 30 minutes ■ Total Time: 2 hours (plus rising)

The blend of herbs and the surprise addition of celery leaves make these loaves extra tasty.

- 1 cup quick-cooking oats
- 1 cup boiling water
- 3 packages (¾ ounce each) active dry yeast
- ½ cup warm water (about 115°F)
- 1 cup milk
- ¼ cup honey
- ¼ cup olive oil
- 1 teaspoon salt
- ½ cup finely chopped onion
- ⅓ cup finely chopped celery leaves
- ¼ cup finely chopped fresh parsley
- 1 tablespoon finely chopped fresh marjoram or 1 teaspoon dried
- 1 tablespoon finely chopped fresh thyme or 1 teaspoon dried
- 1 tablespoon finely chopped fresh sage or 1 teaspoon dried
- 2 cups whole wheat flour
- 4 to 4½ cups all-purpose flour
- 1 large egg white

1. In a medium bowl, combine all but 2 tablespoons of the oats and the boiling water. Let cool until lukewarm. In a large bowl, dissolve the yeast in the warm water. Let stand in a warm place for about 5 minutes, or until foamy.
2. In a medium saucepan, combine the milk, honey, oil, and salt. Heat over medium heat until lukewarm. Stir in the onion, celery leaves, parsley, marjoram, thyme, and sage. Add to the yeast mixture. Stir in the oat mixture and whole wheat flour. Stir in about 4 cups of the all-purpose flour to make a kneadable dough. Let stand for 15 minutes.
3. Turn the dough out onto a lightly floured surface. Knead, adding more flour as necessary, for about 10 minutes, or until smooth and elastic.
4. Grease a large bowl. Add the dough and turn to coat all sides. Cover and set in a warm place for about 1¼ hours, or until doubled in bulk.
5. Divide the dough in half and let rest for 10 minutes.
6. Grease two 9" x 5" loaf pans. Tuck the ends of each piece of dough under and place in the pans. Cover with clean dish towels and set in a warm place for 30 to 45 minutes, or until doubled in bulk.
7. Preheat the oven to 375°F.
8. Brush the egg white over the loaves and sprinkle with the reserved 2 tablespoons oats. Bake for 45 to 50 minutes, or until the loaves are lightly browned. Let cool in the pans on a rack, then transfer to a rack to cool completely.

Makes 2 loaves (16 slices each)

Whole Wheat Nut Bread

Hands-On Time: 20 minutes ■ Total Time: 1 hour 20 minutes

This is a hearty quick bread that is lightly sweetened with honey.

- 1½ cups all-purpose flour
- 1 cup whole wheat flour
- 1 tablespoon baking powder
- ¼ teaspoon salt
- 2 large egg whites, lightly beaten
- ⅓ cup honey
- 2 tablespoons vegetable oil
- 2 tablespoons unsweetened applesauce
- 1 teaspoon vanilla extract
- 1 cup fat-free milk
- ½ cup chopped walnuts, toasted

1. Preheat the oven to 350°F. Grease a 9" × 5" loaf pan.
2. In a medium bowl, stir together the unbleached flour, whole wheat flour, baking powder, and salt.
3. In a large bowl, stir together the egg whites, honey, oil, applesauce, and vanilla extract. Stir in the milk until combined. Add the flour mixture and stir just until well mixed. Stir in the nuts.
4. Spread the batter evenly in the prepared pan. Bake for 50 minutes, or until a wooden pick inserted into the center comes out clean; do not overbake.
5. Cool in the pan on a wire rack for 10 minutes. Remove from the pan to cool completely.

Makes 1 loaf (16 slices)

Variation

For a more solid texture and a bigger fiber boost, use all whole wheat pastry flour in place of all-purpose.

Banana-Walnut Muffins

Hands-On Time: 25 minutes ■ Total Time: 45 minutes

Wondering what to do with an overripe banana? Ponder no more: Whip up a batch of these smashingly delicious muffins. It's the smart—and tasty—thing to do.

Topping

- 2 tablespoons all-purpose flour
- 2 tablespoons ground walnuts
- 2 tablespoons sugar
- 1 tablespoon cold unsalted butter, cut into small pieces

Muffins

- 2 cups all-purpose flour
- 2¼ teaspoons baking powder
- ¼ teaspoon salt
- ½ cup coarsely chopped walnuts
- 1 large ripe banana, mashed (about ½ cup)
- ⅓ cup vegetable oil
- 1 large egg
- ½ cup sugar
- 1 teaspoon grated orange zest
- ¼ to ½ cup milk

1. Preheat the oven to 425°F. Grease a 12-cup muffin pan.
2. *To make the topping:* In a small bowl, combine the flour, walnuts, and sugar. Using a pastry blender or 2 knives, cut in the butter until the mixture resembles coarse crumbs.
3. *To make the muffins:* In a large bowl, combine the flour, baking powder, salt, and walnuts.
4. In a food processor, combine the banana, oil, egg, sugar, and orange zest. Process for 30 seconds, or until well combined. Transfer the mixture to a 2-cup measure. Stir in enough milk to make 1¾ cups. Add to the flour mixture, stirring until just combined; do not overmix.
5. Divide the batter evenly among the prepared muffin cups, filling them about two-thirds full. Sprinkle the topping over the muffin batter. Bake for 14 to 16 minutes, or until a wooden pick inserted into the center of a muffin comes out clean. Cool on a rack for 5 minutes. Transfer to the rack to cool completely.

Makes 12 muffins

Carrot Muffins

Hands-On Time: 20 minutes ■ Total Time: 45 minutes

These miniature carrot cakes are spiced just right with cinnamon and cloves, and then topped with a supersimple cream cheese frosting.

Muffins

- 2 cups all-purpose flour
- ⅔ cup granulated sugar
- 1½ teaspoons baking soda
- ½ teaspoon ground cinnamon
- ¼ teaspoon ground mace
- ⅛ teaspoon ground cloves
- ¼ teaspoon salt
- ½ cup golden raisins
- 1 cup buttermilk
- ¼ cup vegetable oil
- 1 large egg
- 1 teaspoon vanilla extract
- 1¼ cups finely shredded carrots

Frosting

- ¾ cup confectioners' sugar
- 3 tablespoons cream cheese, at room temperature
- ½ to 1 teaspoon milk
- ½ teaspoon vanilla extract

1. *To make the muffins:* Preheat the oven to 375°F. Grease a 12-cup muffin pan.
2. In a medium bowl, combine the flour, granulated sugar, baking soda, cinnamon, mace, cloves, and salt. Add the raisins and toss gently to coat.
3. In a large bowl, stir together the buttermilk, oil, egg, and vanilla extract until well blended. Stir in the carrots. Stir in the flour mixture until just combined; do not overmix.
4. Divide the batter evenly among the prepared muffin cups, filling them about two-thirds full. Bake for 18 to 20 minutes, or until a wooden pick inserted into the center of a muffin comes out clean. Cool on a rack for 5 minutes. Transfer to the rack to cool completely.
5. *To make the frosting:* In a bowl, stir together the confectioners' sugar, cream cheese, milk, and vanilla extract until well blended. Spread over the cooled muffins.

Makes 12 muffins

Sugared Ginger Muffins

Hands-On Time: 15 minutes ■ Total Time: 40 minutes

Tender muffins get their sweetness from crystallized ginger and a sprinkling of coarse sugar.

- 1½ cups unbleached all-purpose flour
- 2 teaspoons baking powder
- 1 teaspoon baking soda
- ½ teaspoon salt
- ¾ cup buttermilk
- ¼ cup (4 tablespoons or ½ stick) unsalted butter, melted and cooled slightly
- 1 large egg
- ⅓ cup granulated sugar
- 2 tablespoons chopped crystallized ginger
- 1 tablespoon coarse sugar (optional)

1. Preheat the oven to 400°F. Grease a 12-cup muffin pan.
2. In a medium bowl, combine the flour, baking powder, baking soda, and salt.
3. In a large bowl, stir together the buttermilk, butter, egg, granulated sugar, and ginger until well blended. Stir in the flour mixture until just combined; do not overmix.
4. Divide the batter evenly among the prepared muffin cups, filling them about two-thirds full. Evenly sprinkle the batter with the coarse sugar (if using). Bake for 12 to 15 minutes, or until a wooden pick inserted into the center of a muffin comes out clean. Cool on a rack for 5 minutes. Transfer to the rack to cool completely.

Makes 12 muffins

Ingredients Note

Crystallized ginger, also called candied ginger, is fresh gingerroot that has been slowly cooked in sugar water, then rolled in coarse sugar.

Chocolate Chip Muffins

Hands-On Time: 10 minutes ■ Total Time: 30 minutes

Who can resist decadent chocolate chip muffins? The good news is that these beauties are lower in fat than the usual suspects, thanks to naturally low-fat buttermilk and applesauce in the batter.

- ¾ cup buttermilk
- ½ cup packed light brown sugar
- 1 large egg
- 1 large egg white
- 2 tablespoons unsweetened applesauce
- 2 tablespoons vegetable oil
- 1½ cups all-purpose flour
- ¼ cup unsweetened cocoa powder
- 1½ teaspoons baking powder
- ½ teaspoon baking soda
- ¼ teaspoon salt
- ¼ cup semisweet chocolate chips

1. Preheat the oven to 400°F. Grease a 12-cup muffin pan.
2. In a medium bowl, combine the buttermilk, brown sugar, egg, egg white, applesauce, and oil. Mix well.
3. In a large bowl, combine the flour, cocoa, baking powder, baking soda, and salt. Mix well. Stir in the chocolate chips. Add to the buttermilk mixture. Stir until just blended.
4. Pour the batter into the prepared muffin cups, filling them three-fourths full. Bake for 12 to 15 minutes, or until a wooden pick inserted into the center of a muffin comes out clean. Cool on a rack for 5 minutes. Transfer to the rack to cool completely.

Makes 12 muffins

Freezing Tip

To freeze, place the cooled muffins on a tray. Put in the freezer for 1 hour, or until solid. Pack in a freezer-quality plastic bag. To use, thaw the number of muffins you need overnight in the refrigerator. Wrap in foil and reheat at 400°F for 5 minutes, or until hot.

Pineapple Muffins

Hands-On Time: 15 minutes ■ Total Time: 35 minutes

Pineapple and coconut jazz up these marvelously moist and scrumptiously sweet muffins.

- 1 can (8 ounces) crushed pineapple packed in juice
- 1¾ cups all-purpose flour
- 2 teaspoons baking powder
- ½ teaspoon baking soda
- ½ teaspoon ground cinnamon
- ¼ teaspoon salt
- ½ cup slivered almonds, toasted
- ¾ cup milk
- 3 tablespoons vegetable oil
- 1 large egg
- ⅓ cup packed light brown sugar
- ¼ cup sweetened shredded coconut

1. Preheat the oven to 400°F. Grease a 12-cup muffin pan.
2. Place the pineapple in a sieve over a 1-cup measure and press with the back of a spoon to remove the excess juice. Reserve the pineapple and ¼ cup of the juice.
3. In a medium bowl, combine the flour, baking powder, baking soda, cinnamon, and salt. Stir in the almonds.
4. In a large bowl, stir together the reserved pineapple juice, milk, oil, egg, and brown sugar until well blended. Stir in the pineapple. Stir in the flour mixture until just blended; do not overmix.
5. Divide the batter evenly among the prepared muffin cups, filling them about two-thirds full. Sprinkle the coconut over the batter. Bake for 12 to 15 minutes, or until the muffins are lightly browned and a wooden pick inserted into the center of a muffin comes out clean. Cool on a rack for 5 minutes. Transfer to the rack to cool completely.

Makes 12 muffins

Sour Cream Muffins

Hands-On Time: 10 minutes ■ Total Time: 30 minutes

Sour cream in muffins? Why not? Here, it replaces the usual buttermilk for a mellow flavor that nicely offsets dried cranberries.

- 2 cups all-purpose flour
- ½ cup sugar
- 2½ teaspoons baking powder
- ½ teaspoon baking soda
- ½ teaspoon salt
- 1 cup dried cranberries or raisins
- ¾ cup milk
- 3 tablespoons vegetable oil
- ½ cup sour cream
- 1 large egg
- 1 teaspoon vanilla extract

1. Preheat the oven to 400°F. Grease a 12-cup muffin pan.
2. In a medium bowl, combine the flour, sugar, baking powder, baking soda, and salt. Add the cranberries and toss gently.
3. In a large bowl, combine the milk, oil, sour cream, egg, and vanilla extract. Stir in the flour mixture until just combined; do not overmix.
4. Divide the batter evenly among the prepared muffin cups, filling them about two-thirds full. Bake for 12 to 15 minutes, or until a wooden pick inserted into the center of a muffin comes out clean. Cool on a rack for 5 minutes. Transfer to the rack to cool completely.

Makes 12 muffins

Italian Flatbread with Fresh Herbs

Hands-On Time: 20 minutes ■ Total Time: 40 minutes (plus rising)

This flavorful bread was made to be drizzled with herb-flavored olive oil. Take your pick of fresh herbs for the bread: Rosemary, sage, basil, and thyme are all excellent, alone or in combination.

- 1 cup warm water (about 115°F)
- 1 tablespoon active dry yeast
- 2 teaspoons honey
- 3 teaspoons olive oil
- 1⅓ cups whole wheat bread flour
- 1⅓ cups all-purpose flour
- ¼ cup finely chopped fresh herbs
- ½ teaspoon salt (optional)
- 2 cloves garlic, slivered

1. In a large bowl, combine ½ cup of the water and the yeast. Stir in the honey and 2 teaspoons of the oil. Stir in the bread flour, all-purpose flour, herbs, and salt. Add enough of the remaining ½ cup water to make a soft, kneadable dough.
2. Knead the dough on a floured surface for about 8 minutes, or until smooth. Place the dough in an oiled bowl and turn to coat on all sides. Cover the bowl with plastic wrap and set in a warm, draft-free place until doubled in bulk, about 40 minutes.
3. Punch down the dough, cover again, and let rise a second time for about 40 minutes, or until doubled in bulk.
4. Preheat the oven to 400°F.
5. Punch down the dough. Place a sheet of parchment paper on a large baking sheet. Transfer the dough to the paper and use your hands to form it into a 14" round that is about ½" thick. Poke the garlic slivers into the dough at intervals. Rub the surface with the remaining 1 teaspoon oil.
6. Bake for 15 to 20 minutes, or until baked through and lightly browned on top. Transfer to a wire rack to cool. To serve, cut into wedges with kitchen shears. If desired, toast under the broiler.

Makes 1 loaf (8 slices)

Nancy's Breadsticks

Hands-On Time: 30 minutes ■ Total Time: 1 hour 5 minutes (plus rising)

Take your choice of any of the three different toppers for these soft and chewy breadsticks. They're ideal alongside a bowl of soup or salad or served with pasta.

- 3 to 3½ cups all-purpose flour
- 1 tablespoon granulated sugar
- 2 packages (¾ ounce each) active dry yeast
- 1 teaspoon salt, plus additional for sprinkling
- 2 tablespoons olive oil or canola oil, plus additional for coating
- 1¼ cups hot water (130°F)
- 1 large egg white
- 1 tablespoon water
- Sesame seeds, caraway seeds, dried dill, or a combination of the three

1. In the large bowl of an electric mixer, place 1 cup of the flour. Stir in the sugar, yeast, and 1 teaspoon salt. Add the oil, then gradually stir in the hot water. Beat for 2 minutes. Add 1 cup of the remaining flour and beat until well combined. Stir in as much of the remaining 1 to 1½ cups flour as you can to make a soft dough.
2. Transfer the dough to a lightly floured work surface. Knead in enough of the remaining flour to make a dough that is smooth and elastic.
3. Grease a clean, dry large bowl. Place the dough in the bowl. Lightly coat the top of the dough with oil. Cover with a clean dish towel and let rise in a draft-free place for about 45 minutes, or until doubled in bulk.
4. Lightly grease 2 baking sheets. Punch the dough down and divide into 8 portions. Roll each portion into a 24" rope. Cut each rope into 6 sticks. Place the sticks on the prepared baking sheets about ½" apart. Cover and let rise for about 15 minutes, or until nearly doubled in bulk.
5. Preheat the oven to 300°F.
6. In a small bowl, whisk together the egg white and water. Brush each stick with the mixture, then sprinkle lightly with salt, sesame seeds, caraway seeds, and/or dried dill. Bake for 25 to 30 minutes, or until golden brown. Cool in the pans on racks for 5 minutes. Transfer to the racks to cool completely.

Makes 48 breadsticks

For a little punch of flavor, add fresh or dried herbs to the dough. Try tarragon, thyme, or oregano.

Focaccia

Hands-On Time: 20 minutes ■ Total Time: 50 minutes

This popular Italian flatbread is perfect alongside an Italian meal, as an appetizer, or used as sandwich bread. It is endlessly versatile: See Variations, below, for ideas.

- 1 cup warm water (about 120°F)
- 1 package (¼ ounce) quick-rising yeast
- 1 teaspoon honey
- 2½ to 3 cups unbleached all-purpose flour
- 3 tablespoons extra-virgin olive oil
- 1 tablespoon chopped fresh basil
- 1 tablespoon chopped fresh thyme
- 1½ teaspoons salt

1. Preheat the oven to 400°F. Grease a nonstick baking sheet.
2. In a large bowl, stir together the water, yeast, and honey. Add 1 cup of the flour. Beat with a wire whisk until smooth and creamy. Let rest at room temperature for 5 minutes.
3. Add 1 cup of the remaining flour, 2 tablespoons of the oil, the basil, thyme, and salt. Whisk hard for 3 minutes or until smooth. With a wooden spoon, stir in the remaining ½ to 1 cup flour, a little at a time, until a soft, sticky dough forms.
4. Turn the dough out onto a lightly floured surface and knead gently for 3 minutes.
5. Place the dough on the prepared baking sheet and shape into a 9" round that is 1" thick. Brush with the remaining 1 tablespoon oil. Bake for 20 to 25 minutes, or until golden brown.

Makes 1 round loaf; 8 wedges

Variations

Savory Focaccia: Replace the basil with 1 tablespoon chopped fresh sage and 1 tablespoon chopped fresh rosemary.

Tomato-Basil Focaccia: In a small saucepan, sauté 1 cup chopped tomatoes and 2 minced garlic cloves in olive oil until most of the liquid has evaporated. Stir in 1 tablespoon chopped fresh basil. After brushing the dough with the oil, use your fingers to make several deep indentations in the dough. Sprinkle the tomato mixture over the dough and bake as directed.

Focaccia with Mediterranean Vegetables: In a small saucepan, sauté 1 minced garlic clove in olive oil for 2 minutes, or until fragrant. Add 2 chopped roasted red peppers, 1 tablespoon chopped pitted kalamata olives, and 1 teaspoon capers; heat through. Remove from the heat and stir in 2 tablespoons balsamic vinegar, 1 tablespoon extra-virgin olive oil, and salt and black pepper to taste. After brushing the dough with the oil, use your fingers to make several deep indentations in the dough. Sprinkle the vegetable mixture over the dough and bake as directed.

Sweet Endings

Vanilla Cheesecake with Strawberry Sauce

Hands-On Time: 30 minutes ■ Total Time: 2 hours 10 minutes (plus chilling)

This cheesecake would be good with any fruit sauce. Go for what looks best in the market. Try raspberry sauce (be sure to strain out the seeds) or peach sauce.

Cheesecake

- 3 large eggs
- 1¼ cups vanilla wafer cookie crumbs
- 3 tablespoons plus 1¼ cups sugar
- 1 tablespoon unsalted butter, melted
- 24 ounces cottage cheese
- 2 packages (8 ounces each) cream cheese, softened
- ¼ cup all-purpose flour
- 1 tablespoon vanilla extract

Sauce

- 2 pints fresh strawberries, hulled and quartered, or 2 pints frozen strawberries, thawed
- 2 tablespoons sugar
- 1 tablespoon fresh lemon juice

1. *To make the cheesecake:* Preheat the oven to 325°F. Grease a 9" springform pan.
2. In a medium bowl, beat 1 egg lightly with a fork. Add the cookie crumbs, 3 tablespoons of the sugar, and the butter. Toss until the crumbs cling together. Press the mixture onto the bottom and 2" up the sides of the prepared pan.
3. In a food processor, combine the cottage cheese and cream cheese and process until smooth. Add the flour and remaining 1¼ cups sugar and process until the sugar is dissolved. One at a time, add the remaining 2 eggs, and then the vanilla extract. Process just until blended. Pour into the prepared crust.
4. Bake for 1 hour 15 minutes. Turn off the oven but leave the cheesecake in the oven for 30 minutes, or until the edges are a light golden brown and the center still jiggles slightly. Transfer to a rack to cool completely. Cover and refrigerate for at least 6 hours.
5. *To make the sauce:* In a medium bowl, combine the strawberries, sugar, and lemon juice. Stir until the sugar dissolves. Transfer 1½ cups of the berries to a food processor or blender and process until smooth. Return the purée to the bowl and stir to mix. Cover and refrigerate for several hours, if desired.
6. Serve the cheesecake with the strawberry sauce.

Makes 8 servings

Dutch Pear Cake

Hands-On Time: 20 minutes ■ Total Time: 1 hour 10 minutes

Use a firmer pear variety, such as Bosc, for this recipe because it holds its shape better. Moreover, its fairly spicy flavor is not overpowered by the flavors of the other cake ingredients.

- ½ cup plus 2 tablespoons chopped walnuts
- ½ cup sugar
- 1 teaspoon ground cinnamon
- ½ cup (1 stick) plus 1 tablespoon unsalted butter
- ½ cup plus 2 tablespoons honey
- 1 cup plain yogurt
- 2 large eggs
- 1 teaspoon vanilla extract
- 2½ cups all-purpose flour
- 1 teaspoon baking powder
- 1 teaspoon baking soda
- 3 medium pears, peeled and sliced

1. Preheat the oven to 325°F. Grease a 12-cup Bundt pan.
2. In a small bowl, combine ½ cup of the walnuts, the sugar, and cinnamon. Set aside.
3. In a large bowl, cream ½ cup of the butter and ½ cup of the honey. Add the yogurt and beat until combined. Beat in the eggs and vanilla extract.
4. In a medium bowl, sift the flour, baking powder, and baking soda. Stir into the butter mixture until well combined. Beat for 3 minutes, scraping the sides of the bowl occasionally with a spatula.
5. Pour half the batter into the prepared Bundt pan. Sprinkle with the reserved nut mixture and layer the sliced pears on top. Cover the pears and nut mixture with the remaining batter. Bake for 35 to 40 minutes, or until a tester inserted into the center comes out clean. Let the cake cool for 10 minutes, and then turn out onto a wire rack.
6. While the cake is cooling, combine the remaining 1 tablespoon butter and remaining 2 tablespoons honey in a small saucepan and warm over low heat. Pour the butter mixture over the cake and sprinkle with the remaining 2 tablespoons walnuts.

Makes 10 to 12 servings

Ingredients Note

Pear slices freeze beautifully. Simply slice fresh pears and toss recipe-size portions into freezer bags or containers, and then freeze. They'll last for about 3 months. Use the slices (no need to defrost) in tarts, cakes, pies, or stewed fruit recipes. Or you may warm them, add spices, and serve with roasted meats and poultry.

Elegant Lemon Roll

Hands-On Time: 45 minutes ■ Total Time: 55 minutes

A tender lemon cake roll encases a creamy filling in this fancy-enough-for-company dessert. There probably won't be any leftovers, but if there are, store them in the refrigerator.

Cake

- 1 tablespoon plus ⅔ cup sifted cake flour
- 1 teaspoon baking powder
- Pinch of salt
- 1 large egg
- ¾ cup granulated sugar
- 1 tablespoon vegetable oil
- 1 teaspoon lemon extract
- 6 large egg whites
- ¼ cup confectioners' sugar

Filling and Topping

- 1 can (14 ounces) sweetened condensed milk
- 1 to 2 teaspoons grated lemon zest
- ⅓ cup fresh lemon juice
- 5 drops yellow food coloring (optional)
- 1 cup thawed frozen whipped topping
- ¼ cup sweetened flaked coconut

1. *To make the cake:* Preheat the oven to 375°F. Lightly coat a jelly-roll pan with cooking spray. Line the bottom of the pan with wax paper. Coat the wax paper with cooking spray and dust with 1 tablespoon of the flour. Set aside.
2. In a small bowl, combine the baking powder, salt, and the remaining ⅔ cup flour. Set aside.
3. In a large bowl, with an electric mixer on high speed, beat the whole egg for 1½ minutes, or until thick and lemon-colored. Slowly beat in ¼ cup of the granulated sugar. Continue to beat on medium-high speed, scraping down the side of the bowl often, for 2 minutes, or until the mixture is creamy and pale in color. Beat in the oil and lemon extract.
4. Wash and dry the beaters. In a medium bowl, beat the egg whites on high speed until soft peaks form. Gradually add the remaining ½ cup granulated sugar, beating until stiff peaks form.
5. Fold or gently stir the egg white mixture into the lemon mixture. Then fold or gently stir in the flour mixture.

6. Gently spread the batter evenly in the prepared pan. Bake for 10 minutes, or until no imprint remains when the cake is lightly touched in the center.
7. Lightly sift the confectioners' sugar on 1 side of a clean dish towel. Immediately loosen the cake from the sides of the pan and invert it onto the towel. Remove the wax paper, then roll up the towel and cake together, jelly-roll fashion, starting from a short end. Transfer to a wire rack, seam side down, and cool completely.
8. *To make the filling:* In a large bowl, stir together the milk, lemon zest, lemon juice, and food coloring, if using. Fold in the whipped topping.
9. Unroll the cake. Spread half of the filling on the cake to within ½" of the edges. Roll up the cake without the towel. Transfer the cake to a serving platter and spread the remaining filling over the roll. Sprinkle the coconut on top. Carefully cover the cake and refrigerate for 1 to 2 hours before serving.

Makes 10 servings

Kitchen Tip

You can also use this cake to make a deliciously simple jelly roll. Prepare, bake, roll up, and cool the cake as above but omit the filling and topping. Spread the cooled cake with ⅔ cup seedless red raspberry jam, then roll up the cake without the towel. Cover with plastic wrap and refrigerate for 1 to 2 hours. Before serving, sift 2 tablespoons confectioners' sugar over the top of the cake.

Devil's Food Cake with Raspberries

Hands-On Time: 35 minutes ■ Total Time: 1 hour 30 minutes

The icing for this chocolate cake should be made just before you plan to use it, or it may become too stiff to spread. If need be, warm it in a microwave oven for a few seconds to soften it.

- 1 cup unsweetened cocoa powder
- 2 cups cake flour
- ¾ cup packed light brown sugar
- 2 cups granulated sugar
- 1½ teaspoons baking powder
- ½ teaspoon baking soda
- ¾ teaspoon salt
- 1 cup brewed black coffee
- 1 cup low-fat buttermilk
- 1 large egg
- ¼ cup vegetable oil
- 2 teaspoons vanilla extract
- ¼ cup water
- 1 tablespoon light corn syrup
- 2 large egg whites
- 2 squares (2 ounces) unsweetened chocolate, melted
- ½ pint fresh raspberries

1. *To make the cake:* Preheat the oven to 325°F. Lightly spray two 8" round cake pans with cooking spray. Lightly dust the pans with a small amount of the cocoa powder, tapping out the excess.
2. In a large bowl, combine the flour, brown sugar, ½ cup of the granulated sugar, the baking powder, baking soda, ½ teaspoon of the salt, and the remaining cocoa. In another large bowl, with an electric mixer at medium speed, beat the coffee, buttermilk, egg, oil, and 1 teaspoon of the vanilla extract. With the mixer at low speed, add the cocoa mixture and beat until just combined.
3. Divide the batter between the pans. Bake for 30 minutes, or until a tester inserted into the center comes out clean. Transfer to wire racks to cool for 10 minutes before turning the cakes out.
4. *To make the frosting:* In a medium saucepan, combine the remaining 1½ cups granulated sugar, the water, and corn syrup. Bring to a simmer over medium-high heat. Cover and simmer for 2 minutes. Uncover and simmer for 2 minutes longer, or until the syrup reaches 245°F on a candy thermometer. Remove the pan from the heat.
5. In a large bowl, with an electric mixer at medium speed, beat the egg whites with the remaining ¼ teaspoon salt for 1 to 2 minutes, or until soft peaks form. While you beat the egg whites, return the syrup mixture just to a boil. With the mixer at medium-high, pour the hot syrup into the egg whites, immediately increase the mixer speed to high, and continue to beat until the mixture is stiff and glossy. Beat in the remaining 1 teaspoon vanilla extract, then stir in the melted chocolate until the mixture is smooth.
6. Transfer 1 cake layer to a plate and frost with ½ cup of the frosting. Place the other layer on top and frost the rest of the cake. Arrange the raspberries on top of the cake.

Makes 12 servings

Fresh Berry Shortcakes

Hands-On Time: 20 minutes ■ Total Time: 35 minutes

Use strawberries, raspberries, blackberries, or a mix of all three for these delicious shortcakes.

- 2 cups all-purpose flour
- 3 tablespoons plus ⅓ cup sugar
- 2 teaspoons baking powder
- ¼ teaspoon baking soda
- 4 tablespoons (¼ cup or ½ stick) unsalted butter, cut into small pieces
- ⅔ cup plus 2 tablespoons buttermilk
- 1½ pints assorted berries
- 2 tablespoons orange juice
- 2 cups vanilla frozen yogurt

1. Preheat the oven to 400°F. Grease a baking sheet.
2. In a large bowl, combine the flour, 2 tablespoons of the sugar, the baking powder, and baking soda. Cut in the butter until the mixture resembles cornmeal. Add ⅔ cup of the buttermilk, stirring with a fork until the dough comes together.
3. Turn the dough out onto a lightly floured surface. Gently pat or roll to a ½" thickness. Using a 3" round cutter or large glass, cut out 8 biscuits. (You may have to pat the dough scraps together to cut out all the biscuits.) Transfer to the prepared baking sheet.
4. Brush the biscuits with the remaining 2 tablespoons buttermilk and sprinkle with 1 tablespoon of the remaining sugar. Bake for 12 to 15 minutes, or until golden. Transfer to a rack to cool.
5. Meanwhile, in a large bowl, combine the berries, orange juice, and remaining ⅓ cup sugar. Allow to sit for 10 minutes to draw out the berry juices.
6. Split the biscuits crosswise in half. Place a biscuit bottom on each of 8 dessert plates. Top with the berry filling and a scoop of frozen yogurt. Cover with the biscuit tops.

Makes 8 servings

Ingredients Note

You can make buttermilk by adding 1 tablespoon lemon juice to 1 cup milk and letting it sit for 10 minutes.

Peach Tart

Hands-On Time: 30 minutes ■ Total Time: 1 hour 50 minutes

You could make this delicious tart with nectarines or plums, if you prefer. Serve with vanilla ice cream, frozen yogurt, or whipped topping.

- 1½ cups plus 2 tablespoons all-purpose flour
- 2 tablespoons plus ⅓ cup granulated sugar
- ½ teaspoon salt
- 4 tablespoons (¼ cup or ½ stick) cold unsalted butter, cut into small pieces
- 2 tablespoons cream cheese
- 3 to 4 tablespoons ice water
- 7 ripe peaches, sliced
- 1 cup coarsely crushed almond-flavored biscotti
- 2 tablespoons chopped almonds
- 2 tablespoons packed light brown sugar
- 1 tablespoon unsalted butter, softened

1. In a food processor, combine 1½ cups of the flour, 2 tablespoons of the granulated sugar, and the salt. Process until blended. Add the cold butter and cream cheese. Pulse until the mixture resembles cornmeal. Drizzle 3 tablespoons of the water over the mixture. Pulse until a crumbly dough forms that will hold together when pressed. If needed, add up to 1 tablespoon more water. Pulse to combine.
2. Turn the dough out onto a work surface. Shape into a disk and wrap in plastic wrap. Refrigerate for 30 minutes.
3. Preheat the oven to 375°F. Grease a 10" tart pan or pie pan.
4. On a lightly floured surface, roll the dough out to a 13" circle. Drape it over the prepared pan. Gently press the dough against the side of the pan, trimming any overhang. Prick the bottom and side of the crust with a fork. Line with foil. Fill with pie weights or dried beans.
5. Bake the crust for 15 minutes. Remove the weights and foil. Bake for 10 minutes longer, or until lightly golden. Transfer to a rack to cool. Do not turn off the oven.
6. Meanwhile, in a large bowl, combine the peaches and the remaining ⅓ cup granulated sugar and 2 tablespoons flour.
7. In a small bowl, combine the biscotti, almonds, brown sugar, and softened butter. Using your fingers, combine to form coarse crumbs. Spoon the peach mixture into the tart shell. Sprinkle with the crumb topping.
8. Bake for 35 to 40 minutes, or until the topping is golden and bubbly. Transfer to a rack to cool. Serve warm or at room temperature.

Makes 10 servings

Streusel-Topped Peach and Berry Pie

Hands-On Time: 15 minutes ■ Total Time: 1 hour

Perfect for summer baking, this one-crust pie shows off the sweet flavor of ripe peaches and fresh raspberries.

Crust

- 1¼ cups all-purpose flour
- ¼ cup old-fashioned rolled oats
- 3 tablespoons milk
- 3 tablespoons vegetable oil

Filling

- 4 cups sliced peaches
- 2 cups fresh raspberries or thawed frozen raspberries
- ⅔ cup granulated sugar
- 3 tablespoons cornstarch
- 1 teaspoon fresh lemon juice
- ¼ teaspoon ground cinnamon
- ¼ teaspoon ground nutmeg

Topping

- ⅓ cup packed brown sugar
- ¼ cup all-purpose flour
- ⅛ teaspoon ground cinnamon

1. *To make the crust:* Preheat the oven to 425°F. Grease a 9" pie pan.
2. In a blender or food processor, combine the flour and oats. Process until the oats are a coarse powder. Transfer to a medium bowl. Add the milk and oil and stir until the mixture resembles coarse cornmeal. Press into the prepared pie pan. Place the pan in the freezer for 5 minutes.
3. *To make the filling:* In a large bowl, toss together the peaches, raspberries, granulated sugar, cornstarch, lemon juice, cinnamon, and nutmeg. Pour into the crust.
4. *To make the topping:* In a small bowl, combine the brown sugar, flour, and cinnamon. Sprinkle over the filling.
5. Bake the pie for 40 minutes, or until the topping is browned and the filling bubbles. Cool before slicing.

Makes 8 servings

Kitchen Tip

On rushed evenings, you might be tempted to purchase one of the ready-made frozen pie crusts. But you wouldn't if you had a homemade crust waiting in the freezer. Stock up on metal pie pans at yard sales. Each time you make a pie, prepare three times the crust. Roll and shape the crusts in the pie pans. Wrap them in plastic bags and freeze unbaked. No need to thaw before using.

Open-Faced Cherry Pie

Hands-On Time: 40 minutes ■ Total Time: 2 hours

Out of season, use frozen tart cherries in place of the fresh.

Pie Crust

- 1¼ cups all-purpose flour
- 2 tablespoons sugar
- ½ teaspoon salt
- 4 tablespoons (¼ cup or ½ stick) cold unsalted butter, cut into pieces
- 3 tablespoons cold vegetable shortening, cut into pieces
- 5 tablespoons ice water

Filling

- 4 cups fresh tart cherries, pitted
- ⅔ cup sugar
- 3 tablespoons quick-cooking tapioca
- ½ teaspoon grated lemon zest
- ½ to 1 teaspoon ground cinnamon

1. *To make the pie crust:* In a large bowl, combine the flour, sugar, and salt. With a pastry blender or 2 knives, cut in the butter and shortening until the mixture resembles coarse crumbs.
2. Sprinkle 2 tablespoons of the ice water over the mixture and toss with a fork. The dough should be just barely moistened, enough to hold together when it is formed into a ball. If necessary, add up to 3 tablespoons more water, 1 tablespoon at a time. Form the dough into a flat disk, wrap in plastic wrap, and refrigerate for at least 30 minutes.
3. On a lightly floured surface, roll out the dough to an 11" circle. Gently lay the dough in a 9" pie plate. Firmly press the dough against the bottom and sides of the pan. Fold the edges under and crimp to form a rim. Using a fork, pierce the bottom of the crust all over to prevent it from puffing up during baking. Place the pie shell in the freezer to chill for at least 15 minutes before baking.
4. Preheat the oven to 425°F.
5. Bake the pie crust for 8 to 10 minutes, or until lightly browned. Remove from the oven and cool on a wire rack. Reduce the oven temperature to 375°F.
6. *To make the filling:* Meanwhile, in a large saucepan, combine the cherries, sugar, tapioca, lemon zest, and cinnamon. Let stand for 5 minutes. Place over medium heat and cook, stirring, for 10 minutes, or until thickened.
7. Pour the cherry filling into the partially baked pie crust. Bake for 20 to 30 minutes, or until bubbly.

Makes 8 servings

Key Lime Pie

Hands-On Time: 30 minutes ■ Total Time: 1 hour 5 minutes (plus chilling)

A gingersnap crust is the perfect complement to a tangy lime filling. If you can find them, use real Key limes (also known as Mexican limes), which have a unique tart flavor that is different than that of conventional limes. Bottled Key lime juice is also sold in some markets and online.

Crust

- 1 large egg white
- 1½ cups crushed gingersnap cookies (about 30)
- 1 tablespoon plus 1½ teaspoons unsalted butter, melted
- 1 tablespoon plus 1½ teaspoons canola oil

Filling and Meringue Topping

- 1 tablespoon grated Key lime zest
- ½ cup fresh Key lime juice
- 1 can (14 ounces) sweetened condensed milk
- 2 large egg yolks
- ½ cup sugar
- 1 teaspoon cornstarch
- 4 large egg whites
- ¼ teaspoon cream of tartar

1. *To make the crust:* Preheat the oven to 375°F. Grease a 9" pie plate.
2. In a medium bowl, beat the egg white lightly with a fork. Add the gingersnaps, butter, and oil. Blend well. Scrape into the prepared pie plate and press into an even layer on the bottom and up the sides. Bake for 8 to 10 minutes, or until lightly browned and firm. Cool on a rack.
3. *To make the filling:* In a large bowl, combine the lime zest, lime juice, condensed milk, and egg yolks. In a small bowl, combine the sugar and cornstarch.
4. In a medium bowl, combine the egg whites and cream of tartar. With an electric mixer on medium speed, beat until foamy. Increase the speed to high and gradually beat in the sugar mixture. Continue to beat until the whites are firm and glossy. Fold ¾ cup of the meringue into the lime mixture. Scrape into the prepared crust. Bake for 15 minutes and remove from the oven.
5. Spoon the remaining meringue over the filling and spread to the edge of the crust. Using a spoon, make small peaks in the meringue. Bake for 10 minutes, or until the meringue is golden brown and set. (If the meringue browns too quickly, reduce the oven temperature to 350°F.) Cool completely on a rack. Refrigerate for 1 to 2 hours before serving.

Makes 10 servings

Apple Pinwheel Cookies

Hands-On Time: 35 minutes ■ Total Time: 1 hour 30 minutes (plus chilling)

Pinwheel cookies usually sport two flavors of dough, typically chocolate and vanilla. But these innovative creations swirl together lemon dough and a thick apple mixture.

- 1 cup chopped dried apples
- 3/4 cup apple juice
- 1/2 teaspoon ground cinnamon
- 1 tablespoon fresh lemon juice
- 2 1/2 cups all-purpose flour
- 1 teaspoon baking powder
- 1/4 teaspoon salt
- 3/4 cup (1 1/2 sticks) unsalted butter, at room temperature
- 1 cup sugar
- 2 large eggs
- 1 teaspoon lemon extract

1. In a medium saucepan, combine the apples, apple juice, cinnamon, and lemon juice. Bring to a boil over medium-high heat. Reduce the heat to low, cover, and simmer for 35 minutes, or until the apples are tender and most of the juice has been absorbed. Let cool slightly. Mash with a fork and set aside.
2. Meanwhile, in a medium bowl, combine the flour, baking powder, and salt.
3. In a large bowl, with an electric mixer on medium speed, beat the butter and sugar for 3 minutes, or until light and fluffy. Beat in the eggs and lemon extract. Beat in the flour mixture a little at a time until well blended. Cover and refrigerate for at least 1 hour.
4. Divide the dough in half. On a floured surface, roll each half into an 11" × 7" rectangle. Spread half of the apple mixture over each rectangle, leaving 1/2" borders. Starting at a long side, roll up tightly. Pinch to seal. Wrap in plastic wrap and refrigerate for at least 4 hours, or until firm.
5. Preheat the oven to 375°F. Cut rolls into 1/2"-thick slices and arrange on ungreased baking sheets. Bake for 10 minutes, or until light brown. Cool on the pan for 2 minutes. Transfer to a rack to cool completely.

Makes about 4 dozen cookies

Cherry Brownies

Hands-On Time: 20 minutes ■ Total Time: 55 minutes (plus cooling)

After tasting these superb moist brownies, you're sure to be forever hooked on the chocolate-cherry connection. An almond-flavored frosting tops the treats.

Brownies

- 1 cup all-purpose flour
- ¾ teaspoon baking powder
- ½ teaspoon salt
- 4 ounces unsweetened chocolate
- ⅔ cup unsalted butter
- 2 cups granulated sugar
- 4 large eggs
- 1½ teaspoons vanilla extract
- 1 cup cherry all-fruit spread

Frosting

- 4 tablespoons (¼ cup or ½ stick) unsalted butter, at room temperature
- 4 teaspoons half-and-half
- ½ teaspoon almond extract
- 1½ cups confectioners' sugar

1. *To make the brownies:* Preheat the oven to 350°F. Grease a 13" × 9" baking pan.
2. In a medium bowl, combine the flour, baking powder, and salt.
3. Place the chocolate and butter in a large microwaveable bowl and microwave on high power for 4 minutes, or until the butter is melted. Remove from the microwave oven, stirring constantly to fully melt the chocolate. Stir in the granulated sugar. Add the eggs, one at a time, stirring after each addition, until well blended. Stir in the vanilla extract and the flour mixture.
4. Spread the batter in the prepared pan. Using a knife, swirl in the cherry spread. Bake for 35 minutes, or until a wooden pick inserted into the center comes out clean. Cool in the pan on a rack.
5. *To make the frosting:* In a medium bowl, combine the butter, half-and-half, almond extract, and confectioners' sugar. Beat until smooth and creamy. Spread over the cooled brownies.

Makes 2½ dozen brownies

Gingerbread Cookies

Hands-On Time: 15 minutes ■ Total Time: 25 minutes

No need to wait until the holidays to make gingerbread cookies. They're a perfect afternoon snack or for taking to a neighborhood cookie exchange any time of the year. Use regular cookie cutters instead of gingerbread ladies and gentlemen, and decorate—or not—as desired.

- 2½ cups all-purpose flour
- 1 tablespoon ground cinnamon
- 2 teaspoons ground ginger
- 1 teaspoon baking soda
- ¼ teaspoon ground cloves
- ¼ teaspoon ground nutmeg
- ¼ teaspoon salt
- 6 tablespoons (¾ stick) butter, at room temperature
- ¾ cup packed light brown sugar
- 2 tablespoons molasses
- ¼ to ⅓ cup water

1. Preheat the oven to 375°F. Grease 2 large baking sheets.
2. In a medium bowl, combine the flour, cinnamon, ginger, baking soda, cloves, nutmeg, and salt.
3. In a large bowl with an electric mixer on medium speed, beat the butter and brown sugar for 3 minutes, or until light and fluffy. Beat in the molasses. Beat in the flour mixture, a little at a time, until well blended. Add the water, 1 tablespoon at a time, to form a stiff but well-blended dough.
4. Divide the dough into 4 equal-size pieces. Roll each piece out to a ¼" thickness. Using cutters of any shape, cut out the cookies. Arrange on the prepared baking sheets, leaving 1" between the cookies.
5. Bake for 7 minutes, or until lightly browned. Cool on the pan for 2 minutes. Transfer to a rack to cool completely.

Makes about 3 dozen cookies

Peanut Butter Cookies

Hands-On Time: 20 minutes ■ Total Time: 35 minutes

Peanut aficionados: Get double the pleasure with these simple-to-make cookies packed with creamy peanut butter and chopped peanuts.

- 1 cup all-purpose flour
- ½ teaspoon baking soda
- ½ teaspoon salt
- ½ cup (1 stick) unsalted butter, at room temperature
- ¾ cup granulated sugar
- ¼ cup packed light brown sugar
- 1 large egg
- 1 cup creamy peanut butter
- ½ teaspoon vanilla extract
- 1 cup coarsely chopped unsalted dry-roasted peanuts

1. Preheat the oven to 375°F. Grease 2 large baking sheets.
2. In a medium bowl, combine the flour, baking soda, and salt.
3. In a large bowl with an electric mixer on medium speed, beat the butter, granulated sugar, and brown sugar for about 3 minutes, or until light and fluffy. Beat in the egg, peanut butter, and vanilla extract. Beat in the flour mixture, a little at a time, until well blended. Stir in the peanuts.
4. Shape the dough into 1" balls. Arrange on the prepared baking sheets and press flat with a fork. Bake for 10 minutes, or just until the cookies start to brown. Cool on the pan for 2 minutes. Transfer to a rack to cool completely.

Makes 4 dozen cookies

Chewy Oatmeal-Apricot Cookies

Hands-On Time: 20 minutes ■ Total Time: 45 minutes

Using fruit purée, such as applesauce or prune butter, instead of shortening provides moisture to cookies, and the fruit's fiber performs some of the same functions in a batter that fat does. In addition, fruit is naturally sweet, so many recipes can be made with less sugar. The fruit/fat substitution works best in simple drop and bar cookies; those that have a fruit or spice flavor are particularly well suited for this fat-saving trick. So why is there still some butter in this recipe? Because of its inimitable taste.

- 1½ cups old-fashioned rolled oats
- 1¼ cups all-purpose flour
- 1 teaspoon baking soda
- 1 teaspoon ground cinnamon
- ½ teaspoon baking powder
- ½ teaspoon ground nutmeg
- ½ teaspoon salt
- ¾ cup unsweetened applesauce
- ½ cup plus 2 tablespoons packed light brown sugar
- 2 large egg whites
- 2 tablespoons unsalted butter, melted
- 1 teaspoon vanilla extract
- 1 cup finely chopped dried apricots

1. Preheat the oven to 350°F. Grease 2 large baking sheets.
2. Spread the rolled oats on an ungreased baking sheet and toast for 8 to 10 minutes, or until lightly browned.
3. In a large mixing bowl, combine the toasted oats, flour, baking soda, cinnamon, baking powder, nutmeg, and salt. Stir well.
4. In another large mixing bowl with an electric mixer at medium speed, beat the applesauce, brown sugar, egg whites, butter, and vanilla extract until well combined. With the mixer at low speed, gradually beat in the dry ingredients until well combined. Stir in the apricots.
5. Drop the dough by level tablespoons, 1" apart, onto the prepared baking sheets. Place both baking sheets in the oven and bake for 10 to 12 minutes (switching the position of the sheets halfway through baking), or until the cookies are lightly browned. Transfer the cookies to wire racks to cool.

Makes 4 dozen cookies

Chocolate Chippers

Hands-On Time: 20 minutes ■ Total Time: 30 minutes

The addition of cream cheese to chocolate chip cookies gives them extra richness.

- 2¼ cups all-purpose flour
- ¼ cup cornstarch
- 1 teaspoon baking soda
- ½ teaspoon salt
- ¼ cup (½ stick) unsalted butter, softened
- 2 ounces cream cheese, softened
- ¾ cup granulated sugar
- ¾ cup packed light brown sugar
- 2 large eggs
- 1 teaspoon vanilla extract
- ¾ cup chocolate chips

1. Preheat the oven to 375°F. Lightly grease 2 large baking sheets.
2. In a medium bowl, combine the flour, cornstarch, baking soda, and salt.
3. In a large bowl with an electric mixer on medium speed, beat the butter and cream cheese for about 1 minute, or until smooth. Add the granulated sugar and brown sugar and beat until light and creamy. Add the eggs and vanilla extract and beat until smooth.
4. Reduce the mixer speed to low. Add the flour mixture in 2 additions, beating just until combined. With a spoon, stir in the chocolate chips.
5. Drop the dough by rounded teaspoonfuls onto the prepared baking sheets. Bake for 9 to 12 minutes, or until golden. Transfer the cookies to a rack to cool.

Makes about 3 dozen cookies

Chocolate-Walnut "Biscotti"

Hands-On Time: 25 minutes ■ Total Time: 50 minutes

Dark and rich-tasting, these simple, once-baked "biscotti" keep well in an airtight container or in the freezer. They are especially good dunked in espresso.

- 1 cup all-purpose flour
- ½ cup sugar
- ¼ cup unsweetened cocoa powder
- ½ teaspoon baking powder
- ¼ teaspoon baking soda
- ¼ teaspoon salt
- 1 large egg
- 1 large egg white
- 1½ teaspoons vanilla extract
- 2 ounces bittersweet chocolate, chopped
- ¼ cup chopped toasted walnuts

1. Preheat the oven to 350°F. Grease an 11" × 7" baking dish.
2. In a large bowl, whisk together the flour, sugar, cocoa powder, baking powder, baking soda, and salt.
3. In a medium bowl, whisk together the egg, egg white, and vanilla extract. Pour over the flour mixture and stir well. Stir in the chocolate and walnuts.
4. Press the dough into the prepared baking dish. Bake for 25 minutes, or until firm. Transfer to a wire rack and cut into 30 fingers. Cool before serving.

Makes 2½ dozen biscotti

Kitchen Tip

To toast walnuts, spread on a baking sheet and bake at 400°F for 8 to 10 minutes, or until lightly browned and fragrant. Keep an eye on them so they don't burn.

Bananas Foster

Hands-On Time: 15 minutes ■ Total Time: 15 minutes

This recipe is traditionally made by flambéing dark rum with the banana mixture. Here, apple juice concentrate is used to keep the dessert family-friendly.

- 1 tablespoon unsalted butter
- 2 tablespoons dark brown sugar
- 2 tablespoons apple juice concentrate
- ¼ teaspoon ground cinnamon
- 3 bananas, halved crosswise, then halves quartered lengthwise
- 2 teaspoons vanilla extract
- 3 cups vanilla frozen yogurt

1. In a medium nonstick skillet, melt the butter over medium heat. Add the brown sugar, apple juice concentrate, and cinnamon. Cook, stirring, until the sugar melts. Add the bananas. Toss to coat well. Cook for 3 to 5 minutes, or until the bananas are tender. Remove from the heat. Add the vanilla extract and swirl to combine.
2. Serve the frozen yogurt topped with the bananas and sauce.

Makes 6 servings

Baked Chocolate Pudding

Hands-On Time: 25 minutes ■ Total Time: 1 hour (plus cooling and chilling)

Chocolate pudding is not just for kids: This velvety baked pudding has a sophisticated semisweet flavor that grown-ups will love. Because the recipe calls for only 1½ ounces of chocolate, you could treat yourself to a fine European brand; however, a domestic semisweet baking chocolate—even chocolate chips—will make an excellent pudding, too. Baking the ramekins of pudding in a pan of hot water protects them from the direct heat of the oven, ensuring that they cook slowly and evenly with little chance of burning.

- 1 cup half-and-half
- 1 cup milk
- ⅓ cup unsweetened Dutch-process cocoa powder, plus ½ teaspoon for garnish
- ¼ cup sugar
- 2 tablespoons cornstarch
- Pinch of salt
- 2 large eggs
- 2 teaspoons vanilla extract
- 1½ ounces semisweet chocolate, chopped

1. Preheat the oven to 350°F.
2. In a small, heavy saucepan, heat the half-and-half and milk over medium heat until small bubbles form around the edges; do not boil. Pour into a large glass measuring cup or heatproof pitcher.
3. Sift the ⅓ cup cocoa into a medium heatproof bowl. Stir in the sugar, cornstarch, and salt. Add the eggs and vanilla extract and whisk until smooth. Gradually whisk in the hot milk. Add the chocolate and whisk until melted.
4. Divide the mixture among four 7- to 8-ounce ramekins or custard cups. Set the ramekins in a 13" × 9" baking pan and add hot water to reach ½" up the sides of the ramekins. Bake for 30 to 35 minutes, or until the puddings are set; they should not jiggle when the baking pan is shaken gently. Transfer the puddings from the water bath to a wire rack to cool until barely warm.
5. Serve the puddings warm or refrigerate for 2 to 3 hours and serve chilled. Dust the puddings with the remaining ½ teaspoon cocoa just before serving.

Makes 4 servings

Apricot Bread Pudding

Hands-On Time: 15 minutes ■ Total Time: 1 hour

Bread pudding was presumably created as a way to use up leftover bread, but the dessert belies its humble beginnings. In a glorified version of French toast, cubed bread is combined with milk, eggs, sugar, and fruit, and then baked into a cakelike confection.

- ⅓ cup snipped dried apricot halves
- ½ cup boiling water
- 2 cups milk
- ¼ cup apricot preserves
- 3 large eggs
- 2 tablespoons sugar
- 1 tablespoon cornstarch
- 1 tablespoon frozen orange juice concentrate
- 1½ teaspoons vanilla extract
- 3 cups crusty bread cubes (½" cubes), preferably French peasant bread

1. Preheat the oven to 375°F. Grease a 9" × 9" baking dish.
2. In a small heatproof bowl, place the apricots and pour the boiling water over them. Set aside to plump for 5 to 10 minutes.
3. Meanwhile, in a blender or food processor, combine the milk, apricot preserves, eggs, sugar, cornstarch, orange juice concentrate, and vanilla extract. Process until well combined.
4. Drain the plumped apricots and place them, along with the bread cubes, in the prepared baking dish. Pour in the milk mixture and mix well with a rubber spatula.
5. Bake for 30 to 35 minutes, or until the pudding is set and the top is puffed and lightly browned. Place the pan on a wire rack to cool slightly. Serve the pudding warm. Refrigerate any leftovers.

Makes 6 servings

Kitchen Tip

Kitchen shears make quick work of cutting up dried apricots. Spray the blades lightly with cooking spray to make the job even easier.

Make-Ahead

Cut up the bread in advance and let the bread cubes dry for a few hours.

Royal Rice Pudding

Hands-On Time: 25 minutes ■ Total Time: 50 minutes (plus chilling)

This elaborate rice pudding uses Arborio rice for creaminess and features two types of fruit and toasted almonds. It's truly a pudding fit for a king (or queen).

- 1 can (8 ounces) crushed pineapple
- ⅔ cup Arborio rice
- ¼ cup raisins
- ¼ teaspoon ground cinnamon
- ¼ teaspoon ground nutmeg
- 1 tablespoon cornstarch
- 2 cups milk
- ½ cup honey or maple syrup
- 2 large eggs
- 1½ teaspoons vanilla extract
- 1½ cups sliced strawberries
- 3 tablespoons slivered almonds, toasted

1. Place the pineapple in a strainer set over a measuring cup. Press as much liquid as possible from the pineapple. Set aside the pineapple. You should have about ½ cup of pineapple juice. Add enough water to equal 1⅓ cups.
2. In a medium saucepan, combine the pineapple liquid with the rice. Bring to a boil and reduce the heat to medium-low. Partially cover and cook for 5 minutes. Stir with a fork. Cover tightly and cook for 10 to 15 minutes longer, or until all the liquid has been absorbed. Stir in the pineapple, raisins, cinnamon, and nutmeg. Remove from the heat.
3. In a large saucepan, whisk the cornstarch with 2 tablespoons of the milk until smooth. Whisk in the remaining milk and the honey. Cook over medium heat, whisking constantly, for about 10 minutes, or until it starts to thicken and just comes to a boil. Remove from the heat.
4. Place the eggs in a cup and slowly whisk in about ¼ cup of the hot milk mixture. Whisk the egg mixture into the rest of the milk mixture.
5. Return the pan to the heat and whisk constantly until the mixture comes to a boil. Remove from the heat and stir in the vanilla extract and cooked rice. Transfer to a large bowl, cover, and allow to cool. Chill for at least 4 hours.
6. Just before serving, fold in the strawberries and almonds.

Makes 6 servings

Ingredients Note

Arborio is a short-grain Italian rice that becomes very creamy when cooked. Although the results will be somewhat different, you can substitute long-grain white or brown rice for the Arborio. The cooking time for long-grain white rice will be the same; the time will increase to about 45 minutes for brown rice.

How to Make All-Purpose Pie Pastry

This recipe makes one 9" pie crust. If you are making a two-crust pie, avoid doubling the recipe. You are more likely to overwork the dough that way. Instead, make one crust, and as that chills in the refrigerator, make the second. To make the crust without a food processor, use a bowl and a pastry blender (or two knives) to cut in the butter and shortening, then stir in the water and lemon juice with a spoon. To bake a two-crust pie, follow the baking instructions of the pie recipe you are using. If you are making the crust for a savory dish, such as a quiche, omit the sugar. If using the prebaked pie shell for a filling that is prone to turning the shell soggy, brush with an egg white immediately after removing the prebaked shell from the oven. This will create a moisture-resistant barrier.

- 1¼ cups all-purpose flour
- 1 tablespoon sugar
- ½ teaspoon salt
- 6 tablespoons (¾ stick) butter, chilled and cut into ¼" pieces
- 2 tablespoons shortening, chilled and cut into teaspoon-size pieces
- 3½ to 4½ tablespoons ice water
- 1 teaspoon fresh lemon juice

1. In the bowl of a food processor, combine the flour, sugar, and salt. Pulse to blend. Add the butter and pulse with six 1-second pulses, or until the butter pieces are coarsely broken up and coated with flour. Add the shortening and pulse with five 1-second pulses, or until the butter pieces resemble small peas.

2. Add 3½ tablespoons of the water and the lemon juice. Pulse 3 times. Add more water if necessary, 1 teaspoon at a time, and pulse 1 or 2 times, until the dough just adheres when pinched between your fingers.

3. Turn the mixture out into a medium bowl and gather the dough into a ball. Press into a disk shape about 1" thick. Wrap in plastic wrap and chill in the refrigerator for at least 30 minutes or up to 24 hours.

4. Remove the dough from the refrigerator and let stand at room temperature for 10 minutes to soften. Spread a 16" piece of plastic wrap or parchment paper on a work surface. Lightly coat with flour. Place the dough on top, lightly dust with flour, and cover with another sheet of plastic wrap or parchment. Roll the dough from the center out into a 12" circle. If the dough sticks to the plastic, carefully unpeel and lightly coat the plastic with more flour.

5. Remove the top sheet and slide your hands underneath the bottom sheet. Carefully invert over the pie pan, centering the dough as much as possible. Lift the dough gently by 1 edge to encourage it to conform to the bottom of the pan. Gently press across the bottom to make sure that there are no air bubbles trapped under the surface. Trim any extra dough so that there is only ½" of overhang. Tuck the dough edge under so that it hangs about ¼" beyond the pan edge. Crimp the edges as desired. Lightly cover with plastic wrap and refrigerate for at least 1 hour.

6. To prebake: Adjust the oven rack to the middle position. Preheat the oven to 400°F. Line the pie crust with foil or parchment paper, fitting it in snugly along the curve of the crust (use another pan of the same size for a very snug fit). Drop dried beans onto the foil, distributing them evenly and fitting them snugly along the curve of the crust. Bake for 18 minutes. Carefully remove the beans and foil. Cook for 12 to 15 minutes longer, or until light golden brown. If the crust begins to bubble, prick with a sharp knife to deflate. Transfer to a rack to cool.

Makes one 9" crust

Grilled Summer Fruit with Berry Sauce

Hands-On Time: 15 minutes ■ Total Time: 15 minutes

Grilling brings out the sweet flavors of fruit, and the bright raspberry sauce gives it a crowning touch of color and flavor.

- 1 cup raspberries
- 1 tablespoon packed light brown sugar
- 1½ teaspoons fresh lemon juice
- 2 apricots, halved
- 2 plums, halved
- 1 peach, halved
- 1 teaspoon vegetable oil
- 2 teaspoons honey

1. Prepare the grill to medium-hot.
2. In a blender or food processor, process the raspberries, brown sugar, and lemon juice until smooth. If desired, strain out the seeds.
3. Brush the cut sides of the apricot, plum, and peach halves with the oil. Grill the fruit, oiled side down, for 2 to 3 minutes, or until lightly browned. Remove from the grill and drizzle with the honey. Serve topped with the raspberry sauce.

Makes 4 servings

Accompaniments

Vanilla ice cream is the natural accompaniment to grilled fruit. You might also want to add some gingersnaps or biscotti.

Baked Winter Fruit

Hands-On Time: 10 minutes ■ Total Time: 30 minutes

Baking fruit concentrates its natural sweetness and creates a moist, tender dessert. For a finishing touch, top with puréed frozen strawberries and vanilla frozen yogurt.

- 2 tart apples, cored, peeled, and each sliced into 4 rings
- 2 pears, quartered
- 16 dried apricot halves
- 2 tablespoons chopped raisins
- 1 tablespoon apple juice or water
- 4 teaspoons maple syrup
- ½ teaspoon ground cinnamon

1. Preheat the oven to 400°F.
2. Tear off 4 large sheets of aluminum foil. Divide the apples, pears, apricots, and raisins evenly among the pieces. Drizzle with the apple juice and maple syrup, then sprinkle with the cinnamon. Seal the packets tightly and place on a baking sheet.
3. Bake for 20 minutes, or until the fruit is tender. Serve on dessert plates.

Makes 4 servings

Kitchen Tip

To make the raisins easier to chop, place them in the freezer for 10 to 15 minutes.

Ambrosia Parfaits

Hands-On Time: 20 minutes ■ Total Time: 20 minutes

Sliced oranges, grated coconut, and confectioners' sugar are combined to make the dessert that Southerners call ambrosia. Traditionalists might see this recipe as gilding the lily, but layering the usual ambrosia ingredients with frozen yogurt does create a truly irresistible treat.

- 2 tablespoons sweetened shredded coconut
- 2 medium navel oranges
- ½ cup halved red seedless grapes
- ½ cup drained crushed juice-packed pineapple, 1 tablespoon juice reserved
- 1 pint vanilla frozen yogurt, slightly softened
- Mint sprigs (optional)

1. In a small nonstick skillet, toast the coconut over medium heat, tossing frequently, for 2 to 3 minutes, or until lightly browned. Transfer to a small plate to cool.
2. Using a sharp paring knife, remove the peel and white pith from the oranges. Cut the oranges crosswise into ½"-thick slices, then chop coarsely. Transfer the chopped oranges to a bowl, add the grapes and the pineapple with its reserved juice, and mix.
3. Divide one-third of the fruit mixture among four 10- to 12-ounce parfait glasses or dessert dishes. Using half of the yogurt, spoon a layer of yogurt over the fruit. Alternate layers of the remaining fruit mixture and yogurt in the glasses, ending with the fruit mixture.
4. Sprinkle the parfaits with the toasted coconut. Garnish with mint sprigs, if desired, and serve.

Makes 4 servings

Kitchen Tip

To easily prepare the oranges for this recipe: Cut off the tops and bottoms of the oranges, then pare downward in wide strips, removing all of the peel and white pith. Cut each pared orange crosswise into slices, then coarsely chop the slices.

Brown-Sugar Baked Apples

Hands-On Time: 10 minutes ■ Total Time: 55 minutes

Tart cooking apples such as Stayman Winesap, Winesap, and Granny Smith taste best in this recipe—buy them in bulk at your local farmers' market or farm stand in late autumn. They keep for several months in a cool place, so you can enjoy baked apples all winter.

- 6 large tart apples, cored
- ½ cup packed light brown sugar
- ½ cup raisins
- ½ teaspoon ground cinnamon
- 1 cup apple juice
- 1 cup sour cream
- 1 tablespoon honey

1. Preheat the oven to 350°F. Place the apples in a 13" × 9" baking pan.
2. In a small bowl, combine the brown sugar, raisins, and cinnamon; stuff into the apple cavities. Pour the apple juice into the baking dish around the apples.
3. Bake the apples for 45 minutes, or until very soft when the tip of a sharp knife is inserted into one.
4. In a small bowl, combine the sour cream and honey. Drizzle over the hot apples and serve.

Makes 6 servings

Kitchen Tip

To core an apple, hold in the palm of one hand and insert a small sharp knife at the top. Carefully cut around the core, but do not cut all the way through the bottom of the apple.

Nectarine and Raspberry Pandowdy

Hands-On Time: 20 minutes ■ Total Time: 55 minutes (plus cooling)

To save time peeling the fruit, choose large nectarines. When fresh nectarines are out of season, make this tart-sweet dessert with unsweetened frozen peach slices.

- ⅔ cup all-purpose flour
- ⅛ teaspoon salt
- 2 tablespoons cold unsalted butter, cut into small pieces
- 2 tablespoons ice water
- ¼ cup frozen apple juice concentrate, thawed
- 2 tablespoons cornstarch
- 1 tablespoon plus 1 teaspoon granulated sugar
- ¼ teaspoon ground cinnamon
- ¼ teaspoon ground mace or nutmeg
- 2 pounds ripe nectarines, cut into ¼"-thick slices
- 1 cup fresh or frozen unsweetened raspberries
- 1 teaspoon milk
- 1 teaspoon confectioners' sugar (optional)

1. Preheat the oven to 425°F.
2. In a medium bowl, stir together the flour and salt. Mix in the butter with your fingers or 2 knives. Stir in enough of the ice water to form a soft dough.
3. Shape the dough into a flat disk and place between 2 sheets of wax paper. Roll the dough out to a 9" circle. Chill the dough while you prepare the filling.
4. In a large bowl, combine the apple juice concentrate, cornstarch, 1 tablespoon of the granulated sugar, the cinnamon, and mace. Add the nectarines and toss to mix well. Spoon the filling into a 9½" deep-dish pie plate and scatter the raspberries on top.
5. Remove the dough from the refrigerator and peel off the top sheet of wax paper. Invert the dough over the fruit and peel off the second sheet of paper. Cut a large X in the center of the dough and turn back the points so they almost touch the edge of the dough. Brush the dough with the milk and sprinkle with the remaining 1 teaspoon granulated sugar. Place the pie plate on a baking sheet.
6. Bake the pandowdy for 12 to 15 minutes, or until the crust is lightly browned. Reduce the oven temperature to 375°F and bake for 15 to 20 minutes longer, turning the dish if the crust browns unevenly. The crust should be crisp and browned and the fruit tender and bubbly.
7. Cool the pandowdy on a wire rack. Sprinkle with the confectioners' sugar, if desired. To serve, cut the crust into 6 wedges. Spoon the filling onto dessert plates and top with wedges of crust.

Makes 6 servings

Plum Compote with Yogurt

Hands-On Time: 10 minutes ■ Total Time: 40 minutes

Compotes can be made with either fresh or dried fruits or a combination of the two. Dried fruits require slow cooking to soften, but you have to be careful not to overcook fresh fruits—such as the plums here—or they may disintegrate. The cooking time will depend on the variety of plums you choose and their ripeness.

- 3 tablespoons seedless raspberry jam
- ½ teaspoon fresh lemon juice
- ½ teaspoon vanilla extract
- 4 ripe medium plums (about 1 pound), cut into ½" wedges
- Half of a 3" cinnamon stick or a pinch of ground cinnamon
- 1 cup vanilla frozen yogurt

1. In a medium heavy saucepan, combine the raspberry jam, lemon juice, and vanilla extract and stir to combine. Add the plums and cinnamon stick. Toss gently with a rubber spatula until the fruit is coated with the syrup.
2. Place the pan over medium heat and bring to a simmer, stirring frequently but gently. Reduce the heat to medium-low, cover, and simmer for 8 to 12 minutes, or until the plums are very tender. Remove the cinnamon stick, if using.
3. Spoon the cooked plums into 4 dessert dishes and refrigerate for 20 minutes. (To save time, you can chill the plums in the freezer for about 10 minutes.)
4. Top each dish of plums with frozen yogurt and serve.

Makes 4 servings

Ingredients Note

Most of the commercially grown plums in the United States come from California. Some of the most popular varieties shipped from that state are Black Amber, Queen Rosa, Santa Rosa, Laroda, Casselman, Simka, Black Beauty, and big, meaty Elephant Heart plum, which is particularly good for cooking. These California fruits are all Japanese varieties, which are generally plump, round, and juicy, with skins ranging from yellow to crimson to black.

Strawberry-Rhubarb Slump

Hands-On Time: 20 minutes ■ Total Time: 1 hour 10 minutes

Slumps are similar to cobblers in taste, but they're topped with soft dumplings that cook into the hot fruit.

Filling

- 2/3 cup sugar
- 2 1/2 tablespoons cornstarch
- 1/4 teaspoon ground cinnamon
- 1 package (10 ounces) frozen strawberries (packed in syrup), thawed
- 1 package (16 ounces) frozen cut rhubarb, thawed

Dumplings

- 1 1/4 cups all-purpose flour
- 2 tablespoons sugar
- 1 teaspoon baking powder
- 1/4 teaspoon baking soda
- 1/8 teaspoon salt
- 1 1/2 tablespoons unsalted butter, cut into small pieces
- 1 1/2 tablespoons vegetable oil
- 1/2 cup buttermilk

1. Preheat the oven to 375°F.
2. *To make the filling:* In a Dutch oven or large ovenproof saucepan, combine the sugar, cornstarch, and cinnamon. Drain the juice from the strawberries into the pan; set the strawberries aside. Stir the sugar mixture until smooth. Stir in the rhubarb and bring to a boil over medium-high heat. Boil for about 2 minutes, or until the mixture thickens and turns clear. Remove from the heat and stir in the reserved strawberries.
3. *To make the dumplings:* In a large bowl, combine the flour, sugar, baking powder, baking soda, and salt. Add the butter and oil. Using a fork or pastry blender, mix until crumbly. Add the buttermilk and mix just until moistened.
4. Drop large spoonfuls of the dough over the fruit filling, spacing them so that they don't touch each other. Cover with a lid or foil and cook over medium heat for 10 minutes.
5. Uncover the pan and transfer to the oven. Bake for 15 to 20 minutes, or until a wooden pick inserted into a dumpling comes out clean. Cool for 10 minutes before serving.

Makes 6 servings

Pineapple Crumble

Hands-On Time: 20 minutes ■ Total Time: 50 minutes

Supermarkets with exceptional produce departments have recently added a real convenience to the fruit aisle—a mechanical device that lets you core and peel a fresh pineapple with the pull of a lever. If this time-saver is not available where you shop, see the Ingredients Note, below, for information on how to peel and core a pineapple.

- 1 fresh pineapple (4 pounds), peeled, cored, and cut into ½" chunks (about 5 cups)
- 3 tablespoons honey
- 1½ teaspoons vanilla extract
- ¾ teaspoon ground coriander
- 1 cup all-purpose flour
- ¼ cup packed dark brown sugar
- ¼ cup old-fashioned rolled oats
- 2 tablespoons shredded sweetened coconut
- ⅛ teaspoon salt
- 3 tablespoons cold unsalted butter, cut into small pieces

1. Preheat the oven to 425°F.
2. In an 11" × 7" baking dish, combine the pineapple, honey, vanilla extract, and ¼ teaspoon of the coriander.
3. In a medium bowl, combine the flour, brown sugar, oats, coconut, salt, and remaining ½ teaspoon coriander. Mix with a pastry blender or 2 knives to break up the lumps of sugar. Cut in the butter until the mixture forms fine crumbs.
4. Sprinkle the crumbs over the pineapple mixture. Bake for 25 to 30 minutes, or until the topping is browned, the pineapple tender, and the juices bubbly.

Makes 8 servings

Kitchen Tip

A pastry blender, made of wires set into a handle, quickly combines butter or shortening with dry ingredients. Two table knives (you don't need sharp blades) can also do the job; use them with a quick chopping motion.

Ingredients Note

To peel and core a pineapple, cut off the crown and bottom of the fruit. Remove the rough outside peel by slicing down each side of the pineapple. Cut the pineapple lengthwise into quarters and then cut away the hard, tough core.

Citrus Ice Pops

Hands-On Time: 5 minutes ■ Total Time: 5 hours

Grapefruit juice makes these grown-up pops tangy and delicious—and much less expensive than store-bought frozen treats. Look for plastic frozen-treat molds at yard sales.

- 1½ cups unsweetened grapefruit juice
- 1 cup sliced strawberries
- ¼ cup sugar
- 1 tablespoon fresh lemon juice

1. In a blender or food processor, combine the grapefruit juice, strawberries, sugar, and lemon juice. Process until puréed.
2. Pour the juice mixture into 8 frozen-treat molds or paper cups. Freeze for 5 hours, or until solid. Dip the molds into hot water before unmolding.

Makes 8 pops

Variation

For more kid-friendly pops, substitute orange juice or apple juice for the grapefruit juice.

Kitchen Tip

If you don't have molds to make the pops, you can use 2-ounce paper cups. Pour the juice mixture into the cups and freeze for 1 hour, or until the pops are beginning to set. Insert frozen-pop sticks (available in craft stores) into each cup so they stand up straight and freeze for 4 hours longer, or until solid.

Gingered Cantaloupe Sorbet

Hands-On Time: 25 minutes ■ Total Time: 25 minutes (plus freezing)

You don't need an ice-cream machine to make sorbet—just a food processor—and you can produce flavors you'll never find at the supermarket, such as this sublime gingered melon ice. It has both pungent fresh ginger and sweet-hot crystallized ginger—lively accents to the fragrant sweetness of cantaloupe.

- 1 large ripe cantaloupe, peeled, seeded, and cut into chunks (about 4 cups)
- ½ cup sugar
- 2 tablespoons light corn syrup
- 1 tablespoon fresh lemon juice
- 1 tablespoon grated fresh ginger
- 2 tablespoons minced crystallized ginger
- Mint sprigs (optional)

1. Place the cantaloupe, sugar, corn syrup, lemon juice, and fresh ginger in a food processor and process until smooth. Add the crystallized ginger and pulse just until mixed. Pour into a 9" × 9" metal baking pan and cover with foil. Freeze for at least 6 hours or overnight, until frozen hard.
2. Remove the sorbet from the freezer and let stand for a few minutes until softened. Break the sorbet into chunks. In batches, place the chunks in a food processor and pulse until creamy and smooth.
3. Transfer the sorbet to a freezer container, cover, and freeze for at least 1 hour, or until ready to serve.
4. To serve, soften at room temperature for a few minutes. Spoon the sorbet into 4 dessert dishes or goblets. Garnish with mint sprigs, if desired.

Makes 4 servings

Ingredients Note

Crystallized ginger is made by cooking slices of fresh ginger in a sugar syrup, then coating it with granulated sugar. This turns the ginger into a tasty confection with a consistency like that of firm dried fruit. The crystallized ginger sold in small jars in supermarket spice racks can be very expensive. Better bets are gourmet or candy shops, or Asian markets, where the ginger is sold by the pound. It's usually much cheaper and also of better quality.

Easy Equivalents

ITEM	THIS . . .	EQUALS THIS . . .
Apples	1 pound	3 cups sliced
Bananas	3–4 medium	2 cups mashed
Carrots	1 pound	3 cups shredded
Cocoa	3 tablespoons plus 1 tablespoon oil	1 ounce unsweetened chocolate
Cornmeal	1 pound	3 cups
Cottage cheese	8 ounces	1 cup
Egg	1 large	¼ cup liquid egg substitute
Elbow macaroni	1 pound	4 cups dry
Elbow macaroni	1 cup uncooked	2 cups cooked
Flour, all-purpose	1 pound	About 4 cups
Garlic	1 small clove	⅛ teaspoon garlic powder
Honey	1 cup	1½ cups granulated sugar plus ¼ cup liquid
Lemon or lime	1	2–4 tablespoons juice
Lemon or lime	1	2 teaspoons grated zest
Lentils	2¼ cups dried	5 cups cooked
Mushrooms	8 ounces	1 cup sliced
Oatmeal	1 pound	5 cups cooked
Orange	1	6–8 tablespoons juice
Orange	1	2–3 tablespoons grated zest
Potatoes	3 medium	1¾ cups mashed
Raisins	1 pound	3¼ cups
Rhubarb	1 pound fresh	2 cups cooked
Rice, white	2 cups uncooked	6 cups cooked
Yeast, active dry	2 teaspoons	1 package

Emergency Substitutions

IF YOU DON'T HAVE THIS...	USE THIS . . .	ADJUSTMENTS
Alcohol (rum, sherry, or brandy), 1 teaspoon	1 teaspoon vanilla extract	Vanilla is strongly flavored, so if more than 1 teaspoon is needed, make up the difference with fruit juice.
Baking powder	¼ teaspoon baking soda plus ⅝ teaspoon cream of tartar	No change.
Bread crumbs, 1 cup	¾ cup crushed crackers	Adjust seasonings to compensate for salt (if any) in the crackers.
Broth (beef or chicken), 1 cup	1 bouillon cube in 1 cup water	Bouillon is saltier than broth, so you may want to dilute 1 cube in 2 cups water.
Butter, 1 cup	⅞ cup vegetable oil	Oil causes a looser crumb in baked products, so work gently to prevent crumbling.
Buttermilk, 1 cup	1 cup low-fat or nonfat plain yogurt	For baking, no change needed. In casseroles, you may want to use ¾ cup, because the yogurt is denser.
Cornstarch, 1 tablespoon	2 tablespoons all-purpose flour	The flour will cause a somewhat duller appearance, so it's best used for gravies, stews, or other mixed combos.
Herbs, fresh, 1 tablespoon	1 teaspoon dried	Dried herbs are stronger, so add them earlier in the recipe.
Lemon juice	Half as much vinegar	This is not recommended for baked goods.
Milk, fat-free, 1 cup	⅓ cup nonfat dry milk mixed with ¾ cup water	No change for baking.
Mustard, prepared, 1 teaspoon	Equal amount mustard powder	Mustard powder is concentrated, so use it sparingly.
Olive oil	Equal amount of any vegetable oil	The consistency will be the same, but the flavor will change.
Roasted red bell peppers	Equal amount of pimientos	No change.
Sour cream, 1 cup	1 cup evaporated skim milk plus 1 tablespoon lemon juice	To speed curdling, microwave on high power for 30 seconds.
Tomato juice, 1 cup	½ cup tomato sauce plus ½ cup water	Tomato sauce has more added salt, so adjust your seasonings accordingly.
Tomato sauce, 1 cup	⅜ cup tomato paste plus ½ cup water	No change.
Vinegar, 1 teaspoon	2 teaspoons lemon juice	Adjust seasonings for changed flavor.

Estimating Food for a Crowd

It's probably not often that you serve 12 guests, but when you do, you want to get the right amount of food. Amounts below are calculated for 12 guests, allowing 2 modest servings each.

FOOD	TOTAL AMOUNT NEEDED
BEEF	
Barbecued brisket	1 whole brisket, about 10 pounds
Flank steak	3 steaks, 2 pounds each
London broil/shoulder steak	10 pounds
Rib-eye roast, boneless	6 pounds
Rib-eye steak	12 steaks, 10 ounces each, halved
Rib roast, bone-in	16 pounds
Sirloin roast	2 roasts, 3 pounds each
Tenderloin or filet mignon steaks	6 pounds
CHICKEN	
Bone-in parts	20 pounds
Breasts, bone-in	24 medium breasts
Breasts, boneless, for stir-frying	6 pounds
Breasts/cutlets, boneless	20–24 boneless breast halves
Whole	4 roasters, 4 to 4½ pounds each
LAMB	
Leg of lamb, bone-in	2 legs, about 6 pounds each
Leg of lamb, butterflied	2 boned legs, about 4 pounds each
Rack of lamb	6 racks
PORK	
Center-cut loin, bone-in	12 pounds
Center-cut loin, boneless	6 pounds
Chops, bone-in	24 chops
Chops, boneless	6 pounds
Ham, boneless	6 pounds
Spare ribs	24 pounds
Tenderloin	6 pounds

FOOD	TOTAL AMOUNT NEEDED
SEAFOOD	
Clams, mussels, oysters, or shrimp, fresh	144–180 pieces
Fish, fresh cleaned	6–8 pounds
Fish, fresh fillets or steaks	4–6 pounds
Fish, fresh whole	9–12 pounds
Lobsters, live	12 lobsters, 1–2 pounds each
Scallops or cleaned squid, raw	3–5 pounds
Shrimp, crabmeat, or lobster meat, cooked	3–5 pounds
TURKEY	
Whole	18–20 pounds
BEVERAGES	
Coffee	8–12 ounces ground beans
Soft drinks	3 bottles, 2 liters each
Tea, hot or iced	5–6 quarts (20–30 tea bags)
SNACKS AND CRUDITÉS	
Broccoli or cauliflower florets	4 heads, 1 pound each
Carrot sticks	1¼ pounds
Celery sticks	2–3 bunches
Chips or pretzels	1¼ pounds
Olives	3–4 cups
OTHER	
Pizza	6 pizzas, 16" each
Rice	6 cups uncooked
Salad, green	6 quarts
Soup	2½ gallons
DESSERTS	
Cake	2 cakes, 13" × 9" each
Ice cream or frozen yogurt	3 quarts
Pie	3 pies, 9" each

INDEX

Underscored page references indicate boxed text or kitchen tips. **Boldfaced** page references indicate photographs.

D

E

F

G

H

I

N

O

P

Q

R

S

T

V

W

Y

Z

Conversion Chart

These equivalents have been slightly rounded to make measuring easier.

Volume Measurements

U.S.	*Imperial*	*Metric*
¼ tsp	–	1 ml
½ tsp	–	2 ml
1 tsp	–	5 ml
1 Tbsp	–	15 ml
2 Tbsp (1 oz)	1 fl oz	30 ml
¼ cup (2 oz)	2 fl oz	60 ml
⅓ cup (3 oz)	3 fl oz	80 ml
½ cup (4 oz)	4 fl oz	120 ml
⅔ cup (5 oz)	5 fl oz	160 ml
¾ cup (6 oz)	6 fl oz	180 ml
1 cup (8 oz)	8 fl oz	240 ml

Weight Measurements

U.S.	*Metric*
1 oz	30 g
2 oz	60 g
4 oz (¼ lb)	115 g
5 oz (⅓ lb)	145 g
6 oz	170 g
7 oz	200 g
8 oz (½ lb)	230 g
10 oz	285 g
12 oz (¾ lb)	340 g
14 oz	400 g
16 oz (1 lb)	455 g
2.2 lb	1 kg

Length Measurements

U.S.	*Metric*
¼"	0.6 cm
½"	1.25 cm
1"	2.5 cm
2"	5 cm
4"	11 cm
6"	15 cm
8"	20 cm
10"	25 cm
12" (1')	30 cm

Pan Sizes

U.S.	*Metric*
8" cake pan	20 × 4 cm sandwich or cake tin
9" cake pan	23 × 3.5 cm sandwich or cake tin
11" × 7" baking pan	28 × 18 cm baking tin
13" × 9" baking pan	32.5 × 23 cm baking tin
15" × 10" baking pan	38 × 25.5 cm baking tin (Swiss roll tin)
1½ qt baking dish	1.5 liter baking dish
2 qt baking dish	2 liter baking dish
2 qt rectangular baking dish	30 × 19 cm baking dish
9" pie plate	22 × 4 or 23 × 4 cm pie plate
7" or 8" springform pan	18 or 20 cm springform or loose-bottom cake tin
9" × 5" loaf pan	23 × 13 cm or 2 lb narrow loaf tin or pâté tin

Temperatures

Fahrenheit	*Centigrade*	*Gas*
140°	60°	–
160°	70°	–
180°	80°	–
225°	105°	¼
250°	120°	½
275°	135°	1
300°	150°	2
325°	160°	3
350°	180°	4
375°	190°	5
400°	200°	6
425°	220°	7
450°	230°	8
475°	245°	9
500°	260°	–